Challenging Professional

A characteristic of professionalism is the obligation to remain up to date in areas of professional expertise. Most professional bodies acknowledge this and require their members to undertake regular relevant continuing professional development (CPD). Unfortunately, CPD struggles within a context of intensification of work, pressure of time and economic restrictions and if the perceived benefits of CPD under such conditions become outweighed by the costs, then CPD can become tokenistic for both the individual and the organisation. Comprehensive research and an evidence base determining which approaches to CPD are most effective and efficient have been sparse.

Challenging Professional Learning fills this research and knowledge gap, exploring the idea that professionals who expect to and are able to continuously learn and unlearn are also able to readily accommodate change as part of their professional development. As the pace of change increases through globalisation and technological innovation the need for CPD is greater. Drawing on a wealth of recent research and evidence, the chapters explore the necessary ingredients for effective and efficient professional learning. They also explore wider implications of these findings and the concept of learning as a collective activity. The text argues that real professionalism cannot be achieved in isolation but instead takes place in a context that has political, social and cultural influences. It links practice around professional learning to both individual and collective professional learning, to organisational learning, leadership and the management of change and offers practical suggestions for improving practices within these areas.

This book will be of great interest to teacher educators and their students at undergraduate and post-graduate levels, as well as anyone who works in higher education and professional development. It emphasises the importance of building both pedagogic expertise and subject specialism. It argues that quality teaching, learning and practice is very much dependent upon professionals undergoing CPD, engaging actively in professional learning activities, generating professional learning communities and building their level of professionalism to meet increasing standards.

Sue Crowley has worked within the FE and skills sector as a teacher, manager and leader for over 40 years; she was a founder member of the Institute for Learning and is its current, elected chair.

Challenging Professional Learning

Edited by Sue Crowley

To John
Who made me learn
to write.

Love
Sue

Routledge
Taylor & Francis Group

LONDON AND NEW YORK

First published 2014
by Routledge
2 Park Square, Milton Park, Abingdon, Oxon OX14 4RN

and by Routledge
711 Third Avenue, New York, NY 10017

Routledge is an imprint of the Taylor & Francis Group, an informa business

British Library Cataloguing in Publication Data
A catalogue record for this book is available from the British Library

Library of Congress Cataloging in Publication Data
Crowley, Sue.
Challenging professional learning / edited by Sue Crowley.
  pages cm
1. Professional education. 2. Continuing education. I. Title.
LC1059.C79 2013
378'.013—dc23
2013005409

ISBN: 978-0-415-81693-9 (hbk)
ISBN: 978-0-415-81694-6 (pbk)
ISBN: 978-0-203-79837-9 (ebk)

Typeset in Galliard
by Cenveo Publisher Services

Printed and bound in Great Britain by
TJ International Ltd, Padstow, Cornwall

Contents

Acknowledgements   vii
List of figures   viii
List of contributors   ix
Foreword   xiii
FRANK COFFIELD

Introduction and overview   1
SUE CROWLEY

1   **What sort of professionalism?**   7
    SUE CROWLEY

2   **Trading places: On *becoming* an FE professional**   20
    DENIS GLEESON

3   **Professional bodies and continuing professional
    development: A case study**   31
    ANDY BOON AND TONI FAZAELI

4   **Interpreting professional learning: The trouble with CPD**   54
    SUE COLQUHOUN AND JEAN KELLY

5   **Evaluating the impact of professional learning**   75
    VIVIENNE PORRITT

6   **Leading and learning in challenging circumstances**   98
    FIONA MACKAY AND PAUL WAKELING

7   **Professional learning and vocational pedagogy**   119
     SUE CROWLEY

8   **Maintaining the challenge and the learning**   134
     SUE CROWLEY

     Glossary   145
     Bibliography   147
     Index   159

Acknowledgements

There are two groups of people without whom I would never have embarked on the journey involved in producing this book. First, are the staff and the membership of the Institute for Learning (IfL). The staff who, in very challenging environments, never lost sight of their commitment to the membership, and members who so willingly shared their hopes, fears and aspirations for the FE and skills sector, for its staff and for the learners that it serves. There are some outstanding teachers and trainers whose personal, interpersonal and pedagogical capabilities, let alone their subject and vocational expertise, are truly amazing, yet they remain modest and still curious about how to improve practice. They are inspirational.

Secondly throughout my 40 plus years in the sector I have been very fortunate to belong to some great teaching teams where we really have been able to engage in high-quality dialogue about pedagogy, professionalism, professional learning, leadership and leadership development. These were the subjects we taught and in the teaching of them we learnt so much more and realised how much more there was still to learn. I am no longer part of a teaching team but these people remain my critical friends and I cannot learn effectively without them.

I hope this book manages to do justice to and impart some of the learning I have gained from my fortunate encounters with these people.

Finally I would like to offer special thanks to Brian Kelly, who is sorely missed by us all, Bill Lucas and Alan Thomson for their careful reading and insightful comments and Dr Matt O' Leary and Dr Rob Smith for their support in editing the text whilst themselves undergoing an Ofsted inspection.

Figures

1.1   A spectrum of professional maturity.   17
5.1   Putting knowledge to work.   80
5.2   The knowledge conversion process.   81
5.3   Professional learning cycle.   82
5.4   Evaluation impact model.   84
5.5   Baseline to impact.   90
5.6   Strategic leadership of PLD.   97

Contributors

Andy Boon is Professor of Law at City University London and former Dean of the School of Law at the University of Westminster, London. He has held research grants on various socio-legal topics and is the author of articles on the legal profession and legal education. He is joint author (with Professor Jenny Levin) of the first academic text to offer an extended analysis of the ethics of the English legal professions *The Ethics and Conduct of Lawyers in England and Wales*, 2nd edition (Oxford: Hart, 2008). He served on the Law Society's Training Framework Review Group which produced 'day one outcomes' for qualifying solicitors. He was educational adviser to the Bar of England and Wales, Chair of the Bar Vocational Course Board and Vice-Chair of the Bar Standards Board's Education and Training Committee. He was recently consultant to the Law Society of England and Wales on introducing legal ethics to the compulsory curriculum for undergraduates and to the Solicitors Regulation Authority on the mandatory scheme for continuing professional development. He is a director of the International Association of Legal Ethics.

Sue Crowley is the current elected Chair of the non-executive board at the Institute for Learning (IfL) (www.ifl.ac.uk). Sue began her career in biochemical research but soon found herself in the further education (FE) system as a part-time biology teacher at an Inner London college. She worked in FE for 17 years as a teacher, manager and staff developer focusing her own professional development on how students learn. In 1988 she moved full-time into teacher education. In 1990 she moved to the Learning and Skills Development Agency (LSDA) developing and delivering national professional development programmes for teachers and trainers, middle and senior managers, principals and CEOs of education and training provider organisations. In 1999 she became the Head of the Centre for Professional Development at the Learning and Skills Development Agency. In 2002 she and her team moved across to the Centre for Excellence in Leadership where she became Director, Quality Improvement in 2006. Sue was a founder member of the IfL and was elected Chair of Council in 2007. Until 2012 she continued to teach on the Aspiring Principals and Senior Leadership Programme for the Learning and Skills

Improvement Service. Her role as Chair of IfL and her teaching commitments have allowed her to keep in touch with the sector at both the practitioner front line and senior leadership levels.

Sue Colquhoun is Head of Professional Status at IfL where she has worked since June 2008, leading on Professional Formation which is the route to Qualified Teacher Learning and Skills (QTLS) and Associate Teacher Learning and Skills (ATLS). She also has responsibility for supporting continuing professional development. She has worked across all sectors, including schools, further education and higher education across three countries and two continents. In her previous role as programme manager in a higher education institution, she was responsible for teacher education and training, in particular for teachers of English for Students of Other Languages (ESOL) in the FE and skills sector. She has co-authored a book entitled, *Diversity and Inclusion: An FE Lecturer's Guide* (Continuum, 2006) and contributed to *Teaching Adult ESOL* (NRDC, 2009) as well as a variety of other journal articles.

She is a member of the Institute for Learning, www.ifl.ac.uk, the National Association for Teaching English and Community Languages to Adults (NATECLA), http://www.natecla.org.uk, and is also a member of the editorial board for their part-peer reviewed journal, *Language Issues* and a trustee of NATECLA's charity, the Ruth Hayman Trust, http://www.ruthhaymantrust.com.

Toni Fazaeli is the Chief Executive of the Institute for Learning (IfL), the professional body for teachers and trainers across further education and skills. IfL members teach or train in diverse settings across further education and skills including in the armed forces, adult education, further education colleges, offender learning, the voluntary and community sector and work-based learning.

As a qualified teacher, Toni has taught in prisons, further and adult education, as well as schools. Throughout her career she has focused on teaching and learning, educational policy and research and writing. Before joining IfL in 2008, she was a senior civil servant with policy responsibilities for further education, was National Director in Quality and Standards in the Learning and Skills Council and was an inspector in the Further Education Funding Council (FEFC) specialising in literacy, numeracy, English for Speakers of Other Languages (ESOL) and humanities across further and adult education. She also was an adult education adviser and officer in Leicestershire Local Education Authority and a development officer with National Institute for Adult and Continuing Education (NIACE). Toni is Chair of Learning for the Fourth Age, a social enterprise offering learning to older people in care homes, and is a college governor.

Denis Gleeson was born in Manchester and was educated and trained as a teacher in London where he both studied and taught in a variety of F/HE institutions.

His teaching and research interests are in the sociology of post-compulsory education, training and employment, across the 14–19 plus age range, including related issues associated with non-school attendance, bullying, academy schools, education leadership, management and governance. He has held professorships at Keele University and at Warwick University, where he is Emeritus Professor of Education. He is currently Professor of Post Compulsory Education in the School of Education Futures, (SEF), at the University of Wolverhampton. He has published widely in areas of education policy and practice in partnerships with schools, colleges, community, trade unions and employers, including international fellowships and funding support from research council and sector organisations in the UK.

Jean Kelly qualified as a teacher in London in 1972 and, after a career in primary school teaching, went as a mature student to Oxford to study English Literature and Language. Her PhD from Queen Mary College, London, and research interests were in the political constructs of medieval literature but her experience of teaching in schools, university and further education has led to her work on teacher training and teacher development programmes both in FE colleges and for national bodies such as the Learning and Skills Development Agency (LSDA), the Centre for Leadership (CEL) and, since 2007, the Institute for Learning (IfL). Jean is the Director of Professional Development at the IfL.

Fiona Mackay is a human resource development specialist with significant experience and expertise in crafting and facilitating learning initiatives for individual leaders, managers, groups and organisations. Fiona's teaching on post-experience programmes is extensive both in higher education and executive education. She ran the highly acclaimed, Aspiring Principals and Senior Leaders Programme for the FE and skills sector for a number of years. She currently works with the executive education team at Warwick Business School on a range of management and leadership programmes in the public and private sectors. She is well regarded for her capability in facilitating groups, action learning sets, as a leadership personal tutor, providing individual Emotional Competence Inventory (ECI) feedback and being an inspired personal coach. Central is her commitment to equal opportunities and to continuing professional learning and development. Her ongoing research interests focus on personal leadership and organisational learning.

Vivienne Porritt is Assistant Director for Partnerships with Schools at the Institute of Education (IoE), University of London. She works with schools and groups of schools on innovative approaches to the development continuum across ITE, CPD, Leadership and evidence-based professional learning. At the IoE she is also the Executive Director of the London Centre for Leadership in Learning (LCLL), a centre which connects research and practice and academics and practitioners to create new knowledge about leadership and how it makes a difference to learners.

Vivienne's professional interests focus on innovative approaches to strategic professional development and its impact on practitioners and learners, working with educational leaders and organisations to support high-impact approaches to professional learning and leadership development. She has published several articles and co-authored the book, *Effective Practices in CPD: Lessons from Schools* with Peter Earley (Institute of Education, 2009).

Following secondary school headship, Vivienne was seconded to the (then) Department of Children, Schools and Families (DCSF) as the London CPD Adviser and the (then) Training and Development Agency for Schools (TDA) before moving to the IoE. Specific projects include consultancy to the London Challenge team, Project Director for the TDA's national research project, Effective Practices in CPD, and a regional consultant for the Leadership of CPD project and authoring the TDA/National College online unit for Strategic Leadership of CPD. At the IoE, Vivienne teaches on MA and MBA programmes for educational leadership.

Paul Wakeling has been Principal of Havering Sixth Form College since August 2006. Previous roles have included Vice Principal at Coulsdon College and Programme Manager at Newham Sixth Form College. He is particularly interested in exploring the relationship between leadership and learning, with a focus on what style of leadership can lead to sustained educational improvement. Paul has completed a research fellowship with the Learning and Skills Improvement Service (LSIS) at the University of Sunderland. Paul attended the Kennedy School of Government at Harvard to study Twenty-First Century Leadership. Other roles have included being a member of the LSIS Council, a board member of Learning Plus UK, a governor of Riverhead Infants' School and an associate lecturer on the Senior Leadership and Aspiring Principals' Programme run by LSIS.

Foreword

I have frequently been told by journalists, even by those of a left-leaning persuasion, that Further Education (FE) is 'not sexy'; 'no-one's interested in FE'; and 'you'll not get your article on FE published by anyone'. It is time to confront head-on the monumental condescension of these journalists, for whom education means schools and universities, because neither they nor their children have ever set foot in an FE college, never mind studied or taught there.

Here is a book which recognises, celebrates and contains new ideas to strengthen teaching, learning and assessment (TLA) in the FE and skills sector, in which around 200,000 tutors educate and train more than 3 million students. The sector provides not only second chance education and lifelong learning for all, but it also confers the wider, social benefits of education in terms of health, social cohesion and active citizenship in the communities it serves. Without a vibrant and successful FE and skills sector, the coalition government's (any government's) educational plans for social inclusion and social mobility and its economic plans for a skilled and productive workforce are set at naught.

This book has the potential to transform the system of Continuing Professional Development (CPD) within this sector. We live in an age where words like 'transformation' are loosely thrown around, when often nothing more than minor modifications are envisaged. But here I use the word advisedly to mean an innovative and much needed change of direction, which most certainly will not be easy or straightforward, but which should prove more exhilarating and liberating than the present, inefficient state of affairs, for all those with the courage to act differently and collaboratively.

Let me back up that strong claim by offering three quotations from the text and discussing three main themes that the authors of the following chapters forced me to think seriously about. I begin with a research finding that has been widely known in the education world since the 1980s but rarely acted on. Vivienne Porritt, in Chapter 5, reminds us of the research on CPD which revealed that 'only 10 per cent of the participants implemented what they had learned and the percentage did not improve significantly if participants had volunteered to learn' (p. 79). This aptly sums up the old system of CPD we need to discard. Second, here is a new principal of a sixth form college describing a very different way of behaving in his first years in post: 'I developed a definition of my role as the "lead learner" in the college, which I shared with all staff at a staff meeting and via my staff Blog ... I find that maintaining the learning dialogue can be challenging ... Many referred to individual reflection as a "luxury"' (Paul Wakeling in Chapter 6, pp. 104–05). I shall have more to say about leadership in a moment.

Third, Sue Crowley, in the final chapter, draws on the following evidence collected by the Institute for Learning (IfL): 'Many staff attending the LSIS Aspiring Principals and Senior Leadership Programme reported that neither the executive team nor the principal ever discussed with them their learning from the programme or how it might suggest improvements in individual or organisational practices ...' (p. 139). Not very professional. Let me, however, offer two possible interpretations of that finding. First, in some FE colleges learning has come to mean something that students and front-line teachers still have to do, but it is a troublesome activity that senior managers can quickly dispense with as soon as they are promoted out of the classroom. Second, is it not more likely that, as Fiona MacKay argues in Chapter 6, senior staff are over-stressed from working in organisations that are over-stretched because the pressures to continuously improve are so intense that they really do not have any time to learn? What structured support are we providing for senior managers to help them cope with all the competing demands made upon them, demands which are becoming well-nigh intolerable?

This brings me to the first of the three main topics which all the contributors to this volume prompted me to think more deeply about, namely, leadership. Tony Edwards argued that the persistent devaluing of vocational education is intimately connected with the long, ignoble and undemocratic tradition in Britain of 'educating leaders but training followers' (1997: 8). If in FE colleges and in adult and community learning centres all governments insist on the overwhelming importance of 'strategic leadership and management' (DBIS, 2011:33), does this not also presuppose the existence of followers whose tactics have to be managed? And is that dangerous divide a recipe for creating a learning organisation or, more likely, a dysfunctional institution, where failures are blamed by those who see themselves as strong, visionary leaders on those they view as incompetent, out-of-date followers, while disillusioned and depressed followers blame what they see as data-driven, uncaring leaders who have become remote from classrooms? In one university studied by Ian McNay 'the executive corridor was known as Battlestar Galactica' (2012:46).

The ubiquitous rhetoric about strong leadership leading to improvement in standards has for years been running way ahead of the evidence (see Coffield, 2012). David Hartley (2007, 2009) has carefully reviewed the extensive literature on this topic and concluded: 'attempts to show a direct causal relationship between leaders' behaviour (be it distributed or otherwise) and pupils' achievement have yielded little that is definite' (2007:204).

A way out of these difficulties is suggested by a number of contributors to this book who convincingly argue for a move from *individual reflection* (which in itself is unlikely to produce organisational change) to *collective, collaborative reflection*, which takes account of the political, economic and internal cultural processes within the highly complex, social world of a large, general FE college.

Sue Crowley begins the book by asking why there is a paucity of learning organisations 'amongst public sector organisations whose focus should be education and training' (p. 1). May I suggest three reasons. The first part of my explanation concerns the unhealthy gap that has opened up in so many schools, colleges and universities between senior management teams (SMTs) and the teaching staff. If SMTs were, however, to become educational leaders as well as business managers and were to return to teaching, then that gap could begin to be bridged.

Another reason why, in my opinion, there are so few learning organisations within the educational world is that the research literature on TLA is not sufficiently well known by many of the executive leaders, who have since incorporation seen their main priority as making and keeping their institutions financially viable. The notion that sound finance is a necessary but not a sufficient condition for success is only now beginning to be discussed and acted upon. FE colleges need first and foremost to be excellent in providing what their name suggests – further education. Achieve that and financial success is more likely to follow.

The third part of my explanation is that instead of leading by example (by teaching students, for instance, or supervising the training of new members of staff or discussing the strengths and weaknesses of their teaching with their colleagues), SMTs manage *not* via education, education, education, but via data, data and even more data. The excitement, the joy and the unpredictable drama of teaching young people or adults are ignored and instead time is wasted on, for example, examining spreadsheets on the soulless, ineffective grading of lessons on a four-point scale.

The second theme which I have chosen to discuss is not only the need to evaluate the impact of any improvement strategies that are adopted, but also knowing how to carry out such an evaluation. We now know, from a considerable body of research done in schools (so little research is carried out in FE), that the main features of effective CPD appear to be: teachers become, in Jean Kelly's memorable phrase, 'the driver and the designer of their own CPD' (p. 57); they are offered a variety of learning opportunities, about which they are given time to reflect; and they learn in collaboration with the colleagues they teach with, as Vivienne Porritt argues in Chapter 5.

Compare that approach with the current, inefficient pattern of CPD in many colleges, which continues to be based on a menu, chosen by management, of courses for the morning and another set of courses for the afternoon. Staff choice is restricted to selecting one session to attend in the morning and another in the afternoon; they then return to work the next morning without ever being given the time to reflect with their colleagues on whether the new thinking or practices they have been introduced to are appropriate and worth incorporating into their own teaching. So the 'best practice' of some outstanding teachers, usually working in ideal conditions, remains just that – someone else's practice which has no impact on one's own.

The final theme I want to discuss is perhaps the most important of all in that I hope it will alter the way we talk, think and act about our professional development as teachers. In what follows I write as someone who still teaches and who is proud to be called a teacher. I refer to what, in retrospect, may well be seen as an historic shift in emphasis from the out-of-date model of CPD (for example, the stress placed on the number of hours staff chalked up) to a broader concern about the quality and impact of their professional learning on students' attainment. Andy Boon and Toni Fazaeli, in a fascinating chapter which compares CPD in the two professions of the law and education, offer a definition of professional learning 'as a process of adjusting practice in the light of experience [and, I would add, research] in order to be more efficient and effective' (p. 35).

The good news is that, according to surveys carried out by the IfL, 'an overwhelming 98 per cent of members were exceeding the minimum number of hours required' (Sue Colquhoun and Jean Kelly in Chapter 4, p. 59), but we now need to find out what changes took place as a consequence in the teaching of the tutor and in the learning of the students.

What, however, are the realistic chances of this becoming the next stage in the evolution of teaching within the sector, when the professional status of its teachers is being threatened by government proposals to employ untrained teachers; and when, as Denis Gleeson points out in Chapter 2, the FE workforce is already 'a casualised and untrained cohort of the wider teaching profession' (p. 23). He rightly points to the reluctance of government to relinquish its control of the pulleys and levers of the vocational education and training (VET) system that Ewart Keep has described as 'playing with the biggest train set in the world'.

Tutors within the FE and skills sector exercise their professionalism within the parameters set by government and management and those parameters are being drawn even more strictly. I want, however, to end on a note of hope. We do not live in a police or a totalitarian state; and teachers, once the door is closed, can still exercise considerable freedom about what and how to teach. One strategy that we could adopt is for us to become powerful, democratic professionals who not only know much more about TLA than government ministers or Ofsted inspectors, but who work collaboratively together with democratic practices and values in the interests of our students. We object to being treated as 'human resources' to be managed by administrators who have never taught; we want to be more than just employees, filling in the hours between 9am and 5pm; we are what no system of measurement will ever capture or appreciate – we are moral agents working to improve the lot of others.

Frank Coffield
Emeritus Professor of Education, Institute of Education, London University
9 April 2013

References

Coffield, F. (2012) Why the McKinsey reports will not improve school systems, *Journal of Educational Policy*, 27, 1, 131–149.

Department for Business, Innovation and Skills (DBIS) (2011) *New Challenges, New Chances*, London: DBIS.

Edwards, A. (ed.) (1997) *Separate but Equal? A Levels and GNVQs*, London: Routledge.

Hartley, D. (2007) The emergence of distributed leadership in education: Why now?, *British Journal of Educational Studies*, 55, 2, 202–214.

Hartley, D (2009) The management of education: from distributed leadership to collaborative community, *Journal of Educational Administration and History*, 2, 1–15.

McNay, I. (2012) Leading strategic change in higher education – closing the implementation gap, *Leadership and Governance in Higher Education*, 4, 46–69.

Introduction and overview

Sue Crowley

An unequivocal characteristic of professionalism is expertise and the obligation to remain up to date in such professional expertise. Most professional bodies acknowledge this and require their members to undertake regular relevant continuing professional development (CPD). As the pace of change increases through globalisation and technological innovation the need for CPD is ever greater. However this CPD is required within a context of intensification of work, pressure of time and fiscal constraint, and the completion of CPD under such conditions can often seem an imposition and its practice can become tokenistic. Much of the research associated with CPD suggests that much CPD is not seen by professionals as valuable, worthwhile or having any impact on their practices.

In order to flourish in the current context of globalisation and fiscal constraints, organisations need to develop creativity and innovation; such capabilities are much more prevalent in organisations and systems that have a very strong learning culture, i.e. learning organisations. There is an irony in the fact that there is a paucity of such organisations amongst public sector organisations whose focus should be education and learning. Brighouse and Moon cite an OECD survey carried out in 2012 across 28 countries: 'Three out of four teachers surveyed reported that attempting innovative approaches in the classroom would not be encouraged by senior managers' (Brighouse and Moon, 2013).

Managerialist contexts and systems, with strong hierarchical and bureaucratic structures and characterised by risk aversion, prevent innovation and creativity and we need to explore different approaches to organisational development in order to foster a learning culture.

More traditional concepts of professionalism are also inappropriate for the twenty-first century and this orthodoxy of professionalism needs to be challenged. By reframing professionalism we may be able to see how a better approach to organisational development than the managerialism characteristic of many public and private sector organisations might be created through individual, collective and organisational learning and development. Professional bodies have a key role to play here.

This book therefore sets out to consider CPD as an ongoing process and to explore what 'blockers and boosters' there are to truly effective and efficient CPD and how they might be addressed. The catalyst for this book was one particular, comparatively new professional body, the Institute for Learning (IfL) but the exploration is relevant to all individuals, teams, organisations and professional bodies who are involved in promoting professional learning.

The Institute for Learning (www.ifl.ac.uk) is the professional body for teachers and trainers working in the further education (FE) and skills sector. The 3 million students served annually by FE teachers and trainers is highly diverse in terms of age, background, the context in which they learn and the programmes of learning that they follow. Many learners themselves will be following professional programmes of study. IfL members are recognised as having 'dual professionalism' in that most begin their careers as subject/vocational specialists and then enter the FE and skills arena to become professional teachers or trainers. They have been required, through legislation, over the last four years, to declare a minimum of 30 hours CPD each year which is usually focused on a balance between their specialism and teaching skills. This CPD was randomly sampled by IfL annually.

IfL wanted to offer an exemplar model for promoting and incentivising the best and most effective professional practices and central to this is professional learning and development. In order to achieve this IfL set out four years ago to collect a vast amount of data about the professional development of its membership to help establish what the professionals themselves identified as effective and efficient approaches to improving professional practices, to feed the findings back to the membership (87,000 in March 2013) and to measure the impact on their practices. This has become an iterative process. The diversity of the contexts in which they practise, their wide range of specialist subject expertise and their understanding of the processes of learning make this group of professionals ideal material for this research and the findings have important repercussions for all professionals and their learning.

IfL shared the emerging findings with a range of other professional bodies, with researchers and academics and with its membership. These others in turn then shared their observations and research findings with IfL. One of the results is this book.

The book focuses on bringing together research and practice around professional learning and links individual professional learning and collective professional learning to organisational learning, leadership and the management of change. Professionals who expect to and are able to continuously learn and unlearn are able to accommodate change readily as part of their professional development, a crucial attribute of twenty-first century professionalism. Whilst CPD is the most prevalent term for the process of updating and improving knowledge, skills and practices, the book refers to professional learning because such previous terms as CPD have been impoverished by the context in which they are applied and enacted and it is important to focus on learning as the key outcome.

Each chapter is different in style and approach, inviting the reader to reframe the challenges of professional learning. Different chapters do not offer solutions so much as a range of perspectives and raise the key questions that we hope help to frame a valuable discourse for all stakeholders around professionalism, professional learning and organisational development.

A powerful theme throughout the book is the concept of professional learning as a collective activity. One cannot be a professional in isolation. It takes place in a context that has political, social and cultural influences. Agents who exert that influence shape which behaviours are perceived as professional and hence our understanding of professionalism. For instance, a political agenda might shape our understanding of standards and accountability; the social context and our peers shape notions of professional identity, status and legacy; the cultural context in which we carry out professional behaviours itself shapes those behaviours so that the organisational health of our work environment and the wider environment affects our ability to practise professionalism. Practising professionalism implies an obligation to professional colleagues and the public good; it is not static but it is ever-changing and always demanding. Implicit in the concept of being professional is a commitment to continuous learning. Understanding how we learn and what influences that learning helps us to learn more effectively. The book explores the range of barriers and enablers to highly effective professional learning.

Whilst the main findings focus on the FE and skills sector the work is highly relevant and transferable to the rest of the education sector and indeed other public services which rely on large numbers of professional practitioners. Given the current situation with the upheaval to school systems and structures (particularly in relation to initial teacher education), the radical changes in higher education (HE) in the wake of the increase in student fees and the governments skills agenda, understanding how to achieve efficient and effective professional learning is crucial to producing a resilient and confident teaching workforce that will make the best of the challenges faced. A range of agents can support and facilitate this learning including individual teachers and trainers, their colleagues, their employers and their professional bodies. Students, parents and employers as well as government will want more reassurance that they are getting the best and most up to date teaching and learning. This is little different to patients expecting their general practitioner to be up to date in their medical practice or clients expecting their lawyer to know the latest relevant legislation and case law.

The book draws on practices in other public sectors to challenge and support its assumptions. It will be very relevant to all those who have an interest in considering what it means to be a professional in the twenty-first century and how to develop and extend professional learning in themselves and their professional colleagues. But it is also relevant to leaders of organisations as it also focuses on how leaders can promote professional learning within their organisations to create a workforce that is hungry to develop and to continue learning, to extend their professional practices and their organisation's capacity for learning and development. Finally, it is also of relevance to those who are the guardians of professional bodies and who lead the thinking around concepts and practices involved with being professional. Learning organisations (Burgoyne, 1999) with expansive learning environments (Fuller and Unwin, 2004b) are best able to adapt to the rapidly changing context in which they function and to ensure they offer the best services possible.

Chapter 1 explores what we mean by professionalism. Introducing a new professional body such as the IfL in the twenty-first century to a diverse sector such as FE and skills has thrown up some interesting challenges. It explores the challenge of introducing a professional body to a sector where managerialism is pervasive and considers how this affects individuals' readiness to engage with a professional body. Many in the sector already belong to a well-established professional body associated with their subject or vocational specialism, others have never belonged to a professional body. Different professional bodies imply different concepts of professionalism leading to potential dissonance. We have a concept within the FE and skills sector of dual professionalism (Robson, 2006) as teachers and trainers in our sector not only have to display professionalism with regard to their vocational or subject specialism but also as professional teachers with an expertise in pedagogy. Tensions and synergies can be created through this dual role. For the Institute therefore a key issue was engaging its membership in dialogue about what the term 'professionalism' means to them and therefore what they wanted their professional body to represent and uphold. This chapter is informed by much of the literature written about professionalism but is also informed by the debate conducted with IfL's members.

Establishing the type of professionalism members of a profession might want and therefore what sort of professional body members require exposes the professional identities that people hold. It tells us where they are on a continuum of the professionalism concept from the technical/rational model through the interpretative/constructivist to the critical and creative model (Boud, 2010). In Chapter 2 Denis Gleeson helps us to understand and respect practitioners' readiness or not to develop and extend their professional identity. He proposes that the concept of professionalism is socially constructed, so is shaped and defined by agency and structure. He suggests that the professional identity of FE teachers and trainers is perhaps more complex and diverse than in many professions and certainly than that of the school and higher education sectors. Professional identity is further contrived by employers and government who have a strong mediating effect between the teacher, their students and the public at large. He suggests that the rhetoric of professional autonomy contrasts sharply with the reality of teachers' lived experiences. This deprofessionalisation, he suggests, has a negative impact on the ability of the education system to support economic growth and social cohesion. He calls for a democratisation of 'pedagogy, professionalism and practice'. Individuals need to be clear about what it means to them to claim their professional status and what has shaped their understanding of professionalism to date. Furthermore, individuals need to understand how their professional identity has been shaped and how that in turn influences their professional behaviours.

In Chapter 3, Andy Boon and Toni Fazaeli give their perspectives on how professional bodies should and can promote professional learning in their membership and the challenges that poses. Some professional bodies have been around for hundreds of years and may have well-established and quite traditional views of what constitutes professional development. Chapter 3 charts the progress of professional bodies as they try to develop more effective approaches to CPD from an input model to an output model, with the challenges and pitfalls created along the way. The authors surface the tensions that can be created within a professional body between its regulatory and its developmental roles and the balance needed between positive incentives and incentives that can be construed as having a negative impact in order to maintain the high standards and quality that belonging to a professional body implies. They consider the interrelationship between professional bodies, employers, the state and the challenges this bring to individual and organisational autonomy. They focus on promoting both individual and collective learning and development that has significant impact on the improvement of professional practices. Finally they consider a range of roles and responsibilities that professional bodies uniquely can take on board to support and enable not just individual professionals but also their employing organisations.

Chapter 4 explores the concept of professional learning. Recent research has suggested that understanding how you learn has a positive impact on the learning process: 'Meta cognition is critical because it leads to the generalised improvement in learning capabilities' (Dixon, 1998: 40). Much professional learning is reactive; we realise (or we are told) we need to know something in order to progress so we find out (or we are told) where to get the information or how to develop the skills. The IfL wanted its members to take a more proactive approach. It wanted to explore with its members what they felt was the most effective and efficient way to carry out professional learning, to support them in identifying what it was they did not know, how best to learn it and then to establish whether it had the appropriate impact on practice and the learners they serve. In this chapter Sue Colquhoun and Jean Kelly chart the progress made to date, the challenges that were met and draws on other relevant research to provide an evidence base for the description of the qualities that characterise effective professional learning. They then consider how to extend individual and collective capacities and capabilities for such professional learning.

The reactive approach to professional learning described above rarely pays attention to the impact it should have on our practices. Something is not right so we do something in response but rarely follow up. Clarity about the impact we want from professional learning helps to determine 'the what and the how' of our learning so we need to be clear about the impact we expect before we embark on that learning journey. When impact measures are developed they are often instrumental and reflect reliability more than validity and this in turn determines what professional learning we focus upon. In Chapter 5, Vivienne Porritt considers different approaches to measuring impact, evaluating its effectiveness and how determining and measuring that impact in itself can be a useful tool for professional learning.

In Chapter 6, Fiona Mackay and Paul Wakeling consider how leaders of organisations can promote professional learning and why this promotion is so necessary to the health and success of the organisation. A meta-analysis of research (Robinson, Hohepa, and Lloyd, 2009) looking for correlation between leadership of educational establishments and learner performance found that the only significant positive correlation was whether the leaders themselves were visibly a learner. Leaders are central through their leadership behaviours to creating a culture of continuous learning so consideration of what those leadership behaviours might look like is essential. There is a great deal of propositional theory about how to create and lead a learning organisation but implementing those theories can be extremely challenging and some of these challenges are surfaced and explored. This chapter therefore focuses not only on individual and collective learning and leadership behaviours but on how these influence organisational health, learning and performance.

In 2012 the government set up an enquiry into vocational pedagogy chaired by Frank McLoughlin, principal of a large FE college. What makes for effective vocational learning is an area of research that has been largely overlooked. Much of the vocational learning that takes place across the country is within the FE and skills arena. Professional learning is a subset of vocational learning but there is an assumption that professional learning applies to teachers and that vocational learning, much of which is also work-based, applies to their learners. In Chapter 7 Sue Crowley examines how closely the two, professional and vocational learning, are aligned, whether findings in one area can usefully inform the other and whether their separation is useful or destructive by perpetuating the disparity between vocational and academic learning. It considers whether, as teachers and trainers establish how they learn best, they might profit from transferring those approaches to their learners.

The final chapter pulls together some of the recurring themes and views them through a range of different lenses: that of the individual professional, collectives that the professional may be part of, their employing organisations and their professional bodies. This final chapter is not a concluding one because we believe the nature of professionalism and professional learning is ever-changing so the dialogue must continue.

Chapter 1

What sort of professionalism?

Sue Crowley

> The challenge to professionalism in the modern world lies in the handling of multiple discourses.
>
> The task of professionalism in the modern world lies in the critical deployment of discourse.
>
> The achievement of professionalism in the modern world lies in the discursive creation.
>
> (R. Barnett)

Overview

The concept of professionalism is highly contested and has changed over time. It has had a range of positive and negative connotations. This chapter charts the journey of the concept and suggests why it is time to revise our understanding of professionalism to meet the challenges of the twenty-first century. The key qualities of expertise, altruism and autonomy remain but these are qualified to reflect the new context of practice, and central to this is the impact of globalisation on current and future approaches to learning.

What sort of professionalism?

Today, a range of social, political, economic and cultural factors shape and influence multiple interpretations of the concept of professionalism. Some writers (e.g. Eraut, 1995) have suggested that the multiple interpretations of the concept have rendered it almost useless but I will argue that we need to understand how these factors have shaped both the meaning and practices of professionalism and that we need to explore ways in which the concept and practices can be redefined to create a useful and productive interpretation for the future. These multiple interpretations of professionals and professionalism reflect the historical legacy of the term and that legacy must be acknowledged and respected but it must not prevent us from exploration of a concept of professionalism that is a better adapted model for the uncertain and rapidly changing context unfolding in the twenty-first century.

This chapter therefore sets out to review the original meaning of professionalism, how and why its meaning has changed over time and why we need to reframe and refresh professionalism and professional practices again in order to meet future social, political, economic and cultural challenges. It then considers some of the barriers to this reframing, particularly in the further education (FE) and skills sector and how these barriers might be tackled.

Introduction

Originally the concept of professionalism grew out of the academy in the Middle Ages and was associated with study and becoming an expert in a particular field such as science, medicine or law. It was associated with scholarly activity. Such professionals strived to be as good as they could be mostly as seekers of truth and critical thinkers. Their expertise was then drawn upon for the public benefit. These assumed qualities of expertise and altruism earned them the right to act autonomously and this right was often enshrined in a code of ethical practices.

The concept was gradually extended to others with high levels of expertise but often associated with more practical work such as nurses, accountants, architects and teachers. Characteristically such professionalism was associated with expertise validated through formal qualifications, a commitment to public service and again, because of this, an earned autonomy and a trust that professionals, with substantial knowledge, skills and experience, would always work in the public interest. Such professionals could be relied upon to give sound, well-informed advice that was in the best interests of their clients, and clients looked to them to make informed decisions on their behalf.

Clearly human nature being as it is some professionals claimed autonomy without earning it; they did not demonstrate the altruism expected of them. They became self-seeking at the expense of their clients, lazy in their approach to updating their expertise but protective and secretive of the knowledge they held, and keen to keep their profession exclusive often in order to attract high fees for the use of their expertise. Thus professionalism became associated, for some lay people and in some fields, with a range of negative connotations.

The evidence of this poor professional practice was powerfully and systematically exposed in the late 1970s and early 1980s and this exposure severely undermined the trust that the general public had placed in professionals. The creation of this lack of trust paved the way and smoothed the path for the introduction of New Public Management (NPM) in the 1980s (Hood, 1991). NPM evolved out of the political pressures to impose a market ideology on public services with an emphasis on competition in order to drive the fiscal pressure for efficiency, effectiveness and economy and to reduce public expenditure. To ensure efficiency, effectiveness and economy it was thought desirable to systematise and routinise professional practices and then to monitor and measure them in order to maximise value for money and ensure accountability. These strategies had worked well for the Fordist, private, mass production industries. Measurements allowed comparisons to be made between individuals, teams and organisations and made public so that the market could decide who should survive. 'There is a shift from trust in the professional and their relative autonomy to an emphasis on measurement and managerialism' (Frost, 2010:19).

The technology of the day meant that quantity and details of measurement could be achieved that were unthinkable previously. Thus the audit society/ culture was created. Highlighting the unprofessional behaviour of the few gave permission to distrust all professional practitioners and justify the introduction of monitoring and auditing for all. This was particularly noticeable in the public sector and was rationalised by the need for accountability to the taxpayer who was funding public services. To oversee this intense scrutiny required large numbers of managers and administrators so that the proportion of professionals to administrators working within organisations was reduced substantially throughout the 1980s and the 1990s. The role of professional practitioners within organisations was greatly devalued in relation to managers such that managers' remuneration packages were larger and the main career path for a professional practitioner was to aspire to senior posts that were predominately managerial. There was a very clear shift in the power relationship between managers and the professional practitioner and this was especially the case in the FE and skills sector.

> With this those charged with improved production resort to increased supervision and bureaucratisation through more detailed rules and regulations, but which only has the apathy-preserving function on the 'workers', which locks the organisation into a vicious circle of repression, subversion and further repression. Nobody wins; neither the managers, nor the professionals, nor clients.
>
> (Bottery, 1996: 187)

The traditional culture of collegiality was diminished. In order to retain the desired appearance of working in the public interest professionals became compliant, conforming, risk averse and more insular. NPM reconfigured professionalism and the culture of the organisations in which professionals worked and reshaped professional behaviours. Professionals were actively discouraged from using their professional judgement, there was an increase in central government control as well as central control within the organisation and great emphasis was placed on the measurement of outputs as opposed to inputs or processes as indicators of quality and effectiveness. Autonomy, a hallmark of professionalism, was seriously undermined. Ironically this might have developed the desired efficiencies but it is at least debatable whether either effectiveness or economies have been achieved. The cost of audit, administration, quality assurance and the managers that monitor these systems arguably outweighed the economies and effectiveness achieved through monitoring the professionals. There has been partial recognition of this by successive governments with the rhetoric of 'bureaucracy busting' initiatives.

Furthermore the professional was no longer looked to and utilised as a resource for expertise, professional judgement, innovation or creativity; for example, curriculum development was shifted away from practitioners to government agency. This is not to say that there was no resistance to these developments. Gleeson and Shain (1999) argue that some middle managers who had previously been practitioners in FE adopted a variety of strategies to undermine top down managerial imposition that they felt was inappropriate. They argued that there were middle managers who rejected managerialism and resisted it, 'unwilling compliers', others embraced it and became 'willing compliers' but the majority responded as 'strategic compliers' who bent the rules and protected their colleagues from the more extreme demands of managerialism whilst remaining focused on the needs of their learners and retaining their professional practices and identity.

Globalisation and professional attributes

Managerialism relies on hierarchical, bureaucratic organisational structures that are characteristically inflexible; its systems of accountability are, by definition, backward looking rather than futures thinking, e.g. occupational competencies are based on the occupation as it has been rather than based on future requirements; effectiveness is measured against past performances in similar systems rather than more creative approaches. However, the new order heralded by globalisation requires new thinking and innovative ways of dealing with rapid change. Managerialism and its associated bureaucracy and hierarchy cannot accommodate such innovation and is, by its nature, resistant to such change. There is a current discourse around organisational development that suggests that the new frame of reference should be 'leaderism' (O'Reilly and Reed, 2010) which emphasises a form of leadership that is collaborative, dispersed and democratic. This can be construed as paradoxical and confusing, as leadership in this context is considered as a quality open to all rather than the quality of an individual even though it suggests an individual may be needed to promulgate 'leaderism'. Much of the discourse around leaderism, however, does point to qualities that might usefully be considered as shaping new notions of professionalism and the organisational development required to sustain this new order.

What follows is an attempt to consider the impact of globalisation and how professionalism needs to be reframed to meet the challenges and opportunities that globalisation brings.

Globalisation is a term used to describe a number of developments that are interrelated and which have profound effects on the way in which individuals and groups now interact across the globe. Many of these developments have emerged through the impact of information and communications technologies. Some key developments include those listed below.

The information explosion

Vast quantities of information are now available to all through the World Wide Web. George Bernard Shaw's description of professionalism as a 'conspiracy against the laity' is now hard to sustain when the laity have such easy access to what was previously considered exclusive knowledge that was only available to the professional.

The uncertain future

Increased speed of scientific and technological discovery and application is unprecedented so that we find it difficult to imagine how we will be working and learning in the near future. We only have to consider the speed of development of the mobile phone which already allows for multiple applications and emailing, access to the World Wide Web, satellite navigation and a mechanism for payment for goods and services. Professional knowledge requires constant updating and we often do not know what it is that we need to know or can know.

The changing nature of knowledge

The nature of expertise is changing as our understanding of knowledge shifts from the idea of uncontestable truths, facts and figures to acceptance of the need to unlearn previous givens, question previous assumptions and recognise the legitimacy of multiple interpretations. Professionals can still lay claim to an expertise but it is less about exclusive knowledge and more about learning processes.

There is a growing awareness that although subjects or disciplines are useful ways of categorising knowledge they are artificial and man-made. Their boundaries can limit our ways of thinking about the world. Sharing the ways of thinking in one discipline with those of another can often lead to more creative ways of thinking, doing and problem-solving. The health service is a leader in this field recognising that starting with and treating the whole person (and sometimes their immediate family) and all of their needs is more successful than focusing on one aspect of their health and welfare. This implies that professionals not only need to understand the nature of their clients more fully but also the nature of their colleagues and to be prepared to work across disciplines as an approach to more creative problem-solving. 'High-level demanding work is not held together by professions or disciplines but by the nature of the work itself' (Boud, in Bradbury *et al.*, 2010: 31).

Multiculturalism and diversity

Increased migration, immigration and social networking are creating more multicultural societies, and globalisation means many of us work if not face to face then remotely with many in other countries and from different cultures. This transnational contact challenges cultural and linguistic norms and leads to different ways of seeing and being. Acknowledging this further increases multiple interpretations and the contestability of knowledge and truth. Working with such diversity can be enriching, stimulating and creative; we are all learning for an unknowable future and need to keep our minds open to other ways of being. So where does this lead professionalism?

Reframing professionalism

Very few of us would be comfortable with being described as unprofessional, it is an undesirable label; it has lots of consistently negative connotations with regard to implied behaviours, attitudes and values. However, its opposite, i.e. professional, is a much more contested term that has multiple constructs and multiple interpretations describing varying behaviours, attitudes and values which may have both negative and positive connotations. The term is currently, as Ginsberg (1996) suggests a double-edged sword.

Ginsberg's concept of 'power with' as opposed to 'power over' can and should be central to a future concept of professionalism and in the current context can claim pragmatism as 'the laity' are in a much better situation with their substantial access to information to challenge inappropriate professional stances. In the case of FE and skills this means power with all the stakeholders in our sector, particularly our students, employers, local communities, third-sector organisations and parents. It means acknowledging that the source of our expertise is not the only valid one. For example, many of us are very aware that our students are more adept at information and communications technology (ICT) than we are, and local communities can teach us much about the teaching and learning needs of learners.

A professionalism that acknowledges the contestability of knowledge whilst retaining expertise and professional responsibility requires continuous updating and development. The concept of 'meister' is no longer possible as the content and context of professional expertise is ever-changing and it is a challenge to keep totally up to date, though this must remain a constant aspiration. Whilst we will retain high levels of expertise in our professional practices we have to acknowledge that the client and other stakeholders will themselves have other relevant areas of expertise or bring different but valid perspectives to the table. We need the expertise of the client to inform our expert perspectives and we have a professional obligation to, as Bottery describes it, pre-arm the client, giving them 'a wider frame of reference by which to understand what the problem is' (Bottery, 1996: 193). We need to seek the ideas and opinions of all stakeholders. We need to understand the cultural perspective of others; we need to engage in interdisciplinary dialogue which requires more listening and questioning and less telling. We need to be open to new ways of perceiving the world and to be prepared to re-evaluate our notions of truth and knowledge. We need to be ready to explore with others from very different backgrounds issues of significance to our professional practices. We need to be networked. This does not mean that we have to reach consensus about how we proceed but it does mean we need to understand why others hold their views and they need to understand why we hold ours and therefore why we practise as we do. We need to respect and value diversity rather than to strive for conformity.

Altruism and expertise are still central to the concept of professionalism as is autonomy but our expertise is not solely knowledge-based and cannot be exclusive and it is an autonomy that comes from interdependence rather than independence. Professional reframing requires a particular understanding of autonomy based on informed decision-making whilst recognising that part of the informing must come from understanding the diverse perspective of others including those whom we serve. Professionals need to be agents in their own work and learning as well as in the work and learning of others.

Bottery suggests that the revision of the practice of altruism for teachers in this new context requires a new ethical framework:

> An ethic of truth disclosure: which must override personal advantage.
> An ethic of subjectivity: for each individual must recognise the limits of his or her perceptions, the individuality of his or her values.
> An ethic of reflective integrity: as each professional recognises the limits of personal perception, of the need to incorporate many understandings of a situation.
> An ethic of humility: as each professional recognises that subjectivity means that personal fallibility is not a failing but a condition of being human.
> An ethic of humanistic education: of the duty of the professional to help the client help themselves.
>
> (Bottery, 1996: 193)

It is against this backdrop that writers have tried to reframe professionalism. A recent report from the RSA, *Rethinking the Importance of Teaching* (2012) written by Louise Thomas, suggests that the concept of the professional teacher as a transmitter of knowledge is inadequate for the current era. It proposes three different models of professionalism – democratic professionalism, activist professionalism, research-based professionalism. These are not seen as exclusive of one another and may overlap but they identify aspects of professionalism that are not encouraged in the present political climate. She suggests that teachers need to develop professional practices that demonstrate their expertise in knowledge and pedagogy, acting in collaboration with multiple partners. Coffield and Williamson (2011) talk of the need for a democratic professionalism to replace managerial professionalism.

> Its core is an emphasis on co-operation between teachers and all other partners in education – students, parents, and business and community leaders. Democratic professionals exercise wider responsibilities than simply being in charge of the education of a group of students, which include working with others to improve the institution they work in, the educational system and their local community.
>
> (Coffield and Williamson, 2011: 72)

Such a model of democratic professionalism they suggest will not evolve from a 'top down' initiative but is more likely to come about with a movement from the grass roots upwards; I would suggest that top down and bottom up is likely to be more successful; it needs a commitment from all stakeholders. Such a movement, however, would need co-ordination and high levels of trust; currently these are unlikely to come from most employers or government but provide a legitimate role and opportunity for a professional body.

The spectrum of professional maturity – the nature and nurture of professionalism

How we view and enact professionalism depends on our prior knowledge and experiences of professionalism, the stage we are at in our professional life cycle and the context in which we carry out our professional practices. It is also dependent on our preferred way of being, including personality traits. It involves both nature and nurture. Some of us respond to managerial professionalism well; we like being told what to do and how to do it; we like the technical rationalist approach for all sorts of reasons. Others may resent the managerialism, the removal of autonomy but relish the opportunity to extend our professional practices, engage with colleagues in professional development, dialogue, continuous improvement and updating activities. Others may want to constantly challenge their own professional practices through study and action research. Coffield and Williamson recognise different professionals will respond differently to change and categorise them as enthusiasts, superficial adopters, unengaged and resisters but this does not explain why individuals respond in these different ways; it explains their actions but not the reasons for their actions and unless we understand what motivates their behaviours it is difficult to move forward.

On entering the profession, we all have an idea about what qualities make a good professional teacher, which of those we inherently possess and which we will need to develop and practise. This concept of professionalism is personal and is primarily a social construct built usually from our experiences as students; we have all watched and experienced teachers we have liked and disliked and have drawn conclusions from that about what makes a good teacher. For most of us that shapes our initial thinking about the type of teacher that we want to be. However what I think is good teaching practice from the perspective of the student may be different to what others might prefer, so our own learning preferences will also shape our idea of professional practices. Some of us like clarity; a clear sense of direction, some of us like surprise; we might like to figure stuff out for ourselves or we might like to be told exactly what to do. So our notions of professional practices are developed through an interplay of nature (our personal preferences) and nurture (our prior life experiences of teaching and learning).

For most of us, when we start teaching or training we are preoccupied with knowing our subject or vocational specialism so well that we can stand up and teach it to others; this is far more demanding than just knowing your subject and as a consequence we focus on 'What am I, the teacher, doing?'. We take the rest of our role seriously and try to do that which is required of us in the preparation of lesson plans usually to a set format, schemes of work, assessment records, etc. As we gain confidence in the teaching material and the programmes we are teaching, most of us shift to 'What are they the students doing?'. It is usually at this point we realise that others have different preferred ways of learning so that the way we like to be taught and have therefore tried to teach may not be the most helpful way for some of our learners. To meet the needs of these other learners we have to move out of our comfort zones as teachers and move into less well-known territory; we have to critically reflect on our professional practices individually but perhaps more importantly with colleagues. We have to engage in professional dialogue about what effective teaching and learning looks like for our students. We have to take risks with unfamiliar approaches to teaching and learning. To do this we need to again engage with colleagues for ideas, perhaps go on teacher development programmes; read up about different approaches to teaching and learning, observe other teachers teaching in other contexts or using different approaches and/or talk to our students about how best to help them. Some of us will want to understand the theory behind the use of different approaches, how students learn, and brain science. Others will want to conduct action research projects with their students individually or as part of a group of teachers to measure the impact of different approaches.

This suggests a continuum of professional practices where at one end we have the technical rationalist approach which is primarily reactive and individualistic; further along the continuum we have an interactive approach to professionalism where we engage with a community of practice to enhance our professionalism, and at the other end of the spectrum we have a community of exploration (Coffield and Williamson, 2011) where perhaps the most innovative and critical approach to professional learning and teaching occurs and extends well beyond the confines of the organisation. This continuum from reactive through interactive to proactive approaches often, but not always, is a reflection of the teacher life cycle. Many of us will enter the profession at different points along the continuum. Some will enter and choose to stay at the reactive end, some start further along the continuum and others may remain at different points along the continuum, but few will start as proactive professionals.

Most individuals who regard themselves as practising professionals do demonstrate some levels of professionalism but they often see this professional behaviour as between them, their conscience and those they immediately seek to serve, usually their students and their employer. They are often preoccupied with the concept of professional meaning an individual expert rather than a collective entity, some are unaware of their responsibility to their professional colleagues and others who are served by their profession but with whom they have no direct contact. They do not acknowledge their professional responsibility to all clients, be they students or patients or the public at large. Most of all they do not acknowledge their professional responsibilities to themselves.

When IfL took responsibility for the government regulation that all FE and skills teachers and trainers should carry out annual continuing professional development, a constant preoccupation of our membership was with what the Institute considered to be professional development; it was extremely rare for anybody to assume that they were best placed to determine this themselves. When working with groups across the country who came to understand this, many would describe it as a light-bulb and liberating moment that they could control their own development. Others, however, felt that by not defining what they should do as professional development IfL was avoiding its responsibility and duty; they were conditioned into being told and not taking responsibility for their own development; they wanted to 'get it right' in the eyes of what they saw as the authority. Maybe they were uncomfortable with the autonomy it offered or just not used to it as individuals developed within the audit culture, maybe they were frightened of failure or just not sure how to proceed.

The crucial questions then are: Why do we all enact different types of professionalism? and How do we encourage and enable each other to adopt a new, more challenging form of professionalism to be not just articulated but enacted? How do we make our behaviours match our good intentions? Where an individual starts and finishes will often depend on the context in which they practise and how conducive it is to change and development. If the reactive approach is the way I am most comfortable with, is the way I would prefer to teach and to behave, is the only way I know, how can I be encouraged to extend and develop my practices? What incentives could there be? And if the culture I work in is one of compliance and blame then my motivation to change is minimal, my resistance to change and development is strong, easily justified and often I interpret change as yet more imposition. However, if I work in an environment where colleagues are supportive, where high-quality professional practices are highly prized and regarded as central to the work of the organisation and where mistakes are recognised as learning opportunities for all then the motivation to share, improve and develop are strong and offer intrinsic motivational rewards through peer and student recognition and job satisfaction. If there is within the organisation a sharing of resources, of thinking and discussion about professional practice and learning and an enthusiasm to explore beyond the confines of the organisation, then movement along the continuum from reactive to proactive is likely to be more prevalent.

The concept of good professional practices is primarily – as explored in Chapter 2 – a social construction and as such can be improved and developed. The improvement and development are led by the individual but can be very effectively fuelled by the students and colleagues around them, the culture of the organisation in which they practise and the steer given by an effective professional body alongside government policy that promotes this approach. As true professionals, we can and should all influence this by encouraging interaction between colleagues and across our professional sector.

	Reactive	Interactive	Proactive
Behaviours	Competent and reliable	Competent and reliable	Competent and reliable
	Willing or reluctant complier	Strategic complier	Strategic complier but challenging with an evidence base
	Dependent on authority for direction	Confident to claim authority	Interdependent 'earned' autonomy
	Individualistic	Social and holistic approach to learning	Maximise all resources available to promote learning
	Risk averse and insular	Risk tolerant, curious and collaborative; wanting impact but not sure why and what – communities of practice	Experimental and measured risk taking with an emphasis on impact and evidence based practice – communities of discovery
	Technico/rationalist approach to accountability	Using more than a tick box approach to accountability	Devises impact measures that are both reliable and valid
	Quality control output orientated	Input and process approach to quality assurance	Total quality approach focused on input, processes and outputs
	Backward looking e.g. benchmarking	Culture of continuous improvement	Futures thinking and continuous improvement
Attitudes	Teacher focussed – individual learning capacity is limited; learning is innate?	Learner focused with some assumptions and biases	Learning focused – suspended judgements, assumptions and perceptions; everyone has the capacity to learn and develop
	What am I doing?	What are they doing?	What are we doing?
Values	Doing the thing right	Doing the right thing	Doing the right thing right
Professional dialogue	Superficial, minimal with restricted use of language	Increasingly challenging with use of powerful questions and analysis of data	Rigorous and systematic with integrated analysis of data
Reflective practice	Spasmodic, superficial, individual and tokenistic	More regular and collective with deeper levels of learning	Collective challenging with a focus on impact

Figure 1.1 A spectrum of professional maturity.

Conclusions

The seeds of distrust about public sector professionals and their professionalism were sown by James Callaghan in his now famous Ruskin Speech in 1976 and were carefully nurtured through the 1980s, 1990s and the early part of this century. NPM has profoundly undermined the trust and original positive attributes of professionalism so that many of us now struggle with the lack of clarity and consequent usefulness of the concept. Perhaps some of the disrepute was well founded but a greater influence was that the traditional concept of professionalism needed challenging because it was no longer fit for purpose in the twenty-first century. Globalisation requires a reframing of professionalism.

- Globalisation is characterised by multiculturism and diversity so that we need to revisit the ethics and values appropriate to the current context.
- Knowledge is now recognised as more frequently contestable so that a professional's expertise and responsibilities are even more crucial and require continuous updating as well as developing a role in what Bottery refers to as prearming the client so that they too can contest knowledge legitimately and productively; this requires that professionals establish a different and equal power relationship with those they serve.
- Globalisation emphasises our interdependence so that professionals can still claim autonomy but an autonomy that is earned through informed decision-making which can only come about by an open sharing of knowledge, assumptions and opinions with multiple and interdisciplinary stakeholders.
- Communication and information technologies continue to develop rapidly so that we cannot predict how we will be working in the future. This creates a need to remain interdependent and networked to one another. It requires us to enable our students to embrace uncertainty and change productively and to be comfortable and inspired by such conditions ourselves.

Professionalism signifies different things to different people at different times. What is important is that we recognise that it is a process rather than a product; it is something that we constantly work upon and is always aspirational. The IfL in 2012 published a summary of a framework for professionalism for the FE and skills sector that drew heavily upon the opinions of our membership and this was summarised 'with three fundamental tenets: the learners' and public interest is central; professionals are dedicated to the highest standards of practice; and professionals uphold ethical values' (IfL, 2012b:2). The values that were also drafted through a consultation process are summarised as: Professionalism, Development and Innovation, Autonomy, Integrity and Equality.

The value of this summary lies not in the summary itself but the professional dialogue that many engaged in through the process of its production (IfL, 2012b). Understanding professionalism has to be an iterative process; as we develop and the context in which we practise alters, our professional priorities shift, but central to professionalism is the commitment to lifelong individual and collective professional learning that becomes more rigorous, deep and systematic in our attempts to continuously improve. We cannot tell what future learning we need to carry out but we are certain that it will be needed. Individuals and groups of professionals are always part of larger systems and these systems, be they employing organisations, professional bodies or governments, need to enable the enactment of a professionalism for the future. Such professionalism will be hard to sustain if organisations remain entrenched in managerialism and the form of accountability it provokes. Enactment of such a reframed professionalism must be built on a sound, well-articulated values base. It must be built on trust. Bottery (2003) describes three levels of trust. First, there is the interpersonal level of trust where being trusted is a manifestation and recognition of personal integrity and trustworthiness so that lack of trust implies a judgement of personal unworthiness. The meso level of trust is the trust we have in our employing organisations; this is often determined by the leaders of such organisations and is a reflection of how well the culture and ethos of the organisation aligns with the values of the individual. Lastly, there is the macro level of trust which occurs between individuals and wider groups such as politicians, the media and senior business leaders. At all three levels trust generation is a two-way process and to develop trust everybody has to be prepared to take risks and believe in the professionalism of those around them; this is where the real challenge lies. Who will take the first risky steps along the pathway to trust?

Chapter 2

Trading places
On *becoming* an FE professional

Denis Gleeson

Overview

This chapter explores the nature and purpose of professionalism in further education (FE) and lifelong learning, in a mainly English context. It explores the way
professional identity is constructed through the prism of competing power relations that find expression in teachers' work. In most developed economies, there
is an ongoing debate about the role educational professionals play in securing
economic prosperity and social inclusion. Equally, there is increasing scrutiny of
the education and training of those professionals, in improving teaching and
learning on the ground. International pressures on economic growth, competition and market reform have intensified that debate in recent years. While policy
attention has been given to successive skills and workforce reform programmes,
little is known about the practitioners who are the subjects of such reform. Recent
attempts to re-professionalise FE practitioners, through mandatory or voluntaristic means, have proved controversial (Department for Business, Innovation and
Skills: 2012a and 2012b). In a sector which has had more than its fair share of
market intervention, this contribution addresses issues of agency and structure
that impact on FE professionalism, in the wider context of public management
reform (Gleeson and Knights 2006). In exploring the role played by practitioners
in this process, the chapter argues for closer integration of sector, community and
stakeholder partnerships, through which professional practice becomes a shared
civic resource, rather than a centrally imposed market option.

Background

What constitutes professionalism across school, further education (FE) and
higher education (HE) practice is an elusive and contested concept. This is partly
to do with divergence in teacher education between the sectors, but is mainly
explained by long-standing cultural and historical traditions. Signs of recent con-
vergence involving school and FE/HE partnerships, associated with the raising
of the school leaving age (14–18+), appear positive but are in the balance, following the election of the Con-Dem coalition (Nuffield Foundation, 2008; Skills

Commission, 2011). However, while the regulatory controls of professionals in education across sectors may differ, they increasingly share much in common in the way invasive market and workforce reforms impact on FE practice. Historically, English liberal individualistic notions of the professions stressed their freedom to define the relationship between themselves and their clients directly, and without any mediation from a third-party employing organisation (Etzioni, 1969; Johnson, 1997). Though self-employed lawyers and, to a lesser extent, doctors and consultants have continued to enjoy the power and privileges of their independence, few today have avoided the erosion and absorption of their independence through the growth of corporate employers, government and the state (Gewirtz *et al.*, 2009).

In terms of locating the source of contemporary professional power, the ability to define the relationship between the occupation and its clients, public service employees, is heavily constrained by the state. However, the inability to define the relationship between the provider and consumer of professional services does not mean that everyone in public service is of the same status (gender, expertise and power), or that relations with learners, patients and clients are hegemony free (Gleeson and Knights, 2006). A major factor turns on the way professionals are viewed, as either part of the problem of modernisation or part of its solution. While the education, training and qualifications of professionals are largely mandatory, though under scrutiny, the power relations of the workplace and market are arguably more significant. The source of such tension has influenced successive government attempts to underplay professional autonomy in favour of institutional accountability, audit and inspection. Outwardly, the policy rhetoric is legitimated through efforts to improve the efficiency of public services that, in practice, include strong ideological and fiscal constraints (Keep and Mayhew, 2010). The process is not new. Essentially, market regulation and governance in education has, since the late 1970s following Jim Callaghan's Ruskin Speech (1976), gradually eroded municipal public authority at local level. The subsequent passing of the policy baton from Thatcher to Blair, on to the current 'Con-Dem' government, is one of a phased incursion of the neo-liberal project, through which centrally imposed market levers regulate the relationship between public professionals and the state. This, as we shall argue, is increasingly open to question as a credible means of growing capability and capacity in the complex relations between education, economy and society.

Introduction

In this context, the chapter focuses on the contested nature of teacher professionalism in FE, which now encompasses a rich field of research, policy and practice. Until recently, FE has been variously described as the 'Cinderella' service or the neglected 'middle child' of English education, due to its voluntaristic and entrepreneurial legacy (Foster, 2005). This, coupled with FE's technical and vocational ethos, has long resulted in it being overshadowed by schooling and

HE as the main avenues of opportunity for a rising middle class. In the past decade, however, FE has expanded to become a significant driver for modernising the UK economy, challenging traditional sector differences between school, FE/ HE and work. The most recent manifestation of this process has been to create a 'new discourse of FE' (Leitch, 2006), with FE at the centre of a *skills race* designed to advance the performance of a flagging UK economy. In this process, considerable importance has been attached to reforming the FE teacher labour force, at the heart of a wider lifelong learning and skills agenda (Brown, 2009; Department for Business, Innovation and Skills, 2012b). This contribution explores the policy rhetoric of placing professionals at the centre of a mainly market and employer-led reform process, and the reality of its implementation by practitioners on the ground. While the chapter focuses mainly on FE practitioners, it draws parallels with wider areas of workforce reform in the public domain, where transitions from old to new forms of public management have been underpinned by both narrow pedagogic thinking, e.g. learning styles, behavioural objectives and skills, and invasive audit and performance cultures (Coffield, 2008).

On becoming

The nature of professional identities in FE is strongly influenced by asymmetrical factors associated with occupational experience, institutional cultures and external requirements, associated with inspection, managerialism and surveillance. Many practitioners entering FE come from established professional and trade backgrounds, accounting, business, catering, construction, engineering, hairdressing, the arts and wider fields. Such expertise often involves considerable work experience with young people and adults, in a variety of work settings. This, coupled with an average age of entry to the profession of 37, partly explains higher teacher retention rates in FE than school, beyond the first five years of professional life. FE teachers' prior qualifications, status and career progression into FE tends to be less linear and more complex than entry into school and HE though not exclusively so. The nature of the transition is marked by strong identities, linked to earlier career and job experience associated, for example, with being an engineer or caterer 'in teaching' (Venables, 1968; Tipton, 1973; Gleeson and Mardle, 1980). Career entry into FE teaching is not clear-cut, however, and is influenced by a variety of factors involving life-course transitions, divorce, illness, redundancy with other changing family circumstances and changing labour markets. If some accounts of practitioners are associated with an altruistic desire to put their expertise and experience back into the community, others talk of 'sliding' into FE through part-time work, often regarded as an unofficial apprenticeship into FE teaching (James and Biesta, 2007).

Such routes into FE are not new and reflect traditional patterns of professional recruitment linked to diverse and engendered occupational fields, which reflect the wider labour market. Overlain with this is a complicated proliferation of roles and job titles that characterise FE cultures and practices, defined as lecturer, tutor, trainer, mentor and work-based assessor. These definitions are also inter-connected with a diverse and fragmented range of academic, technical and vocational programmes, which include a combination of on and off-site work placements. If part-time and casual work practices offer a flexible response in meeting institutional and individual needs, they also reinforce deeper distinctions between core (career) and periphery (part-time) working practices, that impact on the professional lives of FE teachers and their careers. Associated with this are major challenges to do with race, gender and disability in the FE workforce (Colley *et al.*, 2003; Colley 2007), including evidence of homophobic bullying and the ongoing under-representation of minorities in leadership and manage-ment positions (LSIS, 2011: 7). Data from the LSIS *Summary Workforce Diversity Report 2011* reveals consistency over time in differences between part-time and full-time staff, by age, ethnicity and gender, with men remaining over-represented in senior management and technical staff roles. At the same time the gender profile of the sector remains predominantly female.

> Overall the analysis suggests that across the FE college, WBL and ACL work-forces, female staff were more likely to be working part-time than their male counterparts. In FE colleges in 2009–10, 70.7 per cent of part-time and 53.4 per cent of full-time staff were female. There were almost equal propor-tions of male and female teaching staff working full-time.
>
> (LSIS, 2011: 14)

While data relating to the subcontracted delivery of work programmes, within and outside FE, is not readily available, the picture of the FE workforce as a casu-alised and untrained cohort of the wider teaching profession remains largely in evidence. Despite its association with social inclusion, the 'alternative route' and 'second chance' provision, FE students and staff operate in highly segmented and differentiated teaching and learning cultures. With few notable exceptions, the impact and nature of such restrictions has been largely ignored in official reports championing workforce reform in the sector (Department for Business, Innovation and Skills, 2012b). According to Colley *et al.* (2007) (see James and Biesta, 2007; Simmons, 2008), the more noticeable effects of market reform have reinforced rather than challenged gendered and racialised divisions that have had ongoing de-professionalising effects on FE practitioners (Shain, 2013).

Though FE colleges are officially independent of central government control, the sector operates within a context of 'licensed autonomy', with professionals treated as 'trusted servants', rather than as 'empowered professionals' (Avis, 2009). A continuing feature of the market process is that it holds professionals and institutions responsible for the failures of policy implementation rather than acknowledging that the policy itself might be flawed and that, in turn, reinforces government's disenchantment with a public sector policed by self-serving profes-sional interests. The ideological process involved has a deeper purpose in distan-cing accountability away from public and civic values, towards the private interests of a market and consumer-driven economy. In a recent Ofsted report, Coffey (2012) is critical of the influence that subcontractors pose to the quality and accountability of provision:

> accountability challenges linked into governance ... (is) a strong area of concern for us ... all too often we see providers that are delivering more and more qualifications that are clearly not meeting the needs of employers or indeed increasing the individual learner's chance of employment.
>
> (Ofsted 2012: 1)

Professionals operating in such circumstances often have little room for manoeuvre when working on short-term contracts and in the delivery of pro-scribed programmes. At the same time, FE professionalism is pragmatic and situ-ated in a recurring set of unstable conditions and is often highly innovative and adaptable, in spite of rather than because of government policy. Recent research points to the way agency and structure combine in the construction of profes-sional identities, and how practitioners handle diversity and contradictions in the FE workplace, in different ways. As Bathmaker (2006) argues, deficit assump-tions of teachers as dupes or devils, either working with or resisting the system, are overly simplistic. Creative tensions cannot simply be reduced to either or caricatures of the multiplicity of professional roles and identities that are often associated with disruptions and discontinuities associated with the lived profes-sional experience. According to Knights and Wilmott (1999), such experience can equally stimulate creative and potentially innovative practices, in the spaces generated by fragmentation and market failure.

Despite evidence of strategic compliance, which allows professionals to operate within and against audit cultures, the room for discretion is restricted by the own-ership of external inspection and audit cultures (Stronach *et al.*, 2002). Pressure to get results against external performance indicators may not only skew provision but also maintain existential tensions between what professionals believe in, and what they have to do to get by. The processes involved in separating off formal and non-formal knowledge in the teaching and learning environment has contra-dictory effects. At one level, this finds expression in pathologies of creative com-pliance in the form of fabrication and gamesmanship surrounding performance targets, and the need to survive (Ball, 2003). At another level, the sheer pervasive-ness and weight of audit, inspection and funding constraints generates resistance and creative strategies that may make targets work for institutions, but not neces-sarily for improving the teaching and learning processes involved (Beck, 2009).

Wider research in the public sector reveals that such practices are not associ-ated with FE alone. Parallel research in the fields of schooling, HE, legal practice, medicine, nursing, probation and social work, indicates the ways in which expan-sive and restrictive professional practices are constructed through the contested micro-politics of the workplace (Knights and Wilmott, 1999; Kitchener, Kirkpatrick and Whipp, 2000; Clarke and Newman, 2009).

By definition the 'ecologies of practice' involved are likely to vary significantly between different professional fields and practices. A cross section of research indicates how professionalism is influenced by constructions of identity through different processes – 'tacit knowledge' (Eraut, 1994), 'principled infidelity' (Hoyle and Wallace, 2007), 'invisible trade' (Kitchener *et al.*, 2000), 'added value' (Robson, 2006) – and 'cultural/political fit' (Newman and Nutley, 2003; Newman, 2007). One such example, specific to FE, is that of 'underground working practices' that involve the input of vast amounts of unpaid time and flexible working routines, over and above official requirements, to get the job done (James and Diment, 2003). While such working routines form much of the backbone of FE practice, they constitute invisible pedagogies of power (Bernstein, 1996; Bourdieu, 1998), which keep exploitative forms of professional identity and self-governance in place, and away from view. This suggests that officially defined regulatory mechanisms of audit and market control are perhaps less influential than those forms of self-surveillance and governance internalised by professionals in the everyday practice of their work (Foucault, 1997). In these circumstances the question arises about what forms of FE teacher education and training programmes could, or should, bring non-formal pedagogies of practice to the surface, beyond the familiar mantras of skills, standards and delivery.

Though expansive and restricted professional cultures in FE operate alongside one another, evidence of the positive impact of initial teacher training (ITT) and continuing professional development (CPD) on FE improvement remains contested (Department for Business, Innovation and Skills, 2012b; Ofsted, 2012). However, recent research demonstrates how established management and leadership regimes can have a significant impact on professional cultures in FE, as practitioners interact with tutors, teachers and other trainees in college and workplace environments (Nuffield Foundation, 2008; Skills Commission, 2011). At the same time, the construction and shuffling of identities in FE is a complex process. It finds expression in the FE ITT process that is a largely on the job in-service whilst often involving new challenges associated with the demands of academic study, writing and reflective practice. According to Lucas and Unwin (2009) the 'dual identities' associated with being both a teacher and a trainee generate deeper tensions in the gap between the rhetoric of standards and the reality of their implementation in the FE workplace.

One such example is the use made of lesson observation, ostensibly designed to help improve trainee development in the classroom or workshop, through tutor and mentor assessment. In practice, O'Leary (2012) argues that graded lesson observation has become normalised as a performative tool of managerial systems, which now requires a moratorium on its use. The study addresses the need for colleges and tutors to be given greater personal autonomy as to how they go about using observation, allowing them to develop their own systems that place professional learning at the forefront of the professionalisation process. In a related study with Smith, he argues that such cultures have become an integral rather than an accidental aspect of a market-charged environment in which status, job insecurity and redundancy contributed to the low morale of the staff involved (O'Leary and Smith, 2012). O'Leary and Smith's findings run parallel with Lucas and Unwin's research (Fuller and Unwin, 2004a; Lucas and Unwin, 2009) in identifying the way trainee teachers in FE are hampered in completing their initial teacher education (ITE) programmes, due to the often fragmented and restrictive practices in the FE workplace. They point to the shortcomings of senior management in recognising the dualities associated with being both a trainee and a worker, and the failure to provide the adequate time, resources and mentor support necessary to promote expansive professional learning.

Equally, there is evidence to suggest that mandatory standards became used as a performative tool of management, for which they were not initially intended. In such contexts, relationships of power and authority raise wider issues beyond the notion of dual identities, associated with deeper cultural and structural inequalities within the FE workforce (LSIS, 2011). According to Lucas and Nasta:

> The failure of FE teachers to make the transition from occupational to a professional track is complex and has not just been imposed through state regulation. One factor has been the relative weakness of intermediary bodies in FE that could have mediated the standards. Another lies in senior college managers and FE teachers themselves many of whom have been reluctant to be identified with school teachers and have defended their industrial past and differences with other sectors of FE.
>
> (Lucas and Nasta, 2010: 448)

While elements of this assessment ring true, historical ambivalence and resistance towards FE teacher education and training is, however, more in evidence among employers and institutions than practitioners and senior managers (Gleeson and Knights, 2006). Traditionally, such ambivalence is associated with the ownership and control of teacher development by colleges, employer, trade and professional organisations. This, coupled with pressures on senior managers to react more to the externally imposed requirements of state agencies, rather than developing their own strategies and sense of direction, represents a major challenge to leadership in the sector. Wider evidence suggests, however, that when senior managers engage in dialogue with their staff and students, the strategies which follow are more inclusive and productive than those based mainly on replicating external agendas (James and Biesta 2007). More recently, the downward pressure of audit, funding and managerial reform has generated regulatory regimes that continue to restrict autonomous leadership and professionalism, reinforcing a prevailing view that mandatory teacher education programmes have little to do with pedagogic improvement. In tracking earlier developments from the introduction of FENTO/LSDA, to LLUK/SVUK and IfL. Lucas, (2004), Clow (2001) and Harkin (2005) point to a mechanistic approach to standards that too often did not reflect the diversity of FE teaching and learning, and were too closely associated with teacher control.

Following the Lingfield Report (Department for Business, Innovation and Skills, 2012b), the policy landscape has shifted back to a voluntaristic approach to FE teacher professionalism, based on a sector Guild model. This essentially involves the creation of a market coalition of existing sector bodies and associations, bidding to become centres of excellence in the field of FE workforce reform. The report's recommendations to remove statutory requirements and entitlements for staff to achieve teaching qualifications does, however, appear to be at odds with its claims to improve FE professionalism. Such recommendations are not isolated from parallel policy measures designed to employ untrained teachers, which bypass current legislation. Recent proposals to place FE professionalism in the hands of employer and sector-led organisations, whose track record in the field remains in question, represents a major challenge both to present ITT and CPD provision and the independence of new FE Guild. Four initial principles appear to define the Guild's remit:

> The Guild will provide the right environment for employers (i.e. FE providers) to improve their (own) and their staff's capabilities and competences ...
> [It] will act as an overarching body with end to end responsibility for professionalism ... across the sector ... offering institutional and individual membership, both of which will be on a voluntary basis.
> [It] would be closely linked to individual colleges and providers being able to obtain chartered status.
> [It will be] an employer-led partnership drawing in employee representative organisations and sector bodies concerned with workforce development.
>
> (AELP/AoC, 2012: 1–2)

While sector-led self-regulation holds strong appeal, especially among institutions and employers, there has been little consultation with trainers, practitioners and school/HE providers working in the field. Equally, what constitutes FE professionalism appears to be more about membership, standards and chartered status, than the processes associated with improving pedagogic and professional processes and practices. Left unaddressed two main obstacles stand in the way of current reform. The first concerns employer reluctance to address long-standing inequalities associated with casualisaton, segmentation and managerialism. The second concerns the reluctance of government to relinquish its control of the pulleys and levers of the VET system, which Keep (2007) has described as ... 'playing with the biggest train set in the world'. Part of this process manifests itself in successive periods of regulatory and de-regulatory reform designed to meet the order of the day:

- *de-regulation* 1993–97, whereby colleges became independent corporations run on business lines moving from local authority control to institutional/ college autonomy through funding led reform (FEFC).

- *re-regulation* 1997–2001, where checks and balances are put into place to regulate unchecked growth, sleaze and corruption, including the return of representational and community governance.
- *centralised de-regulation* 2001–09, or marginalisation, whereby the planning role of FE governance is replaced by LSC funding and resourcing, based on external inspection, audit, performance and target cycles.
- *centralised self-regulation* 2009 onwards, in which colleges operate through the FE agency, partnership and stakeholder frameworks (FSA, DIUS, SSCs, LAs, DFE, BIS): single-voice and demand-led elements associated with employer, business and third-sector governance.
  (Adapted from Gleeson, Abbott and Hill 2009, cited in Green, 2010: 109)

If such periodisation is not as clear-cut as it appears here, it provides insight into the fast-changing policy gyrations of VET policy, which has impacted on the sector over time. It illustrates the way *policyism* – a form of repetitive strain injury, shorn of independent checks and balances – has become caught up in a cycle of heavily path-dependent state interventions (Gleeson, 2010).

As a consequence, this has reduced the capability of professionals to develop their capacity to act as strong partners in the education and training system and denied access to valuable resources and expertise. In the subsequent void left by a disparate range of initiatives and agencies, *cultures of mediation* have sprung up among managers and practitioners, as a means of making sense of competing policy agendas, with varying degrees of success. While findings from recent research have found that professional identity is challenged in such circumstances, it has contradictory effects, leading both to positive changes in professional expectations (collaborative practices) and negative effects, in reducing discretionary judgement (compliance). This, Grace (1995) argues, is at the heart of democratic professionalism, at a time when governments seek to define what it means to be a teacher, and the struggle over what Ball calls the 'the soul of the teacher' (Ball, 2003). According to Colley *et al.* (2007), the nature of this struggle is not just about professional resistance, but also the way (self-)regulation has become embodied in individuals, as a process of identity control rather than a mechanism for professional development.

Democratic professionalism

In the context of this contribution, the issue challenging teacher professionalism has less to do with regulation or de-regulation, than with democratising pedagogy, professionalism and practice. So long as the dominant market discourse continues to define FE teachers as the *deliverers* of skills and students as the *recipients* of those skills, it limits professional autonomy and independence. At the same time there is increasing recognition that the problems associated with austerity and recession reside more in the economy and neo-liberal policy, than any lack of training and skills provided by FE professionals. The current crisis of a million young unemployed people and the associated costs of poverty and restricted occupational mobility demand a rethink about the way public funding is redirected away from private subcontractors to participative, regenerative and high-value enterprises in the communities that FE serves. In the UK, access to employment through the learning and skills sector is either subcontracted out on a 'payment by results' basis, or by the extended use of the VET system, as a substitute for employment – a process that profits providers rather than learners and society. The failure of government policy to secure high-trust education, training and employment agreements has left a void in which market ideology and employer voice has maintained a restricted view of vocational pedagogy, tied mainly to limited behavioural and learning style objectives, initiated but not supported by employers (Coffield *et al.*, 2007). This has both limited debate about expansive vocational learning and driven some of FE's most innovative professional practices underground. The paradox is, however, that successive governments have chosen to ignore evidence that provides insight into innovative pedagogic thinking, around four key democratic principles:

- maximising student agency
- developing teacher professionalism
- improving pedagogy, curriculum and qualifications
- enhancing positive cultures of learning.

While implementation of such principles is not straightforward, they are achievable in everyday environments where student interests, tutor professionalism and pedagogy are considered together. Insight and evidence from recent research indicates that expansive learning is driven less by audit technologies of measurement and performance management, and more by forms of pedagogy and professionalism, located in communities where 'really useful knowledge' is best understood (ESRC/TLRP Programme, 1999–2009; Nuffield Foundation, 2008, Skills Commission, 2011). In critical and constructionist terms this research draws attention to the ways democratic professionalism can be constructed in the contested contexts and cultures in which FE is situated. If democratic professionalism has much in common with expansive learning, it is also a practical and iterative process that focuses on developing capability and capacity (Sen, 1999). It inhabits different spaces and cultures of work, education and community, and is inclusive of practitioners, learners, managers, stakeholders and participative employers. In contrast with discourses of managerialism and neoliberalism, rooted in a low-skills, low-trust economy, democratic professionalism emphasises reflexive practices located in client, learner and community contexts.

Such a reworking of professionalism is an agentic process that Ball (2003) prefers to call *professionality,* for the way it actively shapes identity, in and through working with others. Like many forms of learning, becoming a professional is informed by pedagogic processes that go beyond subject and technical knowledge, into the wider realms of professionals researching their own practice.

While vocational pedagogies address contested notions of skills, work and employment, the significance of professional autonomy, ethics and trust is central to the improved lives of learners. At present, the UK learning and skills agenda has the effect of legitimating rather than challenging market principles that legislate *on*, not *with* or *for* learners and professionals, who are perceived more as customers and clients than participants and producers of knowledge. The challenge to FE is that it has become increasingly corporate and amnesiac, owing greater allegiance to the pulleys and levers of the market, government and employers than to the communities and civic society that it serves. With the return of yet another and more permanent cycle of recession, the danger is that across the continuing raft of neo-liberal reform, the narrowest notions of autonomy, professionalism and learning will prevail, if left unchallenged.

Chapter 3

Professional bodies and continuing professional development

A case study

Andy Boon and Toni Fazaeli

> Learning consistently takes place when critical thinking is combined with relevance.
>
> (Kindsvatter)

This chapter focuses on the role of professional bodies in relation to continuing professional development (CPD) in two different professional spheres – further education (FE) and legal services. Similarities and differences between these two areas, and in particular the approaches to CPD, are highlighted. The chapter concludes by identifying commonalities and differences in the trajectories, circumstances and regimes of the professions. We consider whether there are key features of CPD that should be common to all professions or whether models of CPD are contingent and dependent on circumstances. We propose a model that covers emerging factors in the conception of CPD. We argue that these findings have applicability to professions and their professional bodies more widely, as well as employers of professionals.

Introduction

Professionalism, the status accorded an occupation with special market privileges, has always been associated with learning, both informal and formal (Larson, 2013). In their early evolution, professions seek a monopoly of knowledge by developing curricula. They consolidate their learning in qualifications and elevate it by association with universities. Ultimately, the special status of this learning is accorded statutory recognition, often in the form of delegated powers to regulate the occupation. These later stages of professionalisation are often marked by an increase in informal education; public and private events, lectures and seminars. Meanwhile, it is assumed that a career in 'professional practice' involves an ideal of a sophisticated process of knowledge acquisition, higher level skill development, increased problem-solving competence and ethical sensitivity, all underwritten by a spirit of public service. For the individual professional, the post-qualification phase of professional learning is typically less formal. Indeed, there is little evidence that most professionals fully meet the ideal. As professions come under increased pressure to fulfil the promise of professionalism, the assumption that continuing development is an organic process is supplanted by formal mechanisms of CPD.

This chapter explores the relationship of professional bodies and CPD. This topic is relatively neglected, at least compared to the attention lavished on what constitutes effective CPD. We argue that it has important political, educational and theoretical dimensions going to the heart of the professional agenda. In this analysis we adopt the view that occupations seeking recognition as professions seldom meet the ideal (Houle, 1980). In fact, they are typically moving towards or away from it. Therefore, while law and medicine in the UK are paradigm examples of professionalisation, their status derives from a popular conception based on a nineteenth-century image; the practice of esoteric art by a closed group of people, each by him/herself, having individual clients and collecting their own fees (Houle, 1980). This image of professionalism, together with those defined by relatively unfettered self-regulation (Johnson, 1972), are in retreat in the UK (Boon, 2010).

In theory, a professional body's involvement with CPD may be limited to designing a framework, or it could include specifying activities, participation in an ongoing process or undertaking assessment of learning. In practice, approaches are potentially extremely varied, reflecting diverse considerations. We speculate that an increasing focus on competence as a driving aim will shift the focus of CPD regimes towards the workplace, placing employers at the centre of the development nexus. This raises questions about the role of the professional body. Will they surrender any role in the operation of CPD and what additional value and challenge function should they bring to the process? We suspect that the solutions to these various problems often reflect diverse factors. These include the professional body's experience of CPD, the particular challenges facing the occupation and the influence of the wider environment, including perceptions of 'best practice'. Understanding how these factors affect professions requires looking in more detail at specific cases.

Professional bodies' approaches to CPD are explored by comparing the experience of CPD in two distinct occupations, lawyers and FE teachers,[1] against a background of CPD development in UK professions generally. Our case studies show the types of roles, behaviours and attitudes that professional bodies hold towards continuing learning and the pressures and needs that impact on adoption and implementation of effective and new practices. They also explore how professions create the community of practice through language, discourse, popular understanding and cultural fabric to support professional learning and concepts of professionalism. While our approach is exploratory at the policy level we are keen to consider what implications, if any, our analysis has for CPD across the professions. In this respect, we are encouraged by Houle's observations that learning processes in different professions are too often considered to be unique.

We take seriously his proposition that '[a] study of similarities could result in an exchange of ideas, techniques, and solutions to problems that would greatly refresh and broaden practice in many professions' (Houle, 1980: 16).

Our data were collected in the course of research projects on the two professions concerned. Material on solicitors and barristers was gathered for a report on compulsory CPD for solicitors. Further material on barristers was published in a report recommending changes in the bar CPD scheme (Bar Standards Board, 2011). Evidence on FE teachers was collected by the professional body, the Institute for Learning (IfL), through interviews, surveys and data from large numbers of FE teachers and trainers, drawing on its published annual CPD Reviews (IfL 2009, 2010, 2012) together with other qualitative data, including material on what constitutes exceptional teaching and learning and CPD (IfL 2010). Our path through the issues is, initially, to outline the context in which the contemporary debate about CPD is set. We examine the professionalisation trajectories of both occupations and the relationship between these trajectories and the functions and forms of their respective CPD regimes. Finally, we analyse emerging trends in the critical relationships between practitioners, employers and professional bodies. We conclude by considering the role of professional bodies in emergent regimes of CPD.

Context

Education is a central activity of professions. Typically, professionalisation of an occupation involves creation of formal initial training usually through a training school, establishment of core knowledge as a higher-level discipline often within universities, establishment of a national association and statutory recognition of the profession by the state. The process of an individual becoming a professional normally involves a mixture of theoretical and practical knowledge, increasingly involving obtaining a degree, or equivalent qualification, and serving a formally recognised trainee period. These stages are developed because breadth of vision is necessary for an individual to exercise unsupervised and autonomous judgement, a key marker of professional practice. Although control of initial training and qualification is a key step in professional recognition and is well established, the expectation of planned, regular and systematic continuing development over a working life is relatively new.

In the UK, professional bodies embraced the idea of CPD during the 1980s (Friedman, 2011). In the adoption phase, professions generally used an 'input' model, measuring the numbers of conferences, workshops, lectures or practice sessions attended, awarding points or hours towards an official requirement accordingly. The first three years post-qualification, which Eraut (1994) calls initial professional education, also follows this template, but is more likely to contain compulsory elements that are theoretical, dense and broad and so unrelated to immediate and specific aspects of practice. In contrast, learning from experience 'on the job' is often supported within organisations, for example, by appraisal, either in the pre-qualification phase or as preparation for new career challenges. While CPD is sometimes used as an umbrella term, incorporating initial professional education or training, subsequent CPD and learning in the workplace, there is potential for these different elements of post-qualification experience either to be formally merged or separated out in CPD regimes.

Nationally, the first generation CPD input model has been roundly criticised for dependence on didactic delivery by diverse and uncoordinated providers (Cervero, 2000; Bolton 2002) and for failure to impact on recipients in meaningful ways. A focus on the need to prove that members undertook CPD drove professions to adopt a restrictive interpretation of what counted. Providers of CPD, often with an accredited status and able to corroborate attendance, were given a captive market. Professionals, often tired after a long day, were forced to attend well-intended but dry lectures on possibly irrelevant areas of practice, while paying through the nose for the privilege. CPD understandably gained a bad reputation with the very people it aimed to inspire, presenting theoretical and practical problems. These were exacerbated by greater awareness, from the 1970s onwards, of the distinctive needs of adult learners (Knowles 1980). In the ideal scenario, the informality of approach harnessed the experience of adult learners, the enthusiasm of instructors and flexibility of the context to instil positive motivation towards learning (Knowles, 1975). This awareness coincided with the emergence of new thinking on how people develop professional skills. The idea of reflective practice (Schon, 1987) offered a parallel path for CPD by focusing on problems that professionals actually faced every day. The notion of self-direction in learning proved to be so powerful that it infiltrated the delivery of university education, but not the assumptions underpinning traditional CPD. First generation CPD did not encourage positive attitudes towards education or equipping professionals to learn from experience.

Schon suggests that the habit of reflective practice can be inculcated through coaching and mentoring professionals by expert facilitators. Professionals able to articulate their approach to the problems of practice, and who think about their experience as they actually engage in it, learn more deeply and profoundly. This is the opposite of the typical, traditional experience of CPD, which functions as 'updating' on a general area without connecting with issues of concern to the practitioner at that time. Schon's theory, that experience, tacit knowledge or 'knowing in action' allows the practitioner to achieve artistry by exceeding the bounds of technical competence, is one of the most cited, as well as often criticised aspects of his work. Detractors focus on Schon's lack of clarity regarding the mechanics of 'reflection in action'. They also criticise 'the readiness of those engaged in professional education to rely so heavily on slogans such as "reflective practice"' (MacIntyre, 1994). Schon followed the increasingly accepted convention that it is learning that is self-discovered and self-appropriated that significantly influences behaviour. New approaches to professional learning have involved moving beyond individual and largely solitary reflective practice to find that collaborative reflective practice is more effective (Boud, 2010).

Learners' motivations towards continuing education tend to be geared to achieving a goal, such as achieving a qualification, an activity, such as the social dimension of the experience of participation, or learning for its own sake (Houle, 1980). The last of these proved to be the most prevalent orientation (Courtney, 1992). Houle conceived of professional learning as a process of adjusting practice in the light of experience in order to be more efficient and effective: eliminating errors, adjusting performance, expanding potential. Eventually these insights might help to reform practices and perspectives. This process is continuous in that learning new or better ways of fulfilling professional roles is an everyday occurrence. Self-directed learning is used by professionals to manage their practice performance as part of ongoing personal development going beyond workplace competence. It extends to the possibility of CPD addressing personal development needs that are not restricted to the narrow workplace performance of the professional, but to broader personal and social needs. This broad conception of CPD is captured in the definition advanced by Madden and Mitchell (1993: 12): 'The maintenance and enhancement of the knowledge, expertise and competence of professionals throughout their careers, according to a plan formulated with regard to the needs of the professional, their employer and society'.

Broader understandings of the role and potential of CPD are reflected in a number of evolutions of the concept. Professions have attempted to convey that personal development activity is not a special event, but a day-to-day activity. A non-exhaustive list of permitted CPD activities for dentists, for example, includes courses and lectures, vocational training or general professional training study days, educational elements or professional and specialist society meetings, peer review and clinical audit, distance learning, multimedia learning, staff training, background research, private study, journal reading and attending conferences. This breadth has driven a more flexible approach to documenting and reporting CPD, with the substitution of more flexible 'verification' requirements. So, for example, dentists must complete 250 hours over five years and 75 hours must be 'verifiable', meaning that it must have concise educational aims and objectives, clear anticipated outcomes and quality control (i.e. provision for feedback). This, in turn, has led to a more open attitude to proof of completion. Satisfaction of dentists' CPD requirements is not checked until the end of the five-year cycle, by a declaration of completion, and only a sample is checked.

The adoption of more flexible approaches to formal requirements is one of several evolutionary changes in CPD. Cervero (2000) noted four trends in the US during the 1990s. First, workplace education had grown to dwarf other kinds of provision. Second, there had been growth in provision by universities and professions, particularly in distance learning formats. Third, there had been an increase in the volume of collaborative arrangements, particularly between workplaces and universities. Finally, there had been an increasing use of CPD to regulate professional practice, including as a basis for licensure and recertification. Similar trends may be occurring in the UK, certainly in the areas covered by our case studies. There has been a growth of in-house staff development in large law firms for example, accompanied by much greater awareness of the economic advantages of in-house training and the opportunity presented to imbue the firm's cultural awareness. Much of this CPD is accredited where possible, offering double value for staff development. Universities have been encouraged to offer CPD within their discipline areas as part of a drive to attract 'third leg income' and there are high levels of activity in some areas. As our case studies show, some professions have explored, if not yet enacted, the use of CPD as a pre-condition of the right to practise or of entry to higher specialisms. Finally, there is growing interest in how the time and resource devoted to CPD might actually be used to enhance performance.

Professional histories and trajectories – lawyers and FE teachers

In theory, professions are distinguished from other occupations by their specialist and sometimes esoteric body of professional knowledge and the indeterminacy of professional judgement. FE teachers are one of many occupations which have a generalised corpus of knowledge. Teaching in vocational areas, especially, needs to be delivered by seasoned and successful practitioners, for example, in retail, construction, engineering, law or new technologies. The IfL has defined FE teachers as 'dual professionals' in subject discipline and in pedagogy. In contrast, established professions choose to conceal a similar division between knowledge and skill in order to maintain the mystery of the professional art (Jamous and Pelloille, 1970). Lawyers and medics have high professional status because, historically, they convinced the state that state regulation is the best mechanism of quality control. Historically, FE teachers have enjoyed relatively little professional prestige, and are therefore more dependent on the professional body in order to achieve it.

Barristers can trace their antecedents to the reign of Henry II (Brand, 1992) while the Law Society, the professional body of solicitors, was incorporated in 1831 (Boon and Levin, 2008). These professions prescribe over half the content of law degrees and vocational courses and insist on extensive training periods in practice (Boon and Webb, 2008). Arising from their roots in the mechanical institutes established in the early nineteenth century, teachers in FE colleges offer a much more recent example of professionalisation compared with law. The relatively low professional status accorded to teachers in FE was partly due to the fact that the sector was dispersed rather than national, with local authorities providing FE funding until 1993, when arrangements were centralised through the Further Education Funding Council. The sector remains relatively marginal in national policy compared with the school system, a fact reflected in the far later introduction of qualification requirements. Qualifications for primary school teachers were introduced as a requirement in 1969, for secondary school teachers from 1973 and for FE teachers in 2001 and updated in 2007.

Until the late 1990s FE teachers had little central organisation or national standards, both of which are usually a precursor of professionalisation. The IfL was established in 2002 by teachers, trade unions and the employers' association, as a voluntary membership professional body. Membership originally numbered several thousand. In September 2007, following an independent review initiated by government (Foster, 2005), a white paper (Department for Education and Skills, 2006) and wide consultation, two sets of regulations were issued. The first required that all FE teachers should be registered with IfL and that they undertake at least 30 hours of CPD a year, to be monitored by IfL.[2] The second set of regulations built on the 2001 requirement that FE teachers be qualified. They also required that, from September 2007, as well as specified initial qualifications, new FE teachers gain the post-qualification professional status of Qualified Teacher Learning and Skills (QTLS), or an associate level for those not holding a full teaching role (ATLS) from the IfL (Department for Innovation, Universities and Skills, 2007), within the first five years of teaching.

Ethics and discipline are two areas often indicative of the later stages of professionalisation. Lawyers are subject to a professional code, formerly upheld by the Law Society and since 2007 by the regulatory body, the Solicitors' Regulation Authority, and, for barristers, by the Bar Standards Board. These codes are underpinned by extensive disciplinary machinery, with power to bar from practice. The government regulations governing FE teaching had no requirement for a code of conduct or ethical standards and no system for removing individuals from practising. In 2008, IfL introduced a code of professional practice, partly as a result of comparisons with other professional bodies and partly to protect the profession and public. IfL's code differs from some other professional codes in that it focuses on professional behaviours and ethics, and not competence, which is left as a domain for the employer to address. The approach was approved in consultation with members. Many evinced pride in professional status and support for investigation and removal of individuals from registration if there was found to be a serious breach of the code of professional practice.

Forms of CPD

In 1985, compulsory CPD was introduced to solicitors in the first three years of practice and extended incrementally to all solicitors from 1 November 1998. The General Council of the Bar introduced CPD a little later than solicitors along similar lines. The original requirement for solicitors undertaking CPD was attendance at 12 hours of approved courses. Currently, all solicitors working at least 32 hours a week must complete a minimum of 16 hours of CPD annually.[3] The only mandatory component is that newly qualified solicitors must attend a Management Course Stage 1, taken between the date of admission and the end of the third CPD year, a clear example of what Eraut refers to as 'initial professional education'.[4] Similar to dentists and doctors, the standard CPD requirement is for completion of 25 per cent of the 16 hours by participation in accredited training courses, from authorised CPD providers, requiring attendance for one hour or more.[5] The remaining 75 per cent can comprise a wide range of activities, such as preparing or delivering courses, legally related research and authorship, coaching, mentoring or work shadowing. The Law Society has launched a CPD Centre providing details of courses counting towards CPD requirements. Solicitors' firms or barristers' chambers often run CPD validated in-house courses. Practitioners can complete online self-assessment exercises, based on law-related publications.

Although the requirements for lawyers' CPD have liberalised, the profession has been quite slow to make a more rigorous link between CPD and competence. The Lord Chancellor's Advisory Committee for Education and Conduct, a generally progressive body, suggested that the lawyers adopt a broad conception of CPD as a 'regular, structured educational activity designed to supplement the practitioner's experience by enhancing any aspect of his professional competence at all the different stages of his career' (ACLEC, 1997: para. 1.13), that there should be an element of reflection and that the Law Society should make appraisal and planning a compulsory element (ACLEC, 1997; paras 1.13 and 4.30). No steps were taken to require reflection, appraisal or planning and the Solicitors' Training Regulations 2009 still define CPD as 'a course, lecture, seminar or other programme or method of study (whether requiring attendance or not) that is relevant to the needs and professional standards of solicitors and complies with guidance issued from time to time by the SRA'.[6] Progress towards recognising the workplace as the focus for the development of competence has also been slow. The Bar Working Group noted that the legal professions are unusual in not recognising that workplace activity can constitute relevant CPD, recommending a move away from accredited courses and towards a more flexible requirement of 'verification' (Bar Standards Board, 2011).

Based on the government regulations introduced in 2007, IfL required each full-time member to carry out at least 30 hours of CPD a year.[7] The CPD strategy was developmental and, in contrast with the legal professions, an 'outcomes model'. Members gauged the impact of CPD on their performance – supported by guidance produced by IfL. The focus on impact rather than hours of input reflects the decision by IfL to support teachers to be the best they can be, up to date in subject or vocational knowledge and in teaching methods, i.e. by moving beyond a threshold competence and a compliance input model. IfL monitors the overall number of hours of CPD carried out each year by each member, gauged by the individual as having an impact on practice, including the proportion of hours relating to teaching methods, and subject or vocational knowledge updating or other areas. Since 2008–09, IfL has sampled members' CPD each year through a combination of examining CPD records, telephone interviews and focus groups. In addition to exploring the nature and range of CPD undertaken, a primary aim of these in-depth interviews is to identify the kinds of CPD that are effective and have had the greatest impact. IfL then publishes findings and shares good practice as a resource for other members and employers (IfL 2009, 2010a, 2012a).

The balance of evidence from tens of thousands of practising teachers and trainers who have declared their CPD, and thousands more involved in IfL's sampling over the last four years, suggests that nearly all teachers carry out about double the number of hours of CPD required each year. They spent an equal amount of time on updating subject knowledge and expertise in teaching methods, activities that may be said to have impact. IfL's research with more than 5,000 members identified what excellent teaching is like and CPD that works (IfL, 2010b). Teachers value sharing critical reflection, testing practice and learning from each other, both within and outside of their place of employment. This led IfL to conclude that collaborative reflection, participating in communities of practice, and individual reflection on professional learning is most powerful and likely to lead to positive change in practice. These findings about the importance of collaborative professional practice (IfL, 2012a) coincide with recent meta-analysis of over 80,000 individual pieces of research weighting the range of teaching interventions yielding the greatest impact (Hattie 2009, 2012). Reflective practice was the most highly rated form of professional learning supporting the development of outstanding practice (IfL, 2010b).

Models: inputs and outputs

Perhaps the key distinction in CPD practice in recent years is between input models and output (or outcomes) models. In this respect, lawyers' and FE teachers' approaches represent different ends of the same telescope. The lawyers' 'input model' attracted concern in that it encouraged a 'box ticking' mentality in attendees and a propensity among course providers for 're-inventing the wheel', often at high cost to small firms (ACLEC, 1996, Gold *et al.*, 2007). Despite high-level encouragement for individuals taking responsibility for their own personal and professional development (ACLEC, 1997: 17), it was not until 2003 that the Law Society Training Committee consulted on the issue, proposing a requirement of more hours within a more flexible system focused on personal professional development rather than hours of activity. While some amendments were made to the solicitors' CPD scheme, the definition of CPD retained the focus on lectures and seminars and this, to a large degree, set the tone.

Solicitors are offered a framework which could provide a basis for a degree of reflection. They are advised to analyse their training needs using a career plan, setting short, medium and long-term goals, setting specific targets for each goal, together with deadlines by which these targets should have been achieved. A suite of forms is provided to help them make best use of the CPD scheme. A development plan template, for example, is in tabular form with columns headed development activity, knowledge or skills to be developed, priority, development strategy/methods, providers, start date/end date [of courses]. Worked examples of training needs analysis forms are attached for those at different career stages. Solicitors are advised to enter on their training record all developmental activity, whether or not it qualifies for CPD credit. Despite the existence of this framework, solicitors' CPD continues to be based on an input model. There is no requirement for planning, reflection, recording or communication and no mechanism to ensure that the various good practice items are followed.

In contrast with the solicitors' approach, the IfL's scheme is 'outcomes driven'. CPD is defined by the outcomes sought; 'maintaining, improving and broadening relevant knowledge and skills in a subject or vocational specialism, and in teaching and training methods so that it has positive impact on practice and the learner experience' (IfL, 2012a: 4). Although government regulations specified that the hours of professional development should be monitored, IfL required focus on hours that had impact rather than the hours spent on an activity. This was a more notional and subjective measure, but it emphasised individual responsibility to identify what they had learned leading to a tangible impact on practice.[8] Evidence collected by IfL suggests that these requirements sparked greater discussion between teachers, and with managers, about professional development and assisted negotiation of development time.

Early experience of the application of IfL's CPD model was not, however, wholly positive. Some employers laid on 30 hours of events a year for their teachers. Worse, some assumed that four days a year of 'development days', leadership briefings on college finances and priorities, motivational speakers, introductions to new administrative systems and a few teaching workshops, fitted the bill. Some FE lecturers therefore shared the familiar CPD experience of many professionals, rail-roaded by employers into events that had little meaning or purpose for them, their learners or their practice. Employers over-managing and over-structuring professional development for their teachers squeezed out the very thing they should seek; effective professional development personalised to meet needs, leading to excellent teaching practice.

Monitoring and licensure

Both legal professions require full completion of CPD requirements as a condition of practice. Solicitors must record their CPD activity in a training record. In the case of courses, providers notify attendees how many hours of credit they attract and the provider's reference. This information, together with the date and course title, must be entered into the training record. The other activities which can form up to 75 per cent of solicitors' annual hours requirement include delivery/preparation of courses, coaching/mentoring, writing books/articles and research. When making an application for an annual practising certificate, individuals are asked to confirm whether or not they have complied with the CPD requirements during the last complete CPD year. If unable to comply they must agree a date by which the shortfall must be made up. The training regulations impose obligations on a solicitor or registered European lawyer to produce the CPD record to the regulator on demand and training records may be subject to random sampling. The emphasis on tracking performance is understandable given the significance attached to the profession's responsibility for quality control of legal services. It is not uncommon that CPD 'laggards' also manifest other professional failings (Houle, 1980).

In contrast to the 'low-trust' model traditionally operated by lawyers, IfL members are trusted to honestly declare their CPD hours. This approach was criticised by some members and others in the FE sector as not being tough enough and not involving tight enough checking. The high-trust strategy was informed by the Institute's own ethical values, developed with members. It is centred on the values of professionalism, autonomy and integrity (IfL, 2011). This is expressed in the aspiration that FE teachers: 'strive for the highest standards in teaching and learning, and high levels of subject or vocational expertise, placing the interests and progression of learners at the very heart of our practice'; they 'should be trusted to exercise informed judgements in the interests of learners'; and to 'use [their] skills and knowledge and resources at [their] disposal wisely to benefit all learners, the public and where [they] work, and are respected and trustworthy members of society' (IfL 2011: 7). IfL argues that the value base for a professional body to monitor CPD is significant, and the methods used for promoting and monitoring reveal the underlying values.

When reporting the CPD undertaken, IfL members are asked for overall numbers of hours of CPD that had impact and the proportions relating to teaching methods and to subject updating and relevant policy knowledge. Some 60 per cent of members choose to enter their individual records of hours online using the eportfolio REfLECT, designed specifically to support teachers' planning, recording and review of CPD. Others use their own electronic or paper systems, or those their employer may provide, or declare their CPD hours to IfL by telephone. IfL aggregates and analyses these data nationally. IfL believes that the professional body has a key role in broadening horizons and publishes or gives access to research findings and disseminates good practice nationally and internationally to support practitioners' CPD.

Changing environments

In the recent past, both of the professional groups under study have undergone significant and dramatic change. The legal professions' longstanding independence was curtailed by the Legal Services Act 2007, which followed a report that was highly critical of the legal professions' regulatory arrangements (Clementi, 2004). The Act created a Legal Services Board to oversee the operation of the legal services market. Professions, formerly operating as 'front-line regulators', were required to create an independent regulatory arm, separate from the 'representative' body. The Law Society created the Solicitors' Regulation Authority and the General Council of the Bar created the Bar Standards Board. Member practising certificate fees went to support the regulatory arm only, while membership of the 'representative' professional body was optional.

The regulatory arms of the legal professional bodies now operate at arm's length from the representative arms. The professional bodies have effectively become one of many stakeholders in the regulation of the occupation. One of the changes urged on the new regulators was the adoption of Outcomes Focused Regulation (OFR), a suite of procedures pioneered in the financial services industry designed to exert tighter control on the day-to-day operation of organisations (Boon, 2010). The bar, however, made the first move towards liberalisation before the review, with barristers' CPD requirements moving away from accredited courses to an extended requirement of 24 hours of which only 12 will be 'verifiable' and with more flexibility around qualifying activity (Bar Standards Board, 2011). The draft handbook defines CPD as improving subject knowledge and keeping up to date with knowledge and skills relevant to practice (Bar Standards Board, 2012). CPD courses for the Bar will no longer be accredited. Declaration of completion will suffice for grant of practising certificates although barristers may be selected on a random basis to produce a portfolio of evidence of completion. The future of solicitors' CPD is in limbo. Policy-makers have registered the pre-existing dissatisfaction with the input model of CPD and are grappling with the implications for CPD, if any, of OFR.

Changes in regulation have caused the legal profession to question and revisit their approach to CPD, but these concerns were parked when the Legal Services Board announced a Legal Education and Training Review to be undertaken by frontline regulators. Possible outcomes of the Legal Education and Training Review include using CPD as a means of post-qualification licensing for areas of work that are reserved to specified legal professions, like providing litigation services and court advocacy. If professions do not set standards and qualifications in these areas the Legal Services Board may seek to do so (Legal Services Policy Institute, 2009). Both legal professional bodies may be pondering whether a new regulatory regime focused on outcomes should have a system of CPD with the same broad objective, with new monitoring arrangements, with a shift in focus from inputs (hours) to outcomes (results), new mandatory requirements to embrace legal skills, legal knowledge, professional values, behaviour and ethics, or to provide specific training for those holding specified roles in the new regulatory structure (Shirley, 2010). One of the implications of aligning CPD with OFR is that mechanisms of monitoring (for example, appraisal) and some mechanisms of enforcement (for example, employment security or promotion) could be focused on employing organisations rather than the regulator.

The professional aspirations of FE teachers potentially have been threatened by recent changes in government policy. The 2007 regulations provided for registration of teachers and payment of their professional body fees. Initially, government agreed to pay the registration fees, putting teachers on the same basis as school teachers registering with the General Teaching Council (England). The three-year period was then extended for a further year to 2011. Confirmation was given in the white paper *Skills for Growth* (2009) and reconfirmed in the skills white paper, *Skills for Sustainable Growth* (2010) that IfL would become self-financing by 2011/12. The risk of negative impact of this change was compounded by the government's subsequent decision to remove regulations requiring registration with IfL, and compulsory CPD, from 30 September 2012. Further, government removed those parts of the regulations requiring new entrants to gain the post-qualification professional status of QTLS or ATLS within five years of initial teacher education. Government also proposed considering removal of initial teacher qualification regulations from September 2013; a very significant backwards step in the professionalisation of the FE workforce as initial training is one of the key hallmarks of a profession.

In autumn 2012, government proposed creating a new Further Education Guild (FEG) of FE employers in partnership with other bodies in the FE sector, by late 2013. The two main employer associations, the Association of Colleges and the Association of Employment and Learning Providers will lead and join with key partnerships including several specialist employer bodies, trade unions and IfL. While it is too early to assess the impact of this move, it represents a significant shift of power to employers, with the partnership between IfL and trade unions a balancing factor. Some elements of the previous regulatory regime may be carried forward by the FEG, for example, the expectation that employers will ensure that teachers are qualified and will provide support for CPD. The IfL continues to offer QTLS, which since April 2012 is also recognised in statute as equal to Qualified Teacher Status (QTS) for teaching in schools as a professional teacher, and ATLS for those seeking associate status. Individuals choose to undergo professional formation to gain QTLS or ATLS with IfL, as there are now no regulatory requirements to gain this professional status.

Analysis

Our brief account of occupational engagement with CPD hints at significant underlying changes in professionalism. From the 1980s, all sectors of the economy became increasingly subject to market forces and, where this did not occur naturally, government intervened. This particularly affected the traditional professions, which had established a high degree of market control by closure of access to the occupational order (Larson, 2013). For lawyers, the process began in the early 1990s with legislative inroads into professional boundaries and culminated with inroads into self-regulation made by the Legal Services Act 1990. The decline of established professions intersected with the continuation of a wider movement towards 'professional society', whereby occupations increasingly used the capitalised value of education, training and experience to command an increasing share of resources (Perkin, 1989, 1996). Some of these occupations gained state recognition and were granted a degree of market control. In the case of IfL, this was established only to be changed within five years. Therefore, we see in these examples that professional status is more threatened and volatile than previously and its rewards more contingent.

Professions are more subject to state manipulation and to mechanisms of state control. This will, we suspect, increase pressure for CPD to demonstrate impact, leading to a stronger focus on the workplace and an ongoing risk of co-option of CPD as a tool of management. Public sector organisations and professions are particularly at risk of a suite of techniques designed to increase efficiency. Gathered under the label 'new managerialism' these regimes establish a narrative of strategic change and operational control subject to external accountability. They aim to capture and colonise professional ideologies and organisational identities in order to release entrepreneurial potential. One impact of new management philosophy on academic labour is through control mechanisms entailing detailed and intensive auditing and continuing evaluation according to externally set performance measures (Reed, 2002). The appearance of freedom within these regimes is deceptive. They produce 'regulated autonomy' for professionals within underlying normative principles (Hoggett, 1996, Deem *et al.*, 2007). The new system of OFR in the legal profession is an example of such a system. Internal mechanisms like appraisal and external mechanisms like audit have the potential to change the complexion of CPD in law firms, emphasising narrow notions of workplace competence at the expense of broader development.

We draw several tentative conclusions from our case studies, suggesting significant evolution and current trends in the development of CPD. First, there seems little doubt that, historically, professions embraced the model of CPD current during the period of adoption. A cynical view of early schemes suggests that the actual purpose was to assure key stakeholders that professions took the issue of competence seriously. Thinking on how this could be achieved was underdeveloped. So, rather than identifying what they want to achieve through CPD, and how best to achieve it, professions tended to adapt the current orthodoxy or 'best practice' to their purposes. This may have had a fortunate consequence for the breadth of CPD schemes, allowing a wide range of activity, accommodating a wide view of professional development and leaving a space for individual choice. One direction for the second generation of CPD schemes is to be more relaxed about content, hours and reporting requirements. This risks increasing pressure to justify any CPD requirements. The other direction involves paying serious attention to outcomes and, hence, performance and competence issues (Bindman, 2010). This risks constraining the breadth of CPD within a narrow view of competence.

Typically, the express purpose of most CPD schemes is the enhanced professional competence of the occupational workforce, but early schemes seldom fit the bill. Professions are increasingly seeing impact as a key feature of CPD. The Academy of Medical Royal Colleges, for example, describes CPD activity as that supporting the development of knowledge, skills, attitudes and behaviour and specific changes in practice (Academy of Medical Royal Colleges, 2010). CPD schemes intended to address deficiencies and those that aspire to excellence in professional performance need to focus much more closely on individuals, their needs and on customised solutions that impact on behaviour. This concern with the everyday experience of the professional can, in general, be seen as a positive development. It meets the practical, contemporary priority that development should contribute to changing practice. It also has the potential for coaching and mentoring, somewhat in line with Schon's notion of a *practicum* for reflective practice. An example of this potential is provided by Gold *et al.* (2007), whose action research provides a rare insight into professional development in a law firm. Citing an example of a tribunal chair demanding a lawyer provide a justifica-tion of a 'taken for granted' assumption, they identify 'hot' action – something discomforting – which can be a catalyst for later learning assisted by articulation and interaction. Learning engendered when routine procedures do not go according to plan is validated and made more meaningful by sharing with others. In this way the lessons of such experience can be elaborated, related to existing practice and refined.

The individual's own practice, and experience more widely among practition-ers in an organisation, provides daily material which has the potential to go beyond 'hot action' in locating the substance of CPD. This recognises Eraut's criticism of Schon that learning often occurs in the neglected routine rather than exceptional cases. Analysis of routine could help 'professionals to reformulate their theories of practice in the light of semi-digested case experiences' (Eraut, 1994: 13). A legal practice example of this routine or everyday experiential learn-ing is also provided by Gold *et al.* (2007) in their case study. They describe how members of the employment department of a law firm eagerly await electronic updates of tribunal decisions, which are analysed daily by the team and related to ongoing cases. This situational learning, which can also draw in the latest practice, research and wider policy contexts, is consistent with growing recognition that for economy, effectiveness and efficiency reasons, employers should foster collabora-tive learning environments in the workplace. Professionals reflecting together have been called 'communities of practice', a term originally coined to explain situated learning, how newcomers to professional communities learned about the social structure of communities from the periphery (Lave and Wenger, 1991).

A strong location of CPD in the workplace, and implicating employers in the process, represents a potentially dramatic change in the focus of CPD for some professions. In the introductory or adoption phase, CPD was generally regarded as a personal responsibility. The lawyers' 'input' model facilitates this by being individualised; CPD was an issue between the professional body and the practi-tioner. Thus, while solicitors are advised to plan their training activity with the needs of their firm and its business objectives in mind, firms or employers are not obliged to pay for or allow time off to attend CPD courses. Similarly, the regula-tions relating to CPD gave responsibility to IfL for the monitoring of CPD and did not specify the responsibilities of the individual – other than a general respon-sibility of at least 30 hours of CPD a year and to record this – nor of the employer. The organisations where the professionals worked had no responsibility for providing or paying for employees' CPD or for ensuring that it was effective, although custom and practice is that FE employers do this though often without a strong focus on individual needs and career development, nor drawing enough on research evidence about the kinds of CPD that work effectively to support positive changes in practice. There were no formal requirements for reflection. For lawyers the regulatory shift to OFR, which will rely on visits to audit the procedures adopted by firms, could be the vehicle for a more pervasive, effective but intrusive CPD regime for solicitors' firms. Likewise, the new FEG may well favour a CPD regime that gives FE employers a more direct role in defining the scope and nature of CPD.

The move to more collaborative forms of CPD organised around the workplace carries great potential and significant risks. In the past ten years there has been growing use of communities of practice in professional bodies and in corporate organisations. These have used the concept in organising employees to build work-relevant knowledge among cognate professional groups (Hara, 2009). One of the issues raised is the somewhat vexed question of the relative responsibility of individuals and employers for driving CPD. There appears to be no single correct balance, but there does need to be some connection between the two to secure the greatest synergies and to reduce conflict. IfL found reflection and dialogue with peers and managers about CPD to be valuable CPD in its own right. Freedom to take responsibility for their own CPD, above and beyond what the employer could expect, is motivational for individuals. One of the risks of organisationally based learning is that processes will become co-opted to the employer's purposes and the more narrow needs of the business.

The role of professional bodies

CPD regimes should, we argue, consider, and if possible balance, a number of competing interests. These might include, for example, the public interest in competent and, indeed, high standards of service, an employer's interest in a productive workforce, a profession's interest in earning status and collegiality and an individual's interest in personal development. The increasing focus on competence, impact and outcomes raises questions about how more diverse interests will be accommodated when increased focus on workplace CPD casts doubt on the role of professional bodies. Both of the professional bodies considered here now operate under considerable regulatory constraints. The Law Society is at arm's length from the SRA, which has regulatory responsibility for designing and implementing CPD. It is merely one of many stakeholders in CPD. IfL now has a voluntary membership and no statutory underpinning or support for its CPD scheme. It will be even more dependent on the commitment and participation of its members. In this new environment, what role should professional bodies seek to play in relation to CPD?

Communication

One of the key roles of professional bodies is communication and engagement. The existence of CPD requirements speaks to various audiences about the ambition and place of the occupation. It offers reassurance to stakeholders, including the public, that the profession takes quality assurance seriously. It also sends an important message to members, providing confirmation that the professional body retains professional aspirations, guidance and programmes capable of realising and sustaining them. This can be a difficult process. The IfL's CPD requirement was perceived by some as an additional burden, both on individuals' busy working lives and on busy organisations. IfL has been leading a counter cultural movement around CPD within FE, questioning old and often not very effective CPD traditions. Unsurprisingly, IfL's approach has met some opposition in achieving this agenda, while at the same time garnering support and enthusiasm.

IfL has sought to convince employers that fostering and supporting CPD that actually helps improve performance appeals to good business sense; it brings a return on investment. From 2007 to the present, some employers, supported by some teachers in FE, expressed a preference for a 'tick box' system for CPD; something that is easy and quick to record. IfL has worked to conceive of the real work of teachers as being more than simply working with students or trainees and that CPD is integral to the work of teaching. However, for some organisations, the developmental of effective CPD may require changes in their own systems and practices and cultures, and sometimes quite significant change. This is because reflective practice involves, for example, collaborative reflection with peers and action research as new and effective ways of using time. Fostering the degree of sophistication needed in approaches to CPD by individuals and organisations is a long-term project.

Engagement

Another key ingredient of normative professionalism is engagement, which professions must work hard to maintain. The removal of compulsion to register with the professional body will test FE teachers' commitment to professionalism. Since 1 October 2012, following the revocation of the regulations relating to registration and membership of the IfL, just over 98 per cent of IfL members chose to remain with the professional body, a total of 77,000 by December 2012. The CPD scheme that IfL will operate will emerge from consultation with members on the ways in which they wish CPD to be supported and monitored by their professional body. It is expected that IfL will seek arrangements that add value to members' professional standing, yet complement any FEG initiative. The extent to which IfL is successful will depend on individual members' commitment to their own CPD and the extent to which they can exercise choice and freedoms for meaningful and relevant CPD in the context of their employment.

Considering purposes, priorities and scope

Professional bodies typically play a significant role in determining the purposes, priorities and scope of CPD regimes. As competence development becomes more firmly located in the workplace, quality assurance mechanisms will need to take this into account. Employers may be more involved in delivery, since their co-operation is fundamental to the success of the scheme, and this creates opportunities for using portfolios as evidence of compliance where compliance requirements are in place.

CPD can also be used for a range of purposes beyond development. Satisfactory completion of CPD activity can be used as a filter for removing members of the profession who are not sufficiently engaged with their calling or as a post-qualification hurdle, for example as a prerequisite for obtaining a licence to conduct particular kinds of work. The nature of the regime should reflect the philosophy of the professional body and the purposes it seeks to achieve by having CPD requirements.

When the legal profession launched CPD schemes the use of the word 'development' suggested that the aims were broader than competence or even 'education', in an old school notion of passively imbibed knowledge. While the purpose of this breadth of focus was never clearly articulated, it was capable of embracing wider but important professional purposes. Philosophically, IfL's aspirational model for CPD seeks congruence with the nature of the occupation; teachers expand the minds and expertise of learners and so too the profession's own CPD should be expansive in nature and intent. IfL's approach to CPD was informed by research and practice across professions that also had begun to critique input models, and to value outcome-focused CPD. IfL sought to avoid the risk of individuals and organisations bypassing thoughtful consideration of experience and falling into the trap of achieving 'minimal compliance if we have to'. It sought to shift the balance away from employers managing employees' CPD experience and to encourage individuals' greater autonomy and freedom as professionals, driving their own professional development. Regimes that are more focused on compliance for practising or licensure requirements may impose greater constraints on autonomy and choice.

Setting standards

Professional bodies can play a significant role in setting standards for CPD. In many professions the national requirement for CPD is described in terms of a minimum threshold linked to competence. IfL's CPD requirements, however, aspired to excellence, producing truly inspirational teachers at the leading edge of their vocational or subject area and their methods of teaching. Research evidence from schools shows that the achievement of excellent outcomes needs quite distinct approaches, ones that go beyond national intervention or compliance which only take developments so far and then plateau, and that creativity, innovation and greater flexibilities and autonomy are needed for practitioners and organisations (Hopkins, 2009). It follows from this that we need to create environments that promote excellence through the value of professional autonomy and seriousness in personal and collaborative endeavours to improve practice. Professional bodies can require elements like reflection which might not otherwise feature in workplace schemes.

Determining strategy

There are numerous factors to consider when designing a scheme of continuing education for professionals. Houle (1980) noted that self-motivated learning is the most effective, but people's propensity for undertaking, or not undertaking, continuing education is often deep-seated. The most likely subscribers are those who have done so before, but any population confronted with new challenges and innovation is likely to include innovators, pacesetters, a middle majority and laggards. Laggards are likely to cause the profession most concern. Professions are likely to have similar practical agendas for CPD schemes – focusing on: 'how to speed up the learning of majority adopters and how to reach the laggards' (Houle, 1980: 164). Merely reaching the laggards does not explain what is then done. According to Houle, the continuing enhancement of professional competence involves constant self-monitoring of practice involving (1) absorption in the task at hand while (2) maintaining the detachment necessary to enable the professional to 'observe the scene in which he or she is an actor' (Houle, 1980: 209). This process is accompanied by introspection, a habit that may be difficult to develop and retain. This difficult challenge requires a strategy for instilling and maintaining the habit of introspection, or critical reflection, which may involve earlier stages of education. Planning how this is done requires a high-level strategy that considers the whole process of training. Professional bodies are ideally situated to carry out this role and to expect it of others with a role in training and professional development.

Defining and defending the space

In FE, there has been an emphasis on in-house workplace CPD as financial pressures impinge on individuals going outside of their institutions for CPD programmes or courses. Much of this in-house CPD is heavily criticised by teachers as being well-intentioned, overly prescriptive, too generic and largely irrelevant to their needs. A tick-box mentality can drive the filling of a staff development day with input 'activity' so that CPD has been done (IfL, 2012a). Many teachers find it hard to get financial support and time from their employer to support CPD that is most relevant to their practice. This is similar in the United States, where teachers, researchers, and policy-makers consistently indicate that the greatest challenge to implementing effective professional development is lack of time and having the right variety of CPD. Teachers need time to understand new concepts, learn new skills, develop new attitudes, research, discuss, reflect, assess, try new approaches and integrate them into their practice; and time to plan their own professional development (Cambone 1995; Corcoran 1995).

Adult learners need both set-aside time for learning, for example, workshops and courses, and time to experience and digest new ideas and ways of working (Cambone 1995). There needs to be time to work in study groups, conduct action research, participate in seminars, coach one another, plan lessons together and meet for other purposes. Professional development can no longer be viewed as an event that occurs on a few particular days of the year; rather, it must become part of the daily work life of educators. The right balance between individuals and peers driving their own CPD, and employers supporting this, both inside and beyond the organisation, is essential. Professional bodies can have a crucial role in identifying the space for CPD, the evidence base for CPD which works and CPD which does not and in defending the necessary space from encroachment.

Providing infrastructure

One of the key roles of professional bodies in maintaining standards is to maintain an overview of CPD on the ground. This allows systems to be adjusted to build on strengths and eliminate weaknesses. There are several ways that this could be done, for example, IfL's surveys, audit visits at which organisations' CPD strategies are discussed or submission of portfolios of evidence. The ease of collation, monitoring and sampling of evidence is obviously assisted by maintenance of substantial databases and sophisticated software. Investment in these tools is an obvious role for professional bodies. They can also to be trusted with the sensitive information that may be created by some CPD activity, which professionals may be reluctant to share with employers. Professional bodies not only have a sufficiently disinterested perspective to handle such data, they can extract and de-personalise it for general consumption and wider benefit.

Protecting autonomy, the ethos of independence and self-direction

For the individual, CPD can be an imposition or a source of motivation towards a stronger commitment to personal development and lifelong learning. It is far healthier for professions if their members are positively motivated towards CPD. This involves professional bodies ensuring that CPD schemes seek to encourage personal curiosity, autonomy and choice. Another task of CPD in the new environment is to resist managerialism. This includes a wide spectrum of activities from standardised and procedural forms of practice often referred to as 'box ticking', to the conception of 'useful' knowledge narrowly as instrumental to the absorption and limiting of CPD into organisational quality assurance frameworks. CPD must retain the potential to develop and inspire. Professional bodies must work to influence and ensure that CPD involves more than the instrumental production of localised knowledge. CPD should also demand the critical use of knowledge of wider frameworks. This may relate to critical depth, examining the assumptions and forms of reasoning influencing circumstances, and critical breadth, locating understanding in a wider, holistic social and political framework (Thompson and Thompson, 2008).

Promoting professionalism

Freidson (1988) identifies core denominators of professionalism as expertise, credentialism and autonomy,[9] suggesting that the exercise of discretion plays a key part in maintaining these distinctive claims of professionalism (Simon, 1988; Nicolson, 2006). It is arguable both that CPD should involve a more conscious effort to develop the capacity to exercise discretion but also a sense of wider professional purposes. For lawyers this could involve, for example, emphasis on professional ethics as an important dimension of discretionary decision-making and consideration of abstract notions such as the importance of the rule of law in pursuing justice. There are strong arguments that professional growth and personal development are achieved most effectively in a co-operative and collegial learning environment (Bebeau, 2008) and that law firms offer an excellent environment for collaborative reflection on ethics in action (Parker and Aitken, 2011). Moves to these more expansive agendas may be at odds with organisational priorities focused on the bottom line, hence the need for professional bodies to champion these agendas.

Redefining professionalism

As our account of aspiring professions demonstrates, professionalism does not stand still. Professional bodies should stimulate work that carries forward the professional agenda, educating about what professionalism is and what it could be. This activity might include inquiry into the occupation's defining functions, how self-enhancement agendas may be served or the formation of occupational sub-cultures, all of which serve important professional functions (Houle, 1980). If, in the future, practising professionals do not define what professionalism means, others will do it for them.

Conclusion

In the first wave of CPD schemes which were invariably input focused, the failure to articulate or prioritise the various potential goals of CPD (or education, or learning) led to an unsatisfactory CPD experience for many professionals. In recent times, many professions have recognised this fact and are now considering, or taking, tentative steps to address the situation. In the UK, across professions, a more liberal attitude to the form and scope of CPD has been accompanied by a more thoughtful attitude to the purpose of development activity. This has two dimensions. First, in addition to CPD addressing issues of work performance, wider issues of professional role and responsibility and wider conceptions of personal development are more likely to be defined within the scope of CPD. Second, adoption of the 'output' model of CPD has seen a sharper focus on the actual effect and impact of professional learning on knowledge, attitudes, perceptions or emotions, behaviour, professional practice and client, patient or employer conditions (Friedman, 2011). Material gathered for the detailed study of the CPD schemes of two professions highlights important practical, operational and theoretical distinctions in available models, and the kinds of circumstances in which they are deployed. For example, the kind of model that aims to inspire positive motivation towards continuing learning may be more difficult where there is a need to demonstrate compliance. We anticipate that the wider purposes of CPD will need to be accommodated within schemes that are much more closely tied to outcomes linked to competence and excellence.

Forms of CPD most likely to deliver changes in practice may be more difficult to control and monitor effectively. Shifts to workplace models may squeeze out professional initiatives to build engagement and a broader professional responsibility. These various factors may be combined within a single scheme, but the process is assisted by a greater and more clearly articulated sense of purpose and possibility. Most importantly, it is necessary to consider the place that practising professionals might have in future CPD regimes, particularly if the location of CPD in the workplace takes more hold. We argue that professions and professional bodies have a vital continuing role in relation to CPD. Scoping activity, such as defining the broader professional rationale of CPD, lies at the core, but there is also a role in defining the scope of employer involvement and gauging its operation and effectiveness for individual professionals. In the new environment for professions and CPD, locating the right balance between individual and employer-led activity, and highlighting the boundaries, is a primary challenge for professional bodies. In summary, our case study shows that government policy has impinged directly on professions, leading, directly or indirectly and intentionally or unintentionally, to changes in the orientation of CPD schemes. Our case study also gives credence to Houle's assertion that occupations are constantly moving towards or away from the professional ideal (Houle, 1980). We predict that CPD will play an increasingly significant role in informing and defining the ideal and moving towards it.

Notes

1 When describing lawyers and their professional bodies we refer to those in England and Wales rather than those in other jurisdictions in the UK. When referring to FE teachers we refer to those in England.
2 This set of regulations were subsequently revoked 30 September 2012.
3 (http://www.sra.org.uk/solicitors/cpd/solicitors.page#cpd-scheme) For solicitors and registered European lawyers (RELs) who work fewer than 32 hours per week, the requirements are reduced.
4 The seven CPD hours the course attracts count towards the annual requirement. Solicitors who qualified by undertaking the Law Society Finals Examination, which was phased out in 1994, or the Qualified Lawyers Transfer Test (QLTT) have a requirement to attend the Financial and Business Skills (not the exam) and, subject to exemptions, the Client Care and Professional Standards modules of the Professional Skills Course (PSC) during their first CPD year. The hours gained from attending these modules will count towards a solicitor's first-year CPD requirement. No hours can be claimed for undertaking the modules prior to admission.
5 'Participation' includes preparing, delivering and/or attending accredited courses. 'Attendance' means attendance at the complete course. Part attendance does not count at all.
  'Course' includes:
  • face-to-face sessions forming part of a course, including those delivered by an authorised distance-learning provider

- a course wholly provided by distance learning that involves assessment by dissertation and written examination
- structured coaching sessions, delivered face to face, of one hour or more, which have written aims and objectives, are documented showing an outcome, and are accredited under an authorisation agreement
- structured mentoring sessions involving professional development, of one hour or more, delivered face to face, which have written aims and objectives, are documented showing an outcome, and are accredited under an authorisation agreement.

6 Regulation 2(3) (Interpretation and Definitions) of Part 1.

7 *Pro rata* for part-time teachers with a minimum of six hours a year.

8 For example, a teacher may attend a six-hour long conference, but gauge that only the one hour workshop session could be legitimately counted as leading to a positive change in the effectiveness of their teaching. By contrast, two hours of reading research on teaching methods and three hours spent reflecting and talking with a fellow teacher about developing and improving teaching methods, when implemented, would count as five hours. CPD is measured by time leading to change, the input that made a difference.

9 Autonomy, particularly in the US, is interpreted as the occupation's independence from the state in internal management, while in the European context, it often refers to the freedom of individual professionals to exercise discretion in their work.

Chapter 4

Interpreting professional learning

The trouble with CPD

Sue Colquhoun and Jean Kelly

> In times of change the learner will inherit the earth while the learned are
> beautifully equipped for a world that no longer exists.
>
> (Eric Hoffer)

Introduction: A professional view of professional learning

From the questions and challenges raised in the previous chapters, it has become
clear that the terms and even the practice of professional learning or development
can be misinterpreted and contested by practitioners, learning organisations and
even professional bodies. This chapter will illustrate how since 2008 practitioners
have articulated their own view of professional learning and how this has been
interpreted by their professional body for teachers and trainers in the further
education (FE) and skills sector, the Institute for Learning (IfL) through the lens
of government regulation.

Context

In 2007 separate government regulations applied to both continuing professional
development (CPD) and the gaining of national professional status, Qualified
Teacher Learning and Skills (QTLS) and so the two parts of this chapter will focus
on (1) CPD and (2) QTLS. The chapter also reflects the views of two IfL staff
leading on each of these areas as to the challenges of aligning professional learning
with government regulation. The first part of the chapter on CPD is an analysis of
how tens of thousands of practitioners responded to the compulsory evidencing
of their continuing professional development and what that might show about the
development of a shared concept of professional learning. The second part, on the
process of Professional Formation in order to gain QTLS, is a description of how,
given more freedom and innovative ways of articulating their learning, teachers
and trainers were able to move from a purely mechanistic model of achieving
status into an understanding of what Michael Eraut termed a transformative state
in both perception and practice (Eraut, 1995). In this interpretation we can see a

more holistic approach to learning and a striving towards 'wider skills for growth' above and beyond political mandate (Lucas, Claxton and Webster, 2010).

The trouble with CPD

A journey is a powerful way of conceptualising the complexity of developing a professional identity and the accompanying process of understanding one's own learning that goes to the very heart of what it means to be a teacher. It is a metaphor that practitioners and teacher educators use all the time to chart progress from the initial stages of the trainee to the seasoned teaching professional. Like all journeys, it can be an unpredictable and sometimes deeply challenging rite of passage.

The real trouble seems to start when practitioners try to make sense of the shift they have to make from professional development to professional learning. In her book, *Realizing the Power of Professional Learning*, Helen Timperley (2011) helpfully distinguishes between professional development and professional learning, where the former is something that may be 'done' to someone so that the teacher is often seen as the passive recipient of this, while in the latter, there is a more active engagement, through which teachers focus on their students' needs and how they can support them more effectively and their motivation for this is driven 'by their need to know rather than someone else's desire to tell' (Timperley, 2011: 14). For many teachers and trainers there is often an abrupt disjunction when the legitimated activity of initial teacher training stops, and the process of CPD starts. It is at this point that many people new to the teaching profession are left either to their own devices or handed a menu of largely irrelevant events put on by their employer that they are required to attend. Indeed Timperley claims 'much professional development has little or no meaning for teachers' (Timperley, 2011: 2) and evidence from four years of IfL CPD reviews would strongly support this view about the irrelevance and poor timing of institutional activity as opposed to individualised and meaningful learning activities.

Why might development be seen as distinct to, and different from, learning? It could be argued that eliding any big idea into a shorthand series of letters diminishes both the concept and the user. The acronym CPD, continuing professional development, should carry the weight of a fundamental principle of professionalism, that learning never stops for the doctor, lawyer or teacher, that continuing learning is necessary for expert practice. However, it has become a reductive description of all that happens to the individual after the learning experience of initial qualification. The trouble with CPD is that we have become over-reliant on one particular acronym and it has lost its meaning. It has become a cypher for more teaching rather than more learning. The implications of 'continuing' have been lost so that the idea of a spiral curriculum of learning in which the teacher continually refines, deepens and broadens understanding, becomes the micro view rather than the big picture and learning is reduced to development which is then equated to a simple list of courses and events to be taken. Professional learning and development become, in this declension, a solitary obligation and even, in the view of some practitioners, a chore. Professional learning and then development of that learning should be about 'active involvement in learning' (Timperley, 2011: 2) and that is why, right at the beginning of the journey, the theory of experiential learning makes so much sense for practitioners in FE and skills. The realisation of 'learning by doing' (Kolb, 1984), the need to examine learning and make it explicit is for some a revelation: student learning and professional learning are actually the same process. For many professionals this is the point at which they become really 'smart people' and understand double-loop learning (Argyris, 1991); they reflect on the multiple processes that occur in any situation, teachers learning from other teachers, teachers learning from their students and students learning from teachers and their peers – the 'visible' learning that gives rise to grounded evidence for improvement (Hattie, 2012).

The excitement of learning about learning in the initial stages of professional qualification (which is mostly about theory into practice) soon gets left behind in the day-to-day busy life of most professional teachers and trainers and practice does not go back to theory as in the Kolb (1984) cycle of experiential learning. The acronyms take over and the time for building on the initial articulation of what learning means can become squeezed into a simplistic version of professional learning – CPD. For some it can be quicker and easier to 'tick the box' rather than spend quality time reflecting on practice back into theory in order to close the loop. Consequently when it comes to meaningful CPD or showing that they are, in the technical term, remaining in good professional standing, teachers and trainers have been pushed into a superficial response to the latter and have interpreted professional learning and CPD as one.

In some ways, therefore, when the IfL was regulated by government to monitor the CPD of teachers and trainers in the FE and skills sector in 2007, the incentive for many practitioners was to make an official record that they were completing the required number of hours per year and nothing to do with the quality of the professional learning they might have been experiencing, or even the impact of what they had done. It was back to single-loop learning for some people in an instant.

In 2008 the IfL was asked by government to review the CPD of its 200,000 members on a yearly basis. The IfL had consulted its elected members on the Advisory Council and were clear about the philosophy it wanted to bring to the sector. The philosophy of CPD was defined as 'maintaining and broadening relevant knowledge and skills in a subject or vocational specialism and in teaching and training methods so that it has a positive impact on practice and the learner experience' (IfL, 2007). From this definition comes a model of CPD that recognises three distinct areas of professional learning:

- vocational and subject-specific knowledge and expertise
- knowledge of effective approaches to teaching and training
- knowledge of how changes in policy and the local context affect teaching and training.

The model was designed to help teachers and trainers think about CPD systematically and holistically and to counter a more conventional tick-box approach or compliance that merely 'clocks up' random development opportunities. This was important when, for the first time, practitioners were being asked to make their professional development available for scrutiny. But to achieve real impact, the use of the IfL model for CPD requires an autonomous, committed and responsible professional to be the driver and the designer of their own CPD year on year.

The IfL considered that a model such as this would give teachers and trainers maximum flexibility in deciding what counted as relevant CPD. In addition, any relevant activities were required to be evaluated through the following questions:

- What professional development activities have you undertaken this year?
- Have you reflected on the learning gained from carrying out these activities?
- Have the activities and the reflection combined made a difference to what and how you teach or train?
- So what….? Can you show evidence of what the difference has been and the impact it has made on your learners, colleagues or the organisation in which you work?

It was always understood by the IfL that the questions were deceptively simple and that the body anticipated that developing a CPD practice that was regulated but also personalised and where the questions could be answered positively and in a confident way by the majority would take several years (IfL 2009: 19).

In fact, what the professional body attempted to do in 2008 was to induct 200,000 teachers and trainers into a different way of thinking about their learning using an experiential approach, starting with their current practice and using dialogue and questioning and determinedly sticking to assessment *for* their own learning when there was pressure (from organisations and regulations) to carry out assessment *of* their own learning (Wiliam and Black, 2006).

This was an enormous task and it was not known what the outcomes would be but it was thought that the methodology was appropriate for adult learners and professionals in the field of education and was scaffolded to enable teachers and trainers to answer the IfL questions through the use of an e-portfolio and peer review and feedback. It was an experiment in changing attitudes to professional learning – a leap of faith in professional judgement and good sense.

Government regulations in September 2007 mandating annual evidence of CPD led initially to some doubt about the value of change, although the majority of teachers and trainers later expressed a view in the annual IfL survey of 2009 that a national rather than organisational recognition of CPD was welcomed. There is always an inherent tension created when a relatively new professional body both supports and encourages personalised and professional learning and simultaneously has to regulate CPD. Indeed, some bodies have split their functions to avoid this. An annual requirement to evidence professional development can be seen by some as a bureaucratic process rather than an opportunity to record a continuous cycle of learning independent of where any teacher or trainer might work. The IfL annual reviews of CPD that followed regulation show what progress was made in conceptualising CPD as professional learning and how practitioners interpreted the IfL model.

The initial year of regulated activity for the professional body (2008–09) was the first time in which a professional body in the FE and skills sector had asked teachers and trainers to 'declare their CPD' as a means of measuring the members' accountability to the regulations and was in many ways a revelation about teachers' readiness to articulate professional learning and lack of readiness to comply with government regulations. The one significant question to the body from members about this process of declaration was 'what counts as CPD', as there was a great deal of concern that they would not get it 'right'. The somewhat revolutionary process of being able to decide for oneself what was relevant, meaningful and impactful, and to be trusted by the professional body to do this, left many in a difficult position. They could see the logic of the personalised model and the need to trust the professional, but it was the formalisation of the declaration process that was seen by some as a barrier or even negation of that trust. All members were asked to declare the hours and type of professional development they had completed throughout the year and inform the IfL of this information before the deadline of 31 August 2009 (a requirement and a deadline set by government in statute). The collation of data was both to comply with government regulations and to provide an evidence base of CPD for IfL, but it seemed to many to be contradictory and at odds with a genuine trust in the professional judgement and honesty of practitioners.

The IfL tried to counter this perceived imposition of bureaucracy with a choice in the means to complete the formal declaration of completion of CPD for the year. There was a simple self-declaration process members could do online (a straightforward summary sheet) or the IfL's recommended option, the use of REfLECT, a bespoke e-portfolio which had been developed for the purpose of allowing teachers and trainers to access and share, if wished, their own personal and private webfolio record. This e-portfolio was scaffolded, in the sense of webpages prompting critical reflection, evaluation and self-assessment (assessment for, not of, learning) and a storage space for keeping visual, aural and written learning materials. All we asked as a summary was:

- the number of hours' CPD completed (based on their total number of teaching hours)
- whether teachers, tutors and trainers had shared their CPD with their employer or peers
- a breakdown of hours spent on subject or vocational specialism, teaching and learning and local and policy context.

The beauty of the REfLECT e-portfolio was that it was a benefit of membership, a private and personal space for teachers and trainers to collate and evaluate their own learning throughout the year. The only part of the portfolio that members needed to share with the IfL or with their employer was the summary sheet; everything else could be kept private or shared with other colleagues. The IfL had hoped that this would encourage real professional dialogue and the building of a community of practice that gave many isolated teachers and trainers an opportunity to engage with and learn from others. The e-portfolio had been designed and developed by teacher education tutors at the University of Wolverhampton as the Pebble Pad system and was in use with all their trainee teachers. The success of this system was well documented and evidenced and the development team of Pebble Learning agreed to create a bespoke version for the IfL – REfLECT. In some ways this was also breaking new ground as the take-up of e-portfolios and sharing learning online was, according to BECTA, an e-learning organisation at the time, very underdeveloped in the FE and skills sector.

In the 2008–09 cycle of CPD, 82,000 members accessed REfLECT and 51 per cent of members used it to record their professional development activities which showed a rather unexpected enthusiasm to participate in new technology, but the IfL could not expect all members to either have access to such technology where they worked or even where they lived. The decision, therefore, was to make the use of REfLECT optional as it was recognised this too was a development that would take several years to bring to fruition the notion of sharing and collaborating online. It was a system ahead of its time; the rapid development of Facebook and LinkedIn technology since then would make an introduction of this in 2013 much easier to promote and adopt.

All that teachers and trainers had to do in August of 2009 was to complete a summary sheet either on the website or in REfLECT and send to IfL. We then intended to sample the total number of declarations after the deadline by area of the sector and ask the individuals selected as part of the random sample from our database to share more details of what they had done with us. It was thought this would give IfL a better picture of CPD in different parts of a very complex sector than the statistics would ever do alone.

The review of the findings this first year were very positive in one sense, an overwhelming 98 per cent of members were exceeding the minimum number of hours required so they, or their organisations, were obviously committed to undertaking conventional professional development, but also worrying in the sense that only 44 per cent had shared what they had carried out for their CPD with a colleague. A growing body of research has shown that the kinds of professional development that make the most difference to practice are based on professional dialogue about teaching and learning but there was disappointing evidence of learning with and through others at this initial stage (IfL, 2009).

What was more concerning was the evidence that was sent in by the randomly selected groups. There were 593 portfolios submitted in total and these were all reviewed by trained peer reviewers who read the evidence with three criteria in mind:

1   Relevance: was the evidence commensurate with the job role of the member?

2   Sufficiency: did the hours declared tally with the number of hours evidenced and required?
3   Authenticity: did the details confirm the member information on the database?

All of the members in the sample received feedback from their peer reviewer; this process was not an assessment but peer review. Everyone received critical and detailed feedback on what could be improved. However, the evidence that was seen varied enormously from the detailed and massive portfolio sent special delivery at some considerable expense, to a torn-out sheet from a lined exercise book with a few notes on 'things I went to'. There was a great deal of going on courses, but little evidence of the impact of professional learning.

The real concern was that, despite some brilliant examples of CPD event-going, there was little evidence of the difference the development activity had made. There was confusion about what counted as CPD and what the IfL would accept, and so we had, with great reluctance, given a list of what could count (a hugely varied list ranging from reading an article in a professional journal to acting as an external assessor to formal courses and programmes) trying to make this as loose as possible but all the time bearing in mind the 'so what' question attaching to every activity, the reflection on the impact of professional learning.

As a professional learning team within the professional body, a great deal from this first experiment with evidence of CPD in this form had been learned. In the second year of monitoring CPD, an attempt was made to make an explicit link between professional learning and excellence in professional practice. So IfL looked back, using Ofsted findings and current research into teacher training, at what had been a common practice in the sector of providers offering menus of disparate CPD opportunities, and in this second report determinedly looked forwards to a growth in understanding that professional learning was a way of systematically maintaining and improving knowledge, skills and competence throughout a working life (IfL, 2010a).

IfL took the same route to discovery as before (with the random sample selection), finding in this second year an increase in the amount of hours completed and, more significantly, an increased interest in sharing CPD with and beyond the profession – 64 per cent said they shared their CPD with a colleague; 67 per cent with an employer. But, this year, as well as peer review on evidence IfL followed up the sample with telephone interviews to try to dig beneath the surface evaluation to get to the richer soil where learning happened – and why.

The phone interviews were partially successful and IfL learned a great deal more about how individuals combined their 'dual professionalism', their understanding and approaches to pedagogy and their updating of their subject specialism or industrial updating, but still little about the impact on themselves and others. IfL were trying to take the notion of Argyris's (1991) double-loop learning further and to foster an understanding of triple-loop learning. Learning is not just about problem-solving or single-loop learning but about reflecting on how teachers often perpetuate the problems through their own behaviours, double-loop learning. IfL wanted to go a stage further and to critically collaborate to promote further learning in both self and others:

> When we declare that we have made a commitment to CPD; when we show evidence of what we have achieved and how we have made a difference to our own and others' learning; when we are able to reflect on feedback from our peers, then we are participating in a cycle of professional dialogue and development that is enriching and ennobling for the profession and our learners.
>
> (IfL 2010a: 10)

There was clear difficulty still about the interpretation of what professional learning was and how important it was to 'profess' it. Many members in the phone interviews were suspicious and found it hard to express what they had done – 'Why are you ringing me – is it to check out what I have already told you?' or 'Oh, does that (a professional dialogue with colleagues that led to experimentation and changes to practice) really count as CPD?' It was never the intention as a professional body to police or mandate certain types and forms of CPD but rather to trust the professional and his/her own accounts of learning, but this was proving harder to articulate than had been realised.

The review in cycle 2 closed with the clear realisation that it required a different methodology if IfL wanted to get to a better understanding of what constituted professional learning for our members.

In cycle 3 the professional development team had grown, and consisted of the in-house CPD team and the many associates to IfL of peer reviewers and regional advisers and together all had learned from the first two years about the magnitude of what IfL were trying to explore by talking to each other and using each other's expertise and knowledge. IfL had established a community of practice which enabled us to interrogate the data and establish a basis on which to move forward. In the third year IfL asked for the same declaration of CPD and did the same random selection of members, but this time IfL split the groups regionally and held a series of face-to-face focus groups in the nine regions in order to try to get beneath the surface but also establish similar communities of practice with local groups. IfL tried networking in its broadest sense – both to build relationships between practitioners but also between groups of subject specialists and teachers in specific areas of the sector – there was also an online community for everyone, even for those who had not been able to meet face-to-face at the group meetings.

This approach recognised the experience of the previous years, the importance of collaborative professional learning, the importance of communities of practice in which an individual can 'profess' their knowledge and understanding of practice with others. The individual, lone practitioner is vulnerable and often isolated and the coming together of people with a shared experience helps to fertilise ideas, thoughts and change – it provides a space for the public articulation of tacit professional learning:

> The new professional is often a networked professional, having to co-operate and communicate with a wide range of colleagues within and outside their chosen profession … this reconstructs the space for reflection – it takes place in shared and networked situations.
>
> (Frost, 2010: 18)

IfL's methodology therefore evolved to facilitate and reconstruct these spaces for professional learning. The methodology also models ways in which participants can see 'new paradigms of investigation' and use them with their learners in their own context of CPD activity. A number of face-to-face dialogues were organised around the country in which members could exchange ideas about professional learning and deepen the understanding of the networked professional within a variety of communities of practice.

During the course of these focus groups, IfL heard that the best moments of professional learning were always with other people so it follows that for maximum impact every teacher and trainer needs to discuss, critically reflect and co-construct their professional learning with colleagues.

IfL also listened to the views that if self-directed professional development activities and learning experiences give rise to the most meaningful results (which the vast majority of our respondents agreed was the case), then any organisation employing teachers and trainers needs to create what Fuller and Unwin (2003a) term a more expansive and less restrictive working environment so that learning at work becomes valued and valuable (Fuller and Unwin, 2003a). Expansive workplaces encourage teachers and trainers to work creatively as teams taking responsibility for their own professional development, and they facilitate and reward innovation and experimentation in teaching and learning.

The publication of the IfL 2011 review of CPD (IfL, 2012a) drew attention to several recommendations about the interpretations of professional development and learning:

- Sharing the outcomes of CPD is excellent professional learning in itself so there is a need to create more time for this. If collaborative learning and collective and critical reflective practice on what works and the impact on learners is key to improving teaching and learning then organisations could help to create communities of CPD practice to model focus groups and outcomes.
- More planning time and time for effective personalised and collaborative CPD is essential as directed and mandatory CPD is not necessarily effective and yet employers seem to invest mostly in this.
- CPD is vital to career development and readiness for new teaching and learning opportunities.

- The impact of CPD is insufficiently theorised or prioritised and action research and supported experiments get the teacher beyond surface evaluations and to deep learning about teaching and learning strategies that work.

(IfL, 2012a: 9)

It could be argued that in early 2011 the IfL reviews had generated discussions about professional learning and that was, in one sense, very positive. Everyone was talking about professionalism and learning opportunities and models: the government, the trade unions, employers and employer bodies and associations. However, running alongside this big conversation were concerns, in particular from one trade union, about regulation itself, the compulsion to declare professional learning and even the legitimacy of the professional body itself. The government set up an independent review panel on professionalism, and, after consultation on the recommendations of the panel, the 2007 regulations on the need to join a professional body and evidence annual CPD were revoked by the government in 2012. The current political will is to recognise the importance and benefits of professionalism but to let professional learning be 'employer-led' rather than individually planned in conjunction with organisational need. It may well be significant that members of the review panel also saw a 'degree of fearfulness' expressed by many practitioners and a 'confidence deficit' which is unsurprising given this undermining of professional autonomy (Department for Business, Innovation and Skills, 2012: 13).

This 'confidence deficit' was also seen in the early findings of the IfL review of 2012. The focus of this review was on the impact of CPD, how to measure it and how to apply the learning gained from it. Although everyone who took part in the 2012 focus groups was asked to provide examples of something they had undertaken which 'made a difference' and was able to articulate the benefits of their CPD activities, there was little hard evidence of specific, measurable learning that was then used to improve the outcomes for learners. Many of the respondents said that they did not always know what they would learn from any development activity and agreed that if learning itself is not predictable, why should professional learning be any different? It could be argued that the ongoing and often heated debates about regulation and the perceived 'imposition' of having to share evidence of CPD took away the confidence that had been steadily growing over the previous three years. In the absence of clear government decisions around who or what should review CPD, many teachers and trainers were unsure of their ground and their own professional autonomy.

Perhaps it is the question of who or what interprets the difference between types of learning: professional, vocational, applied or academic, that is the reason for the trouble with CPD. Or perhaps it is because, for some, professional development is perceived to be all about teaching and not about learning. The IfL has found over the four years it has been monitoring the professional development of teachers and trainers in the FE and skills sector what could be argued to be the beginning of a shift in an attitude to professional learning and a change in the nature of the discourse about CPD. It could be said that only an independent national professional body can nurture this in a way that an individual employer cannot. It remains to be seen whether fundamental changes to the sector in the form of an employer-led FE Guild will continue this shift in the philosophy of professional learning. The second part of this chapter examines how well the philosophy around Professional Formation stood up to changes in regulation.

The opportunities of Professional Formation

As the name suggests, Professional Formation is the beginning of a journey into professionalism, usually but not always, following an initial teacher training/ education (ITT/E) course or programme, leading to an ITT/E qualification, such as the Diploma in Teaching in the Lifelong Learning Sector (DTLLS), Postgraduate/Professional Graduate Certificate in Education (PGCE) or Certificate in Education. According to the regulations of September 2007, the IfL was given responsibility for conferring the status of QTLS and was instrumental in the design and development of the new process for gaining the status, the model of Professional Formation.

If experienced teachers and trainers remain largely unconfident about interpreting and grounding their professional learning in evidence, those people new to the sector, the 'unformed' in pedagogy though experienced in their own subject area, who put themselves forward for Professional Formation begin their journey somewhere on a continuum from unconfident novices in the field of learning (although highly experienced in their own subject specialism) or as somewhat overconfident experts in teaching and training. On their way to demonstrating their status as a professional, they learn much more about themselves and the worth of what they have done in the past and will do in the future than they could imagine. This process makes transparent the paradox about the continuum from novice to expert that underpins initial teacher education (Dreyfus and Dreyfus, 1986). For the majority of teachers and trainers in the FE and skills sector, professional learning does not articulate with a linear journey at all, it requires an opportunity for expression that is altogether more sophisticated. The process of Professional Formation that was developed by the IfL offers one such opportunity.

The notion of Professional Formation had first been suggested by the newly formed IfL in the sector consultations on professionalism and was endorsed by the then Labour government as a concept (Department for Education and Skills, 2002). Once government regulations were finally in place in 2007 to mandate this approach, work began to develop a model of evidenced professional learning that teachers and trainers would recognise and support as professionally relevant and sufficient to gain the status of QTLS which would be on a par with lawyers, doctors and, indeed, teachers in the school sector who already had a system for gaining QTS (Qualified Teacher Status). From the outset, in discussion with peers and drawing on the learning from the first ever pilot review of CPD in June 2008, Professional Formation was developed as an online process to be completed in the specially designed webfolio in REfLECT in which newly trained teachers could demonstrate the application of the theory covered in their initial teacher training to their practice in their teaching appointment/s.

As such, it provided a broad scaffolding of standardised requirements, such as:

- certificates of ITT/E qualifications and appropriate demonstration of level 2 skills in literacy, numeracy and information and communications technology (ICT)
- a self-declaration of suitability to practise
- a supporter's statement;

alongside more personalised elements, based on the 'dual professional' model (Robson, 1996) adopted by the IfL and underpinned by the notion of reflective practice, namely:

- subject specialist expertise and updating
- knowledge of teaching and learning
- self-evaluation
- professional development planning
- reflective practice.

Unlike the competence-based assessment model used in most ITT/E qualifications, the webfolio was designed to provide scaffolding and an opportunity for individuals to tell the story of their personal journey into teaching, for example, when, where and how they started teaching, to reflect on the learning involved in their ITT/E course and its application to their current practice in terms of their professional needs and future career development directions.

In contrast to CPD, Professional Formation was an entirely new way of making professional learning underpinned by reflective practice explicit. It enabled tacit knowledge to be articulated and applied, so that it could be shared with peers. Inherent in CPD is the notion of extending learning, updating, refreshing and improving practice, most effective through professional dialogue, networking and sharing good practice, while Professional Formation was an original and exciting route which provided a pathway to extended learning, simultaneously looking back as well as forward and leading to the recognition of professional status. The excitement was generated by a new way of thinking and doing, opening up spaces and allowing participants and reviewers to explore and recognise their learning and its impact on their practices. Some of this excitement is captured in the comment below.

> I enjoyed reading the stories and felt privileged to share the journey. What a fascinating opportunity. I have carried out online assessments and this has been the most organised and supportive!
>
> (Peer reviewer, July 2012)

The how and why of Professional Formation

In the first ever cycle of Professional Formation offered from September 2008, IfL fellows were invited to participate in the research and development phase of the process in order to inform and shape its structure. To be graded as a fellow of the IfL, members would need to be highly experienced practitioners holding Masters or higher degrees in Education, demonstrating specialist knowledge of teaching or training, research and development and its application within the sector.

Fellows were specifically invited to lead this development because of the likelihood that their knowledge and experience would have given them the confidence to exercise autonomous professional judgement. As fellows they would be most likely to have the capabilities to experience the process, effectively evaluate its impact and offer suggestions for improvement of both the experience and its impact. Fellows conducted peer review of each application in setting and agreeing the required standards and expectations of sufficiency, relevance and authenticity. One hundred and nineteen applicants were involved and 90 were successfully awarded QTLS in March 2009.

Central to development of Professional Formation was the exercise of peer review and the agreement that an holistic approach be adopted so that this was distinguished from assessment and involved a personal, professional judgement of the evidence provided, rather than a decision based on a deficit model of what might be lacking. The purpose of professional learning is not about securing minimal levels of competence but about striving for excellence, as indicated in Chapter 5 in the case study which compares CPD in FE and skills and the legal profession.

Without too much digression into the literature surrounding competence and competence-based assessment, a conscious decision was taken to avoid reducing everything to minimum generic levels of performance. The decision was to adopt a more flexible, sophisticated and personalised approach which would be able to recognise and capture the multifaceted nature and complexity of each individual's learning, experience and professional development.

What IfL was attempting to achieve was a form of what Dylan Wiliam refers to as assessment for learning (AfL) as opposed to assessment of learning. AfL is an ongoing process of identifying where individuals are in their learning journey, where they are travelling to and how they are likely to get there, while assessment of learning is more like an end product, looking back on what has been achieved, once someone has arrived.

Although in the development of Professional Formation, the five key strategies of AfL, identified by Wiliam (Wiliam, 2011) were not consciously followed, they influenced the design of the elements within the webfolio and were implicit in implementation of the process. Professional Formation mirrored these key strategies, placing QTLS applicants and their reviewers in the position of learners, not always in a classroom, engaging in professional learning. As Wiliam (2009) in his work on formative assessment has made clear, AfL cannot happen through 'tick box' assessment and IfL was equally convinced that neither could professional learning through the process of Professional Formation. This process was sometimes as much a revelation for the reviewers as it was for the participants.

> This process has taught me so much about taking the holistic view and has informed some of my practice.
>
> (Peer reviewer, March 2012)

It was decided to opt for peer review as opposed to assessment and to make explicit the distinction between holding an ITT/E qualification which, once achieved would be permanently retained and holding the professional status of QTLS, which would depend on an ongoing demonstration of remaining in good standing as a professional, keeping up to date with ever-changing circumstances through reflecting on practice, engaging in professional dialogue with peers and professional learning. This, however, was often elided with CPD, and as indicated by the concerns expressed earlier in this chapter, this conflation of terminology needs to be challenged as it may have implications for evaluating impact.

In contrast to CPD which invited members to use REfLECT to record their CPD as described earlier in the chapter, for Professional Formation, the use of REfLECT was recommended as the prescribed route with exceptions being granted in a small number of cases where legitimate reasons for not being able to follow this route were able to be provided. The use of REfLECT was grounded in the notion that it would be anomalous to award professional status to teachers in the twenty-first century unable to demonstrate a basic working knowledge of the application of technology. Although ICT had been identified in the regulations of September 2007, there was no specific government driver to support how this might be achieved, but it was considered by the IfL to be critical in advancing and securing professional learning through the medium of Professional Formation.

Linked to this and the peer review approach, was the agreement not to provide exemplars of evidence or to prescribe word lengths as each individual's evidence was regarded as unique and to be judged on its own strengths. The lack of prescription was seen as important to ensure that each individual would take responsibility for and make professional judgements about the integrity and robustness of the evidence they had selected to demonstrate their professionalism. Some found this particularly challenging and this was a reflection of IfL's experiences with CPD when members were given the freedom to choose what might count as appropriate CPD.

Fellows had provided their own evidence in their Professional Formation applications to be reviewed by their peers and this has been central to the review of all Professional Formation applications for QTLS and remains an essential and continuing requirement in the training of all new peer reviewers of whom there are now in excess of 130; they are all QTLS graduates. Furthermore, at the end of each cycle of Professional Formation, all reviewers and moderators meet for the Final Evaluation meeting to discuss, review and revise procedures and any new developments in order to inform the future shape of Professional Formation so that it is an ongoing, developmental model of professionalism, responding to ever-changing situations.

Central to the integrity of the process is the continuing professional dialogue of all involved in Professional Formation, including peer reviewers, moderators, applicants and wider IfL colleagues. The purpose of the professional dialogue was to stimulate further learning.

> If teachers are prepared and committed to engage in the risky business of problematising their own practice, seeking evidence to evaluate in order to judge where change is needed, and then to act on their decisions, they are thus engaging in assessment for learning with respect to their own professional learning.
>
> (Pedder and James, 2012: 41)

Key elements of professional learning for all are emerging in the model adopted by Professional Formation: namely, scaffolding (Bruner, 1966; Vygotsky, 1978) in supporting applicants to tell their story and support the development of communities of practice (Lave and Wenger, 1991) through peer review and professional dialogue of each Professional Formation application. Engagement in Professional Formation has enabled members to gain confidence in directly questioning and challenging what it means to be professional and involved them in 'professing' in communities of practice and providing rich opportunities for professional learning, not from a position of arrogance, but rather as mentioned earlier in the chapter of double-loop learning, teachers as learners, learning from other teachers and also their learners, actively engaged in a continuous cycle of learning and continuing to learn.

From my own experience as a teacher and teacher-educator, what has been exceptional and highly unusual about Professional Formation has been its ability to work outside prescriptive competence assessment boundaries and to enable professionals to take autonomous decisions about the applications of their peers for QTLS and this has only been possible because of the reviewers' personal involvement in Professional Formation, first as applicants themselves, and then later as reviewers exercising the ability and opportunity to engage in ongoing peer discussion and dialogue, to profess on what it means to be a professional.

Professional Formation has been released from competence-based assessment to a more open, holistic and new dimension of the discussion of professionalism in terms of the evidence individual applicants have chosen to provide, which is not criterion based, but individualistic and personalised. This invites freedom of expression, the exercise of personal autonomy and professional judgement of peers so that it activates and operates in a completely different sphere of personal trust which is something rare, sometimes messy and untested in current manager-ialistic paradigms, but which has been the driving force in taking forward the success and achievements of members holding the professional status of QTLS, of whom there are currently more than 13,000.

Professional Formation aligns very well with the concept of building professional capital as described by Hargreaves and Fullan (2012). They suggest that professional capital combines three elements of capital, namely, human, social and decisional with the first, human, focusing on individual knowledge and training, but for this to be further developed; the second, social, is necessary and refers to the way in which interactions with others provide access to their human capital, enabling this knowledge to be shared.

Central to this process of working together and sharing knowledge is relationship-building and trust, but even these are not sufficient for professionalism. The final dimension is decisional capital which involves making discretionary judgements. Decisional capital may be defined as:

> the capital that professionals acquire and accumulate through structured and unstructured experience, practice and reflection – capital that enables them to make wise judgments in circumstances where there is no fixed rule or piece of incontrovertible evidence to guide them. Decisional capital is enhanced by drawing on the insights and experiences of colleagues in forming judgments on many occasions.
>
> (Hargreaves and Fullan, 2012: 93–94)

The completion and review of Professional Formation is one such example of a complex process of which in teaching there are an infinite variety. It involves a wide range of individual teachers from diverse areas with peer reviewers reaching decisions based on the evidence they have provided in order to be awarded the professional status of QTLS, which might have life-changing consequences and outcomes with implications for future career directions.

This review of Professional Formation is built on collaboration, dialogue, trust and sharing and it is far from a box-ticking exercise, but involves highly experienced practitioners, many of whom are teacher educators who have themselves gained QTLS, acting as peer reviewers, making judgements about complex situations for which there may be no categorical certainties and taking difficult decisions about individual applications. There are no simplistic 'right' or 'wrong' answers and decisions are refined through teamwork and professional dialogue with other reviewers and moderators involved so that decision-making is also a learning experience for all, as reflected in the comments below.

As usual, this was interesting and enjoyable. It never ceases to fascinate me the different routes by which people enter the Lifelong Learning sector, and the range of subjects that were taught. Overall, I had fewer queries than I have had in the past, but then I had new queries which I had never encountered before – such as someone attaching an observation indicating that they were an inadequate teacher!

(Peer reviewer, March 2012)

For me and others involved in developing Professional Formation, it has provided the motivation and opportunity to begin moving along the professional continuum outlined in the spectrum of professional maturity in the first chapter, from reactive through interactive to proactive, developing skills required for informed autonomy, powerful dialogue, rigorous reflective practice and an understanding of the potential impact of professional learning.

Different people have started from different places, and in a way Professional Formation has been the vehicle which has enabled members to begin the journey into what it means to be professional, often only partly understood, but providing opportunities to engage in professional dialogue, to grow in confidence and assertiveness, to 'profess' based on evidence and professional judgement, which is something that is not always encouraged by a managerialist approach.

Professional Formation has created opportunities for IfL members to apply these ideas and to put them into practice, shaping their own professional development and contributing to that of the sector with implications for their learners. Professional Formation has mirrored the steps of the IfL, as a relatively young and emerging professional body for teachers in FE and skills and exemplified the wider notion of professionalism espoused by the IfL.

Reviewers new to the experience describe it as a wonderful opportunity in which they feel privileged to participate in recognising the professionalism of their peers within the sector and the rich diversity of the experience which they bring to their roles.

It is genuinely a privilege to undertake this work and assist my fellow professionals to attain ATLS or QTLS status. I always take the opportunity to promote this designate whenever I have the opportunity to do so as I believe it is so worthwhile.

(Peer reviewer, July 2012)

In order to maintain consistency and reliability of the Professional Formation process, rigorous moderation and quality assurance procedures were implemented.

Thank you for all your hard work ... to ensure that we as reviewers can deliver the highest levels of professionalism and consistency for applicants.

(Peer reviewer, July 2012)

From comments such as these and based on my own experience of Professional Formation, it would seem that professional learning is a journey of specific stages, not necessarily linear but highly individualised, depending on personal situations and starting points and wider conditions of employment, often beset with obstacles, setbacks and opportunities and there comes a time when it feels right for an individual to make a conscious choice to move beyond where they are.

> As part of the Professional Formation process, I undertook a SWOT [Strengths, Weaknesses, Opportunities and Threats] for self-evaluation, then built a development plan built on that evaluation. As a result I noticed the need to develop and practise a wider range of teaching and learning activities and techniques which would particularly benefit those who have a more visual, non-linear approach to their learning. I did this and embedded it in my teacher education classes, so that my trainees also became aware of 'non-standard' approaches which worked well in the classroom. In our Ofsted inspection, the inspectors remarked on the way our trainees 'used a wide range of teaching approaches and are not afraid to experiment'. We received a grade one from Ofsted.
>
> (QTLS Graduate, 2012)

Sometimes the choice is not always of the teachers' own making. Factors within their current job role have indicated that change is necessary so that they begin Professional Formation, working individually, or possibly collaboratively with a group of people, and as they proceed, it becomes apparent that this is not about knowledge and skills transfer but rather a personal journey, requiring deep personal awareness, providing space to choose, to ask questions, and about choice and autonomy in terms of collecting and collating relevant evidence highlighting their teaching biography.

Everyone's journey is unique, may involve pain, and learning how to live with ambiguity and the realisation that achieving professional status is not an end point, but the beginning of lifelong involvement in professional learning and reflective practice. Furthermore, being a professional is not solely about subject specialist knowledge, but learning and about taking responsibility for choices and being accountable. It is about continued learning and development and the most effective learning in this is ultimately, shared and collaborative.

> I now have that flexibility and work with schools as well as FE colleges because of QTLS. and I'm treated like an equal. Now I have my sights on IfL fellowship.
>
> (QTLS Graduate, 2012)

Teachers have a specific responsibility for learning which might make their professional learning different from that of other professions. They are 'dual professionals' needing to learn not only about their subject specialist base but the business of learning. The business of learning is highly complex and creative and depends on the practice of teachers in the classroom and/or on their interaction with learners. Teachers do not create learning, learners do, but teachers create the conditions in which learners learn (Wiliam and Black, 2006) so that investing in the professional development of teachers is critical to the improvement of learning and achievement.

In the FE and skills sector, which is key in driving forward wider productivity and economic renewal, professional learning ought to secure government commitment. However, given recent directions towards self-regulation, employer responsibility for initial teacher training qualifications and CPD rather than a legal national minimum of ITT/E qualifications and CPD (Department for Business, Innovation and Skills, 2012b), opportunities for securing a foundation for professional learning might look somewhat bleak.

Having generated a process that encourages and recognises professional autonomy and creates spaces for professional capital, there are serious concerns about the way in which removing this will also take away the gains of exercising newly acquired autonomy.

It is central to the professional learning of teachers to work within the context of professional capital, drawing upon human, social and decisional capital so that teachers feel confident about being accountable and taking responsibility for making judgements which impact upon their learners and others. This is becoming even more important in the current political climate and Professional Formation has provided such a model, enabling teachers through their engagement in peer review and dialogue and supporting their professional development to be autonomous, flexible and to exercise choice, while at the same time taking responsibility for justifying their decisions and remaining accountable.

The most telling views on professional learning, shared publicly at awards ceremonies and in other communications, are those of the practitioners themselves and their articulation of the experience of undertaking Professional Formation and gaining QTLS. For example:

> The achievement of Professional Formation I see as the successful completion of a complete career change. It has made me more disciplined in the need to go through the process and the supporting testimonial from my tutor has really given me the confidence that I am now a thorough professional in my new role.
>
> (A member's view on his experience of gaining QTLS)

I believe QTLS very important, gives recognition for all that I have done, recognised under one banner. So important, encouraging my colleagues to do QTLS and assisting them with the process.

(QTLS Graduate 2011)

I just wanted you to know that as a result of your help in gaining my QTLS, I had my time working at Harrogate, that led to a national commendation for my work and that coupled with the QTLS assisted me in gaining entry into a Masters Degree in education, which will conclude in October.

(QTLS Graduate, 2011)

Furthermore, following the publication of the Wolf review of vocational education in 2011, in which the recommendation that all FE trained teachers with QTLS should be regarded as equivalent in status to school teachers with QTS, IfL surveyed members about the proposed changes in December 2011 and received over 2,500 responses. Of these just under 1,800 were QTLS holders, 10 per cent of respondents also already held QTS, 97 per cent supported QTLS holders being able to teach in schools as qualified teachers. Those with QTLS commented on the benefits they could see their experience bringing to learners in schools, and others who are already working in schools could describe the benefits they are bringing to learners and colleagues. Below are a few examples.

With the vocational expertise we hold we can inspire and challenge thinking far beyond the classroom. Many FE teachers have worked very hard to move from industry to the classroom and the skills we have brought with us are extremely valuable to our younger generation who are fighting for college places and employment.

My school now recognises my QTLS! The most significant difference for me has been in how my colleagues view me, now they see me as an equal and I feel they respect my opinions and views more. I have also moved to the QTS pay scale, which is great!

I think that it is essential in the best interests of pupils that QTLS holders with their vocational and pastoral expertise of working with young adults be able to teach in schools. As schools develop their vocational curricula QTLS teachers will have the essential skills and expertise to support both the vocational and employability aspects of such teaching.

If schools are to take on the challenge of vocational learning, then they need teachers who can demonstrate the dual professionalism that characterises the vocational teachers in the FE and skills sector, as reflected in their comments above.

It seems fitting to close this chapter with not only what practitioners have learned but also our own learning from the experiences at IfL working with CPD and Professional Formation systems. They (these examples) have illustrated that regulating professional learning does not make a teacher or trainer professional. We knew even before the regulations were introduced in 2007 that professional learning is something altogether more complex than either the declaring of CPD or the gaining of professional status might reveal – it is something more spontaneous, unpredictable and personalised – affirmative of what it means to be a professional.

This requires creating a space for collaboration and professional dialogue so that teachers feel secure in their practice, confident about making decisions and exercising autonomy as well as being valued for their professional judgements which contribute to the development of positive learning environments that will have a beneficial impact on their learners and wider society.

The paradox of the regulations was that, through the mechanism of securing compliance, they gave us at IfL a critical mass of data to analyse and reflect back to the sector. IfL thought it was using the regulations as a means to an end in terms of enhancing the professionalism of the sector, but the consequences of a compliance culture undermined what IfL was trying to achieve. The articulation of professionalism, of being able to profess one's practice and one's philosophy, can be commensurate with a managerialist system of accountability (lawyers manage it after all) but it is a huge challenge and one that requires several years, even decades, to meet and resolve.

Final thoughts

The two views of professional learning in this chapter illustrate a significant area for future work. As an independent professional body, IfL remains committed to supporting the professional learning and development of its members and, drawing on the experiences of both regulated professional development and Professional Formation, is engaged in researching the impact of professional learning in the FE and skills sector, an area which has been under-researched and insufficiently theorised. If through this research we can identify what is relevant, what is meaningful and what will have the most impact on teachers' and trainers' confidence and practice, then the challenge will have been worthwhile.

Chapter 5

Evaluating the impact of professional learning

Vivienne Porritt

We cannot solve problems with the same thinking that generates the problems.
(A. Einstein)

Introduction

In Chapter 1, Sue Crowley offers a picture of a proactive professional and suggests this is 'where perhaps the most innovative and critical approach to professional learning and teaching occurs'. I support such a picture and this chapter focuses on a particular aspect of being a proactive professional and, I would add, a proactive profession. Sue suggests a proactive professional maximises resources available to promote learning in ways that focus on evidence-based practice and impact. This includes permission to challenge existing practices and take measured risks and suggests a parallel focus on quality and continuous improvement – on 'doing the right thing right'. In particular, this requires a rigorous and systematic approach to evaluating the impact of professional learning with integrated analysis of data.

How close are we to being able to evaluate the impact of professional learning in a way that matches Sue's powerful and welcome picture?

I would suggest educational organisations are struggling to know how to evaluate the impact of professional learning and indeed most educational improvement strategies. This struggle is whilst operating in a climate that requires regular and often instant judgements on the impact of professional learning on learners. This chapter draws on experiences of supporting leaders in the school and health sectors to address accountability demands as well as to develop the quality of professional learning through an innovative approach to evaluating impact.

This chapter therefore has three parts. First, it suggests that we need to unpick the kind of impact we want to *achieve* from professional learning. Secondly it considers why leaders and practitioners struggle with *evaluating* the impact of professional learning and argues that evaluating impact is both a learning tool as well as a way of evaluating outcomes. Finally it outlines some possibilities for progress in *evidencing* impact and shares examples from schools which are developing a new approach to this thorny issue.

Achieving impact

To articulate what kind of impact we want to achieve from professional learning we need to unpick what we understand by 'professional learning'.

In the schools sector, it is first worth noting the range of terminology in use, all of which probably means the same thing to most teachers and educational leaders. There is still some use of the word INSET. It means In-service education and training and was first introduced over 25 years ago by means of the ring-fenced INSET grant, the purpose of which was to train teachers by sending them on courses and to gather together in the school hall for an INSET day. This reflects schools that do not exist anymore (doesn't it?) and needs to be consigned to history. Most schools certainly refer to 'INSET days', their label for their five closure days and the time most schools still devote to collective opportunities for professional learning. I suggest rebranding these days as professional learning days would help teachers, leaders and parents understand better what is intended for these 30–35 hours.

In the FE and skills sector teachers and trainers were from 2007–11 expected to carry out a minimum of 30 hours mandatory CPD per annum (pro rata for part-time teachers) but there was lack of clarity about whether these hours were to be provided by the employer, whether individuals developed their own annual programme or whether there was a mixture of both. CPD is no longer mandatory, although many organisations encourage staff to engage.

The majority of schools and colleges do use the term CPD – continuing professional development (except for INSET days!) to refer to engagement in professional learning opportunities. Few teachers or leaders know why the phrase begins with 'continuing' and lots refer to 'continuous' which implies no time off even for good behaviour. 'Continuing' actually refers to development after initial teacher education and the qualification phase. To emphasise the importance of a coherent development continuum, some organisations now prefer 'professional development'.

The title of the book chooses the phrase 'professional learning' whilst the Institute for Learning's (IfL's) website uses the acronym CPD and indeed CPD is used in differing ways by contributors to this book. It is likely that IfL members see the terms in the same interchangeable way as school practitioners – does this matter? I think it does. This variance in the use of the terminology reflects some of the tensions in thinking that still exist around professional learning and professional development. If we do not yet have a sharply defined language and understanding as to what we call professional learning, it is no surprise that we are still working towards how to evaluate its impact and how best to lead this in educational organisations.

Of course, changing language is pointless unless thinking, practice and leadership also change. A team of colleagues at the London Centre for Leadership in Learning (LCLL) at the Institute of Education, University of London, specialises in working with leaders of professional development. Teachers and leaders explore with them the implications of the terms 'professional learning' and 'professional development' and whether re-conceptualising these words leads to better design, strategic leadership in this area and, fundamentally, more effective learning and impact for teachers, leaders and learners. I suggest we can look at these as distinct and yet interconnected processes.

Professional learning

Professional learning encompasses all the opportunities offered for colleagues to, for example, learn something new, update their skills, be informed of new developments, explore a new technique or resource, refresh subject-specific knowledge, improve teaching quality, develop more independent learners. These opportunities can be offered in a wide range of ways; courses, workshops, seminars, learning walks, reading articles, visits to other organisations, action research, Masters qualifications, peer observation, collaborative planning. Such opportunities can be offered and facilitated in-house by colleagues in the same organisation or from other colleges, the IfL, a higher education institution (HEI), private provider or an independent consultant. The variety of such professionl learning opportunities is better than ever and many organisations are also personalising such professional learning to avoid the historical one-size-fits-all approach and responses such as this: 'It appears that in planning organisation-wide CPD, too often the principles of good teaching and learning are abandoned and what could be a valuable opportunity to learn away from day-to-day pressures is diminished' (IfL, 2012a:12).

It is particularly frustrating when opportunities are offered that do not reflect the extensive body of research into what makes effective professional learning. From Joyce and Showers (1980) through to the four EPPI centre reviews (Cordingley *et al.*, 2003–07), there is a wealth of research that highlights key elements that support effective learning. Building on the research by Curee in the EPPI centre reviews and, as confirmed by the national Effective Practices in Continuing Professional Development project for the Training and Development Agency for schools (TDA), Earley and Porritt (2009) identified the quality of professional learning opportunities would be further improved if participants:

- had ownership of such opportunities
- engaged with a variety of professional learning opportunities
- were offered time for reflection and feedback
- learned in collaboration with other colleagues.

Such factors need to be designed into the opportunities for learning offered and pose challenges to many of our historic and current ways of working in educational organisations. Some schools and colleges have found ways to re-engineer existing time for reflection, and to enable colleagues to take ownership of their own professional learning, especially through collaborative learning opportunities such as coaching, enquiry-based learning, lesson study and such examples as Paul Wakeling's learning blogs as described in Chapter 6. Such opportunities also bring the added benefit of harnessing the tacit knowledge exhibited within colleagues' excellent practice and therefore the organisation. Tacit or unspoken knowledge (Nonaka and Takeuchi, 1995) is seen in the habitual practices that educators use every day and refers to things that we know how to do but do not always articulate. One of the questions the 2010 Ofsted report into good professional development asks is: 'How well do we know, value and use the expertise of our staff?' This is further supported by a key recommendation of the latest IfL review into CPD which states that 'More planning time and more time for effective personalised and collaborative CPD is essential' (IfL, 2012a: 9). Most of the learning that colleagues need to improve their practice is contained within the organisation already and a key way to improve the quality of professional learning is for colleagues to learn from and with each other. Whilst external specialist input might prove valuable, it is talking with colleagues and having a professional dialogue that promotes effective professional learning. However this professional dialogue needs to be practised, must be rigorous and, most importantly, teachers themselves need to identify what they and their learners need to learn to promote development and improvement.

Yet Helen Timperley notes: 'Much professional development has little meaning for teachers' (2011: 2) and Russell Hobby, General Secretary of the National Association of Headteachers, in a webinar for the Teacher Development Trust, suggested:

> There's a gap between practitioners and researchers on this [topic], in the sense that I suspect that not all school leaders do know what effective CPD is, or are confident that they know which aspects of CPD will help them deliver their priorities.
>
> (Hobby, 2012)

The first imperative in evaluating the impact of professional learning is, therefore, for leaders and teachers to engage in professional learning that has the potential to achieve impact and, in spite of research into what such professional learning looks and feels like, there is still some headway to be made. This means when designing high-quality learning opportunities a key priority should be to evaluate the impact of professional learning. To put it another way, if we start by offering low-impact professional learning, is it worth trying to evaluate it? The four factors above are indicators for strategies that contribute to high-quality professional learning and offer the opportunity to design high-impact professional learning opportunities. They also offer a test for educational leaders looking to maximise their investment into professional development – does the professional learning offered in your organisation start from, and always include, these factors?

The IfL's definition of CPD is: 'Maintaining, improving and broadening relevant knowledge and skills in a subject or vocational specialism and in teaching and training methods so that it has a positive impact on practice and the learner experience' (IfL, 2010a: 4).

This is an important definition as it prioritises the impact of the professional learning opportunities rather than the opportunities themselves. The next consideration is thus to consider how much of the available organisational time and energy is spent organising opportunities for colleagues to learn and what proportion on embedding such learning as improved practice, evaluating the impact of the new practice or supporting other colleagues to benefit from this new practice. In working with school colleagues around the country, the average answer is 80 per cent of relevant leadership time is spent on organising professional learning: everyone wanted to have a more equitable balance between the quality of learning and ensuring its impact on adults and learners.

This reflects the starting point for Joyce and Showers' work in the 1980s, based on extant evaluation of training which revealed that only 10 per cent of the participants implemented what they had learned and the percentage did not improve significantly if participants had volunteered to learn. Well-researched curriculum and teaching models did not find their way into general practice and thus could not influence students' learning environments. In a paper for the Education Endowment Foundation, Campbell and Levin state:

> a considerable body of evidence shows that the seemingly simple objective of putting knowledge to work is in fact very difficult to attain. For all kinds of reasons, it is still difficult to change organisational practices to be consistent with research knowledge, even when the lessons of research are strong and clear. What we have learned from several decades of research on this question is that research findings do not automatically inform or shape policy or practice, and that without specific efforts to strengthen those connections, even the most powerful research evidence will have only limited effect.
>
> (Cambell and Levin, 2012)

'Putting knowledge to work' is a powerful way of articulating the importance of ensuring that professional learning has an impact.

Professional development

The professional development process or stage is then about building on positive engagement in professional learning. Thomas Guskey's key message about being able to achieve impact is: 'It's not the training, it's the follow up' (Guskey, 2005).

The 'follow up' to professional learning is about converting what colleagues have learned into improved and sustained practice. Professional development should mean that teachers and leaders have changed and improved their existing practice.

This improved practice then needs to become embedded in their everyday inter-actions with learners and it is then we can say there has been professional develop-ment. Timperley argues for a shift from the prevailing term of professional development which she feels 'has taken on connotations of delivery of some kind of information to teachers in order to influence their practice' (Timperley, 2011: 4) towards professional learning. Whilst agreeing with the importance of profes-sional learning as the process for 'solving entrenched educational problems' (Timperley, 2011: 5), there has to be another stage after learning something valu-able. It takes time to put new understanding, strategies, techniques, skills into practice and takes longer for the improved practice to become habitual and embedded. I would argue we should see professional development, not as the activity being offered but as the embedded practice we look for as a result of professional learning.

This is a complex process that takes time and can have the following stages:

- learning something new
- reflecting on what has been learned
- trying out new learning in the classroom, taking risks
- developing new practice, embedding what works so it is habitual
- evaluating the impact of new practice on students' learning
- sharing what supported such impact with other colleagues
- other colleagues reflect on what they have learned … and the virtuous circle continues.

It is in this systematic process where innovation is needed to enable us to put the building blocks in place to evaluate the impact of professional learning and development effectively. At the moment CPD is a catch-all phrase that incorpo-rates both opportunities for colleagues to learn as well as supporting and evaluat-ing the process by which this learning is converted into developed practice, better learning and raised standards. Whilst they are clearly integral to each other, if we separate out the learning stage and the follow-up or development stage, we are better able to put in place the organisational processes and systems that would allow our colleagues to innovate and flourish. Nonaka and Takeuchi explored four stages whereby the knowledge and skills of an individual can become organ-isational knowledge. Applying such thinking to our organisational systems helps us to explore a more effective way of supporting the professional development stage and harnessing such potential knowledge. In essence, this is a way to put professional learning and new knowledge to work so it becomes developed

Figure 5.1 Putting knowledge to work.

practice that can be shared across the organisation and then, and only then, be evaluated for the difference it makes. Nonaka and Takeuchi's four stages support the movement from professional learning to professional development and thus to impact.

1   *Socialisation* – tacit knowledge, sharing what we know, in an informal way in corridor conversations, team meetings.
2   *Externalisation* – reflection on and articulating learning, examining it, sharing it with others in a formal way so it becomes *explicit*.
3   *Combination* – taking newly acquired *explicit* knowledge and combining it with a systematic approach to transporting this knowledge to all parts of an organisation where it can improve practice and learning.
4   *Internalisation* – *explicit* and regular practice of this new, improved knowledge enables it to become part of an individual's own knowledge base, makes it possible to use it habitually, becomes *embedded practice* that has an *impact* on the *learners*.

It is the explicit and systemic nature of the third and fourth stages that have the potential to achieve demonstrable change and development as a result of professional learning. It is at these stages that the new knowledge is put to work and practically applied in order to achieve impact. It is this demonstrable development that I see as impact. For professional learning and development to be effective and so have an impact that can be evaluated, the process must be seen in terms of the consequent development of knowledge and expertise, which may (or may not) result from participation in a wide range of learning opportunities. The goal is the change effected in the thinking and practice of our colleagues so that such change improves quality for learners. Of the three words within *continuing professional development*, we need a stronger focus on the *development* that comes from engaging in CPD activity: this complements the quality of the activity.

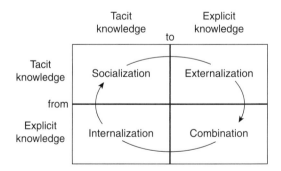

Figure 5.2 The knowledge conversion process.

Source: adapted from Nonaka and Takeuchi, 1995, http://nicsord.hubpages.com/hub/Nonaka-takeuchi-knowledge-management-cycle, accessed 15 May 2013.

Helen Timperley offers a complementary cycle whilst still emphasising the centrality of learners' needs to professional learning (Timperley, 2011:115).

Timperley sees professional learning as important as it 'challenges previous assumptions and creates new meanings' and offers a way to solve 'entrenched educational problems' (Timperley, 2011: 5). In addition, I suggest we need a more effective process for ensuring that such valuable professional learning leads to sustained professional development and impact on the practice of teachers and, subsequently, on outcomes for learners. This is what I see as demonstrable impact and it is to this that we now turn.

Evaluating impact

If teachers and leaders have yet to apply fully the research available into what effective professional learning and development (PLD) look like, it is even more the case that existing knowledge as to how to evaluate the impact of PLD is underutilised, in spite of significant evidence based on research in schools.

There are many models and theories about how to approach evaluating the impact of PLD. Impact evaluation approaches have been characterised as input-based or output-based. The former is simpler and led to approaches that measured what can be measured easily. This approach is deployed when teachers are asked to record how many times they have attended CPD opportunities, how many hours they have engaged in CPD, how effective the facilitator was, how satisfied they were with the learning opportunity. Input measures can (at best) demonstrate that something was done or was done for a length of time or for a

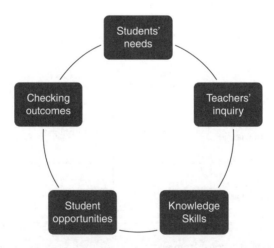

Figure 5.3 Professional learning cycle.
Source: adapted from Timperley, 2011: 25.

number of times. Such measurement has a use in being able to say that a certain percentage of teachers have engaged for a specific number of hours or in a type of opportunity. However, the value or impact of that activity for teachers or learners cannot be known from such data and does not necessarily indicate that anything has been learned, or that CPD will lead to any change in practice. This is a concern I have with the requirement in some sectors or professions, including FE, to log a number of hours of CPD, the number of points gained or the nature of the CPD opportunities with which teachers have engaged. The effort required in obtaining such data could be better directed to ensuring professional learning is effective and leads to professional development that has an impact on, first, the teachers engaged in professional learning and then, secondly, has the potential to have an impact on learners. The purposes and impact of PLD are multiple and complex. Any model that can be used to guide impact evaluation must allow for these complexities. For the purposes of PLD, learning should not simply be a measure of an increase in knowledge; it must be focused on what is done with this new knowledge. We need to guard against loosely defining impact as whatever emerges from PLD. We need an approach that recognises complexity whilst being able to be applied simply and with rigour.

Output approaches developed as a way to obtain objective evidence of learning or change in professional behaviour and so try to offer evidence of the effectiveness of such learning or changed behaviour: in an educational context this would include developed teacher practice and improved outcomes and well-being for learners.

Bubb and Earley (2007) provide an account of approaches to these evaluation models. A useful academic overview of relevant evaluation literature is given by Coldwell and Simkins (2011) who consider the strengths and weaknesses of various models, including what they term the 'levels' approach which combines input and output approaches and which they argue can be used in a number of ways. Both cite Kirkpatrick's (1959) pioneering work on evaluation which identified impact on four levels: reactions; learning; behaviour; outcomes. Thomas Guskey (2000) further developed this thinking for education and introduced a significant focus on evaluating CPD through learning outcomes for young people. Guskey's model is well known in academic circles, yet seems little known and less applied in schools and colleges. This model sees impact from CPD as being achieved at five potential levels:

1   participants' reactions
2   participants' learning
3   organisation support and change
4   participants' use of new knowledge and skills
5   student learning outcomes.

Crucially, as well as a useful framework for evaluation, Guskey (2002a) suggests that reversing these five levels enables better planning for CPD opportunities that have the potential to have an impact on teachers' practice and improved standards for learners. He offers the following questions:

- What impact do you want to have on learners? How will you know that you have had this impact?
- If that's what you want to accomplish, then what new practices do you need to develop and implement?
- What does the organisation need to do to support that, e.g. what time/ resources do people need?
- What learning and knowledge do people have to have and what skills do they have to develop to implement and embed these new practices?
- What professional learning opportunities do people need to gain those skills or knowledge?

The reversal of these levels begins to help significantly in evaluating the impact of PLD.

In *London's Learning*, a resource for CPD leaders in London, Porritt (2005) applied Guskey's (reversed) five levels stating that to be able to evaluate the impact of CPD, 'it is vital that anticipated learning outcomes, for teachers and learners, are explicit from the beginning' (Section 7). In 2007, the TDA published eight principles for impact evaluation which built on Guskey's work and other evaluation frameworks, notably the Harvard Family Research Project's Logic Approach (Weiss and Klein, 2006). The TDA noted the importance of clarity around the key principles underlying effective evaluation of the impact of

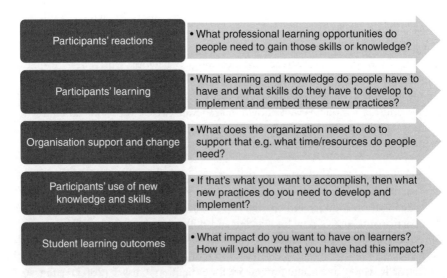

Figure 5.4 Evaluation impact model.

CPD. The principles include the importance of planning, focusing on what participants learn and agreeing the evidence base and the success criteria for the evaluation of impact (TDA, 2007).

Such principles were explored in depth in the Effective Practices in Continuing Professional Development project (2007) commissioned by the TDA (as then), which worked with over 600 schools, colleges and other organisations within 230 projects over 3 years. In the overall project's framework, Earley and Porritt, the co-directors, built on and further refined Guskey's approach by stressing the need to develop an evidential baseline to enable impact evaluation. Participants were asked the following three questions at the start of the project:

- What is your current practice/baseline now?
- How do you know this is the case?
- What evidence can be drawn upon to show this?

I will return to the significance of these questions as a way of both evaluating and evidencing impact.

The above models highlight the importance of both learners' and professionals' learning. The latter has also been raised by Frost and Durrant (2003) who made a helpful distinction between three sorts of impact on staff: classroom practice, personal capacity and interpersonal capacity. They also discuss the impact of CPD on learners in terms of distinguishing factors such as their enjoyment in learning, attitudes, participation, pride in and organisation of work, response to questions and tasks, performance and progress and their engagement in a wider range of learning activities.

A range of impact evaluation models, theories and frameworks therefore exist yet research and inspection evidence suggest that educational leaders are still to employ such tools effectively.

Such research has consistently shown that educational organisations lack experience, skills and tools to evaluate the impact of CPD (e.g. Goodall *et al.*, 2005; Ofsted, 2006, 2010; Bubb and Earley, 2007; Bubb., 2009). *The Logical Chain* (Ofsted, 2006) noted that: 'Few schools evaluated the impact of CPD on teaching and learning successfully', a situation which appears not to have improved much according to more recent inspection evidence (Ofsted, 2010) and research. Pedder *et al.* note in their *State of the Nation* report that CPD evaluation was seen as 'instinctive and pragmatic with reference to outcomes that are insufficiently specified and insufficiently linked to pupil learning outcomes, school, improvement and self-evaluation' (Pedder *et al.*, 2010: 18). The impact of CPD on student learning was rarely evaluated by schools and, if it was, was rarely executed very effectively (Porritt, 2009a; Ofsted, 2010). The IfL review of CPD highlighted that, 'The impact of CPD is insufficiently theorised or prioritised' (IfL, 2012a: 9).

Timperley states that 'there is little evidence that [professional development] has had an impact on teachers' practices or on student outcomes' (Timperley, 2011: 5).

Eun cites Frechtling *et al.* (1995) in identifying that the literature 'does not offer much on the impact of professional development at the classroom level' (Eun, 2011: 319) and it is this lack which means leaders continue to use input-based approaches and focus on measuring rather than evaluating. This leads to 'teachers [who] do not see that engaging in professional learning necessarily means making changes to practice.' (Timperley, 2011: 71) Timperley offers an approach based on cycles of teachers' inquiry and knowledge building which 'can improve students' engagement, learning and well-being' (Timperley, 2011: 10). We need to articulate that changing, improving, refining practice must be a result of engaging in PLD as this is essential to improve the quality of the experience offered to learners. Once this is understood and implemented, we can address the challenge of evaluating the impact of CPD in a way that teachers and leaders are able to apply effectively. As O'Brien notes, 'there is clearly a need to follow-up and follow-through CPD interventions so that clear links are established between CPD provision for teachers leading to enhanced teacher quality and the attainment and achievement of students' (O'Brien, 2012: 160). The approach we have developed at LCLL takes us towards realising this need.

We see impact evaluation as consisting of two stages: first, a design tool to enable effective PLD to have an impact and, secondly, a process of evaluating and evidencing such impact. Primarily, it must be a process that designs more effective professional improvement and development processes that have greater potential to ensure impact is achieved. As one CPD leader stated: 'This will focus my planning and give me much greater clarity on what I want to achieve. It will sharpen my attention to specific steps in my support for colleagues.'

This means that impact evaluation should be a 'powerful method to raise the quality of learning and standards' (Porritt, 2009a: 9–10) with value for money and accountability being helpful benefits rather than the purpose. This is an important point to me. I believe educational leaders have tended to view impact evaluation as about demonstrating external accountability and so have not looked to experiment and improve in this field. If we see impact evaluation as a high-quality learning tool, as well as a way of evidencing and evaluating the difference we have achieved, we can bring about a step change in its application. We can also provide evidence that justifies new approaches to learning and development.

One of the other reasons educational leaders often give as to why it is so difficult to evaluate impact is because they believe it will take several years to be able to see results. This expectation is based on a traditional view of impact evaluation and often an academic approach including longitudinal analysis. The Harvard Family Research Project cites concrete data by the district's research and evaluation unit and the Massachusetts Department which demonstrated 'Compelling evidence of effective professional development in Murphy School in Massachusetts through significant reductions in the numbers of students who failed the state math exam over 3 years' (*The Evaluation Exchange*, 2005/2006: 5). Such specialist evaluations are extremely valuable at a system level yet they run the risk highlighted earlier that educational leaders are not aware of the evidence built up in such research or believe they cannot apply such an approach without external support and a long-term study. Leaders in schools and colleges cannot always engage in long-term studies and need to be able to improve what they do 'by focusing on better use of what we already know' (Levin, 2012: 22). Guskey's framework offers teachers and leaders a way of both designing effective PLD approaches and opportunities and evidencing impact. This framework can then be applied in any learning environment and benefit the learners with whom teachers work every day.

The approach to impact evaluation that the LCLL developed was therefore used to underpin the Effective Practices project. The approach is a very practical one that is simple in concept yet rigorous in the difference it can make. The initial thinking behind this approach was first highlighted in *London's Learning* (Porritt, 2005; Porritt *et al.*, 2006). This resource explored Guskey's key concept that evaluation issues should be 'an integral part of discussions during the earliest stages of professional development planning when ... goals are defined and activities specified' (2000: 250).

Traditional impact evaluation tends to be at the end of a development activity yet 'all initial planning as to the potential impact of CPD should be undertaken *before* CPD activity starts' (Porritt, 2009a: 9–10), for example, stating *specific* changes in a teacher's classroom strategies or clarity about a changed approach by a middle leader to addressing variation in teaching quality in his/her team. In terms of learning outcomes, it should be agreed at the outset what the differences will be in how learners learn as a result of proposed professional learning – for example, *learners will move from using closed questions to the use of higher order questioning*. This is a simple concept to agree yet requires a significant change in the PLD practice of many individuals, groups and teams and organisations.

It is important to know what sort of impact is being sought. To support their developing understanding, the leaders of the *Effective Practices* projects were encouraged to look at impact evaluation in terms of three separate yet progressive areas – *products, processes* and *outcomes/impact*. Products might include policies or resources. Processes are new or improved systems.

We will look at these three separate yet related areas – *products, processes* and *outcomes/impact* – in more detail.

Products can be seen as a focus on tangible outputs from development work, e.g. an improved policy, a new strategy document, a directory/database of available CPD opportunities, a newsletter, an ICT tool to support performance management, a workshop, the creation of a development programme, the establishment of a network meeting, production of consortium action plans, etc.

Processes are the *new or improved systems* in the organisation, e.g. improved alignment between CPD and performance management, investigating what aspects of CPD staff feel to be effective, full involvement of staff in CPD processes, development of new knowledge and skills, creation of a new approach to needs analysis, etc.

However, do such products and processes really make a difference to colleagues' practice and learners' outcomes and experiences? Are these not classic examples of input approaches to CPD; something that can be easily measured? Earley and Porritt suggest that impact can best be seen in terms of:

> the difference that is made by using the product or experiencing the process has made to the learning and the experience of colleagues, the teams and the school and therefore to the learning and experience of the children and young people.
>
> (Earley and Porritt, 2009:8)

For example, producing a new CPD directory – a product – has the *potential* to have an *impact* but creating the directory is not what makes the difference. Rather, it is how teachers and leaders feel about and use the opportunities to which they now have access (*process*) that may make a difference. The *outcome* would then be the difference their feelings or newly developed practice makes on their teaching or the way they carry out their role and ultimately, the difference this makes to the learning and experience of the learners.

This difference can best be expressed as *impact*. It is often harder to quantify this difference, yet we are all striving to be able to say how we know we are making/have made a difference. *Impact* is the difference in behaviours, attitudes, skills and practice demonstrated by teachers and leaders as a result of the professional learning and development in which they have engaged. Ultimately impact is also the difference in the learning and experience of the *learners* as a result of the change in colleagues' practice. Bringing about an improved outcome for all learners is what enables us to say that professional development of staff has had an impact.

In the first phase of the Effective Practices project it was clear leaders struggled with articulating improved outcomes on their own learning, their practice or the learning of the students in their charge. The key was to plan the expected specific impact at the outset and be able to articulate the baseline practice and quality of learning. This required project leaders to have a clear picture of what teachers' practice and the quality of learning were like and what improvement they wanted to achieve *before* engaging in any CPD activity.

So we now suggest the key questions for impact evaluation are, first, and as suggested previously:

- What is your current practice/baseline?
- How do you know this is the case?
- What evidence can be drawn upon to show this?

to which we add:

- What difference have we made (as a result of engaging in CPD activity) to the practice of the staff, the organisation and to learners?
- What evidence is telling us that we are making this difference?

Evidencing impact

> Knowing that teachers make a difference is not the same as knowing how teachers make a difference.
>
> (Thompson and Wiliam, 2007)

Educational leaders are searching for practical ways to know what has worked and what does not work to make the most effective use of their greatest resource, human capital or people. Thompson and Wiliam expound further:

> We need to identify features of practice that when teachers engage in these practices, more learning takes place, and when they do not, less learning takes place. Second, we must identify features of teaching that are malleable – in other words, we need to identify things that we can change. For example, to be an effective Center in basketball, you need to be tall, but as one basketball coach famously remarked, 'You can't teach height.'
>
> (Thompson and Wiliam, 2007)

To know what works and what doesn't, we need to be able to evidence impact. Two particular aspects are worth consideration to help us to do this:

- the importance of establishing clear baseline and impact narratives with supportive evidence
- understanding evidence sources and asserted or substantiated evidence.

Establishing baseline and impact narrative and evidence

We have established it is crucial to impact evaluation to take the time to be clear about current professional practice and learner experience (baseline) and the impact on practice and learning that the teacher wants to achieve *before* engaging in sustained professional development activity. The most significant benefit to such clarity is to enable an effective match between the need for improvement and the type of professional development activity that will best effect such change: this then is high-impact professional learning.

This approach can be exemplified through coaching case studies from the Effective Practices project (see Bubb, 2009, Illingworth, 2009; Porritt, 2009b). The starting point (baseline) in one project, as in Figure 5.5, was a narrative of low-level pedagogical practice which was limiting learning and the impact desired included a rich narrative of the ways in which improved pedagogical practices would support improvements to students' learning. It is at this point that the most appropriate professional learning activity – coaching – can then be selected.

An example of the improved practice from baseline to impact is given below.

	Before coaching – baseline	After coaching – impact
Impact on practice of teacher	Focused on skills of subject, with literacy being incidental.	Literacy now more explicit through starters which are devoted entirely to developing literacy, through the subject context, helping to highlight the importance of the literacy elements.

	Before coaching – baseline	After coaching – impact
Performance of pupils	Pupils writing in paragraphs which linked sentences on the same topics, with little overall structure or use of signposting.	Focus on openings and connectives has helped pupils to produce more rounded paragraphs.

Figure 5.5 Baseline to impact.

Source: adapted from Illingworth, 2009: 77.

Lloyd (Earley and Porritt, 2009) offers an alternative example in another of the project's case studies. A focus on student outcomes was implicit throughout the specific project with improvements to student learning expected to result from the findings of enquiry walks – structured visits to participating project schools to enquire into specific aspects of practice. Enhancing student learning was always a core aim for the participating head teachers who felt that this project was about enabling and equipping them to do so more effectively. However, it was difficult for the participants to evaluate the specific impact of the enquiry walks on student outcomes. This was because the latter needed to be more explicit in the project design from the outset for participants to be able to capture evidence as the project progressed and at the end of the project. The next stage for this case study would be to identify the intended impact on student learning to which the specific leadership and learning behaviours gained in this project would now lead.

This is a simple concept yet the implications for practice are far-reaching. This approach requires greater levels of understanding as to the intended purpose of PLD activity for both individual colleagues and their team leaders. It requires higher levels of professional dialogue, especially in the needs analysis stage of PLD and in the performance management process, before the most effective PLD activity can be determined. Another hurdle is that the purpose of PLD often tends to be explicit only in terms of the needs of adults, i.e. the teachers or trainers. It is rare that clear improvements for learners are explicitly articulated at the outset as the true purpose of PLD. If this link is made, it tends to be, in the school context, only at the level of a whole-school attainment target (e.g. 70 per cent 5A*–C grades) or expressed in terms of levels or sub-levels to be achieved. The development of individuals and teams brings about improvement in the learning of separate groups of learners in separate classrooms at first and it is at this level where impact on learning needs to be sought. Only then can such improvements be aggregated to the organisational level.

To further support the baseline and impact approach to evaluation, we need to add another dimension, which is to be clear on the desired timescale by which the impact of professional learning will be seen. The examples above highlight the value of a specific focus and goal for PLD activity. To be most effective in supporting impact evaluation, achieving the goal needs to be aligned to clear timescales.

Understanding the stages and time needed to bring about real learning and to embed this learning to support change is crucial to effective PLD. Professional learning initiatives can flounder without working out the stages needed to improve and ensure consistency in the practice of all colleagues so that all learners benefit. This process is also powerful, even within a short period of time. A good example of this was seen in one of the Effective Practices case studies (Porritt, 2009b) whereby change in the classroom practice of individual teachers was achieved within the short timescale of a coaching trios' cycle as this 'gave urgency to the process, gave it a specific focus and goal and spurred participants to achieve small-scale success' (Porritt, 2009b: 64).

Clarity as to intended impact within a specified timescale thus supports not only short-term and individual goals as above, it is essential to embedding change and success on a whole-school level.

One school that participated in the Effective Practices project applied the baseline and impact thinking which, when aligned with a focus for CPD and clear timescales, enabled the leaders to evidence significant medium and long-term impact. The co-leaders of Kaizen Primary School, Newham, London, were challenged by the project to articulate their baseline professional development practice. This changed their thinking with regard to planning to put professional learning at the heart of school development and enabled them to determine the change in practice, the real innovation, they needed to move forward.

In January 2007, Ofsted stated, 'The head teacher has a clear vision of how she wishes the school to develop'. Some areas for development were identified, such as:

- some teaching was satisfactory
- pupil achievement was satisfactory and sometimes good.

This baseline was developed further through identifying specific issues and possible outcomes to be explored leading to key questions that would support collaborative, action research projects, one of which was:

Year 4 – How can we develop children's abilities in mathematics by the use of higher-order questioning skills?

Rebekah Iiyambo, as project leader, was realistic that this would take time:

We anticipate two to three years before we see real returns.

The focus on the learning needs of the students supported an increase in opportunities to reflect on practice in professional learning sessions that were more personalised to the baseline issues. Every colleague created a Professional Improvement Plan (PIP), directly linked to the school's improvement plan. The plan focused on how adults maximise their impact on students' learning, through reflective professional dialogue, observation and review with a PIP leader throughout the year. This was a shift away from previous performance management interviews and colleagues became more engaged and clear as to what they wished to develop and how.

> I identified mental maths oracy as an area of pupil need for my class. I then completed a PIP form outlining the actions I wanted to take. In this instance I observed the numeracy coordinator and then worked with them to develop my own practice.
>
> (Porritt, Mulholland and Iiyambo, 2011:37)

Teachers and leaders in the school stated they were much clearer about what success needs to be and what it looks like. Staff were able to ask specific questions about how professional learning opportunities supported their focus and to be clear of this at the beginning of each learning opportunity. They gained a greater understanding of how professional learning is planned, how processes and structures fit into the overall structure for school improvement and of their own professional learning and development needs and what the school could do to support them.

All staff found the shift challenging initially. Now, the type of professional learning opportunities most requested are coaching sessions or experience in team teaching situations and are related to the issue pertinent to their current class, year group or team. Colleagues are engaged in action research and there are also more explicit examples of taking responsibility, such as the Year 2 team taking action to redress the slow progress of learners towards expected outcomes. They did this by working with the numeracy leader to ensure that the adults working directly with the learners fully understood the subject requirements and expectations. Learning leaders (such as subject co-ordinators, etc.) gained better leadership skills from working with specified year groups during a topic.

> I have gained valuable experience from talking about problem solving skills in numeracy, to people involved in every stage of the child's learning, from parents/children to leadership teams and advisers.
>
> (Porritt *et al*, 2011:39)

The school has taken a long-term approach to professional development and the evaluation of its impact. However, improved outcomes for students arrived more quickly than expected. For example, the focus of one of the curriculum development projects was 'Reluctant writers' where 48 per cent achieved Level

2b or above in 2006/07. As a result of the new ways of working outlined above, achievement increased to 71 per cent Level 2b or above in 2008 which was recognised in the Ofsted report: 'The school has been successful in improving attainment and accelerating progress in writing and mathematics' (Ofsted, 2010: 4). The quality of learning is also now good overall.

It is thus clear that the following aspects support the most successful approaches to PLD:

- including a focus on learner outcomes in PLD activity
- establishing clarity of purpose at the outset in PLD activity
- specifying a focus and goal for PLD activity aligned to clear timescales.

The three factors above are essential to support a rigorous approach to impact evaluation. They can be added to the four factors established earlier as essential to professional learning that supports the potential for impact.

To many Effective Practices project leaders, the aspects above represented a new way of thinking about CPD activity and were a significant challenge to their usual practices. They initially found it difficult to:

- be clear about what they wanted to improve *before* engaging in CPD activity
- be clear as to what was possible in a specified time frame
- identify the appropriate CPD activity to improve their starting point and so change and improve practice.

Consequently, they struggled with evaluating whether they had achieved their intended outcome through engaging with CPD activity.

Understanding evidence sources and asserted or substantiated evidence

This second aspect seems to cause the greatest concern. When working with CPD leaders, the evidence cited for both the baseline practice and impact achieved was the source of the evidence only, not the detailed evidence itself. This included line management meetings, lesson observations, interviews with staff, coaching conversations, attendance or attainment data, surveys or questionnaires. The statements that tend to be offered as evidence of impact are often vague assertions such as *'inconsistencies in practice'* as a baseline, *'teachers worked more collaboratively'*, *'effective systems and processes'* for impact. It was rare for actual evidence to be offered from these sources as to what, for example, *'inconsistencies in practice'* actually were, what *'more collaboratively'* looked and sounded like in changed practice or what the *'effective systems and processes'* were – for either the practitioners or the students. In one case in the Effective Practices projects, for example, the following was offered as evidence of impact: *Use of questionnaires to ascertain what pupils like about the club.* What is really interesting is to interrogate the evidence source as to what the pupils actually liked, what does the analysis of the questionnaires say? This then offers either a baseline from which to improve practice or a repeated questionnaire evidences changed levels of satisfaction – impact.

The need to investigate the evidence source and interrogate the evidence to interpret what it suggests about impact was especially marked when impact on adult practice or pupils' learning was cited. In the majority of Effective Practices projects, this evidence was asserted:

- The outcomes for teachers included improvements in planning and pedagogy – *such as?*
- Incremental improvement in reading ages – *from what to what?*
- Teaching and learning in this school had clearly improved overall as seen by more personalised learning and improvements in the questioning skills of teachers – *such as?*
- The speaking module for GCSE shows improved results – *from what to what?*
- The quality of teaching in the sixth form improved – *from what to what?*

(Earley and Porritt, 2009: 114)

Project leaders were mostly reliant on asserting gains they had achieved at the conclusion of their project and found it difficult to use qualitative and quantitative data as evidence to substantiate such gains. This is surprising as schools, as are colleges, are awash with data, yet practitioners in the project's case studies shied away from highlighting the precise data which would have highlighted links between the professional learning activity and improved outcomes for colleagues and pupils. This finding is common in all of our work in this area. Why is this the case?

It was clear that project schools felt the evidence was available and they were proud of their achievements, yet they had not seen the value of offering this to the case study researchers and the data were often inaccessible except by, for example, further mining of the spreadsheets. Schools seemed reluctant to do this and yet there is immense value in being able to celebrate the impact of PLD on quantitative and qualitative improvements to colleagues' practice and substantiated improvements in the quality of learning as well as attainment.

In one of the project's case studies, data were offered as evidence of CPD activity leading to improved attainment. The project's leader cited a marked improvement in terms of children's achievement in maths at all three key stages:

- 10 per cent increase in pupils achieving level 4 or above in the KS2 SATs
- 24 per cent increase in pupils achieving level 2 or above in KS1 SATs
- 23 per cent increase in pupils achieving six points or more in the aspect of Calculations in the Foundation Stage Profiles.

(Mulholland, 2009: 98)

This was a very helpful step forward and the participants were rightly proud of these achievements: this is something to celebrate. A significant development would have been to reference the particular baseline and the period of time over which improvement was achieved. In terms of the baseline, are the figures given above based on last year's cohort or the prior attainment of the particular pupils involved in the project? The difference is important as it highlights the starting point for the improved attainment of the learners. It is also valuable to reference the timescale so the size of the accomplishment is also noted and a judgement can be made on the relative investment of time.

A key lesson to learn then is why practitioners shy away from using the data they have gathered to highlight successful outcomes to PLD activity. One reason may be that identifying, gathering and citing baseline data and practice is not the norm in educational organisations. It is then difficult, if not impossible, to capture valid interim and final data as there is a lack of clarity as to what impact will look like and meaningful comparisons cannot be made, hence the vague assertions highlighted earlier. Also, possibly there is still an assumption that impact is only appreciated when quantifiable evidence is given. Impact can also be seen in other terms as in attitudes, perceptions and feelings and then images such as a photograph or words from quotations or interviews may be more useful. Evidence can also be gleaned from qualitative sources, yet again, teachers and leaders often devalue such evidence or believe quantitative data is what is required.

An interesting example comes from working with a group of middle leaders on an Aspiring to Leadership programme. Participants are supported to choose a focus for change and improvement and to bring this about within the defined timescale of the programme. I support them to create baseline narrative and data of the practice in their chosen focus area and then to mirror the same evidence in terms of the impact they wish their leadership to achieve. In the final session, participants share their baseline and impact narratives and data with others to celebrate the change they have supported. One middle leader was supporting a group of newly qualified teachers to take a leadership role in a whole-school project. She created a word picture using Wordle to capture, from their group conversation, their baseline perceptions about their role and what they could achieve at the outset of the project. The words with the greatest frequency were:

know, get, sure, done, first, need, give, check.

Such words reflected their anxiety and the need to be told what to do rather than to take ownership and leadership.

At the end of the five-month project, the word 'picture' was repeated based on their evaluative discussion and the words with the greatest frequency were:

together, involved, ideas, group, development, worthwhile, learning, grow.

This is qualitative evidence of impact at Guskey's level four and the two Wordle pictures are substantiated, rather than asserted, evidence that the middle leader had had an impact on the teachers' skills to lead in a whole-school way.

A third reason why practitioners eschew existing data may be that they are not yet experienced enough in seeing the link between PLD activity and improvements in practice and learning and that these improvements are essential before there can be impact on attainment and measured results. This can be explained by the current focus in most educational organisations on the range and quality of PLD *activity* rather than a balanced focus on both quality of provision and impact on practice. If PLD is to effect change and improve practice in the classroom, and so outcomes for learners, there is also a need for a strong focus on evaluating impact through the concepts outlined in this chapter.

This would indicate that further development is needed in supporting leaders of PLD to interpret and analyse what the evidence source highlights in terms of the changes to practice and learning to be achieved through engaging in development. This would offer a coherent understanding of the current situation and practice at the beginning of the proposed development, an improved ability to select appropriate baseline and impact evidence and increasing efforts to interpret and analyse this evidence. Case study projects found it hard to use *actual* qualitative or quantitative evidence to illustrate and substantiate their starting position. This ability is crucial in being able to identify appropriate PLD activity to bring about the consequent change and improvement and then to evaluate the impact of such activity. Further work should continue in this respect: in particular, teachers and leaders would benefit from seeing data used positively to determine a subsequent course of action and to demonstrate success and achievement.

This means we can add a further two factors to make nine in our menu of what is required to ensure that impact evaluation is not an end in itself but a way to improve the quality of the intended outcomes. We need to:

- develop the strategic leadership of professional learning and development
- understand how to evaluate the impact of PLD.

Conclusion

The nine factors offered by Earley and Porritt as a result of the Effective Practices in CPD project can be re-ordered and categorised. The effect of professional learning and development activity is maximised if its leadership.

I argue that there are two essential factors to ensure PLD has an impact. First, educational organisations and their leaders need to understand how to design professional learning activity to ensure impact is achieved. Secondly, that PLD activity needs to have a strategic focus and this needs effective leadership. These two factors are then underpinned by the remaining seven above which support the strategic purpose and impact of PLD through focusing on clarity of purpose for PLD and importance of the needs of learners and, crucially, when such impact

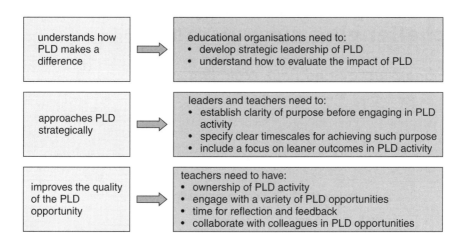

Figure 5.6 Strategic leadership of PLD.

could be evaluated. When such a framework is established, shared and understood across the organisation, the final stage is ensuring high-impact opportunities for professional learning are in place.

Traditionally, the process above starts with, at best, putting learning opportunities in place and, at worst, imposing learning. And we know the latter does not work so why is this still happening? This is the challenge to much of our current professional learning approach and activity. The opportunity open to us is to be able to demonstrate and evidence the real difference, the significant impact our learning and development has on outcomes for learners.

Chapter 6

Leading and learning in challenging circumstances

Fiona Mackay and Paul Wakeling

It only takes a good follower to do nothing for leadership to fail.

(K. Grint)

Introduction

This chapter considers the role of leadership within a developing learning organisation. The chapter seeks to contribute to the debate about 'how' leadership is accomplished through a conversational approach between a leadership facilitator Fiona and a principal, Paul. The chapter is based on reflective discussions on our practice. Fiona was engaged in running the sector programme Aspiring Principals and Senior Leaders Programme (APSLP), and Paul contributed a session on leadership as part of the programme for several years. The approach is based on action learning which is collaborative, its research focus is with people and ourselves, we therefore are not seeking consensus but rather dialogue and difference (Vince 2001). Both concepts include learning from action and experience.

We wanted to intersect two voices: one considering the ideas presented in the literature alongside a voice of a leader reflecting on his practice. The juxtaposition was experimental and raised further questions which were later inserted into the main text and generated some further reflections. We have drawn on social learning theory that considers learning as a process of identity formation within and through participation in a social practice. And we drew on a social perspective of organisational learning. With this lens Fiona reviews the concept of organisational learning, reflection and leadership. Paul reflects on the ways in which the ideas of organisational learning can be supported in practice. We acknowledge that the way leadership is experienced will inevitably impact on how leadership is enacted in the organisation as a whole. Paul openly reviews his personal learning and how organisational learning can be promoted. Lastly, Fiona considers the implications for the design of leadership programmes to support the development of organisational learning capability.

PAUL: Many people in leadership positions across education, the public sector and, indeed, the private sector are reporting that currently the circumstances that they are facing are the most challenging of their career. In my own particular college we are facing a programme of sustained cuts (at least 14 per cent actual cash cuts per learner over four years); a continued economic downturn resulting in financial issues for staff and students; increased competition; a declining demographic; a tougher inspection regime; changes to the curriculum and methods of assessment; and sustained industrial action. Whilst the college is coping well with these circumstances, we have suffered from a decline in achievement this year.

There is incredible pressure, often unsaid but very intense, to abandon the values and the learning approach. Results have to be fixed straightaway, the inspectors are coming and young people only get one chance. The temptation is to move back to a command and control regime, micromanaging staff in order to ensure improvement.

FIONA: To what extent are you aware of the serious external challenges destabilising internal learning and development processes?

PAUL: There are 2,700 fulltime students in the college, every one of them is on an examined course and almost all of those courses are one year. This means that there is incredible pressure every year in terms of results. Everything becomes measured in one-year frames because we naturally see them as appropriate. Actions are described as successful and having impact if results improve, or unsuccessful if results go down. What we often forget is that many change programmes take a lot longer than a year to have an impact. Unfortunately this means that we often abandon things before they have had a chance to succeed, or worse, we scale things up that we think have had an impact, only to find that the action-impact link was false.

Recent educational theory and research into the Learning and Skills Sector focuses on developing the culture of educational organisations such as colleges. The Teaching & Learning Research Programme (TLRP), the biggest research programme into the Learning & Skills Sector, has found that the best way to improve learning, for example in a college, is to improve the learning culture of that college.

Thus, all members of that college: leadership, teachers, support staff and students should be committed to learning. James and Biesta link this to models of leadership and management arguing that command and control management, characterised by the objectives model of setting targets and then achieving (or not) those targets, is not an effective way to improve learning. They argue that '[t]he dominant form of learning management at the moment is a version of the objectives model. The ... research show(s) that, in the context of shortage of resources, it often makes things worse' (James and Biesta, 2007: 150). So let's just admit it. The idea that we can take specific actions that result in measurable learning objectives is highly suspect. Teachers know that the cause and effect link between particular teaching action and identifiable student outcome is tenuous, at best probabilistic. At worst the insistence on this link is harmful. When particular actions are identified as having the causal effect of improving student out-comes our sector has rushed to scale up and we implement throughout a college or locality. Before we know it, before careful trial and educational evaluation, we have surveyed every learner in the country regarding their learning style, insisted on using six different thinking hats or 'accelerated' everyone's learning. Before we know it we have wasted money and time but are no further on with understanding how to make things better. A real com-mitment to leading learning would explore what happens when we move away from this objectives model to a process model where staff are given time to focus on their own learning and the teaching and learning of the students in the college.

FIONA: I notice in more current writers an acknowledgement that leadership in difficult times requires rethinking. These writers link the levels of societal and global change and the implications for new and emerging views on leadership. The popularity of the charismatic leader has been challenged by relatively recent events; the collapse of corporations such as Enron and Lehman Brothers in the US, the evolving revelations in the British banking sector. Any review might now place more emphasis on models of authentic, collaborative, values-driven leaders to best cope with new challenges and new uncertainties. We know that when an organisation's brand is based on a value base, it encourages greater employee commitment and is a useful guide to behav-ioural norms and standards. Leaders need to foster a climate in which values are shared and are enacted inclusively as part of the prevailing culture. Bolden *et al.* offer a generously broad definition of leadership. For them it is:

1   a process
2   of social influence
3   to guide, structure, and/or facilitate
4   behaviours, activities, and/or relationships
5   towards the achievement of shared aims.

(Bolden *et al.*, 2011: 39)

This definition is useful as it sees leadership as a process not necessarily housed within one individual alone; it is a process of influence and it implies leadership is an attribution made by others. It also allows for distributed and shared leadership. Whilst shared or dispersed leadership is attractive to the education sector the underlying power relations inherent in organisations can limit its potential. As they acknowledge, this definition fits well with a discursive perspective cited by Fairhurst (2007). Pedlar, Burgoyne and Boydell posit that the Learning Organisation suggests there are two chal-lenges for leaders:

•   The personal challenge of leading and behaving differently to stimulate learning in yourself and those around you

- The organisational challenge of mobilising change and learning on a more systematic basis throughout the enterprise.

(Pedlar *et al.*, 2004: 136)

Personal learning as a leader

PAUL: In my first year as principal of a college I attempted to engage the teaching staff in what I thought would be a good collective learning initiative. I ran some staff training sessions that all teachers attended on teaching and learning. My aims were to change the direction of teaching and learning in the college and to signal my interest in teaching and learning, ensuring that it was high priority. The sessions asked staff to focus more on student learning, making lessons more active. Much of the content was based loosely on ideas about accelerated learning.

   The sessions created quite a buzz, the college principal actually cared about teaching and learning! However, in truth, the sessions were experienced by most staff as the principal telling them how to teach. Various defensive responses resulted. Some staff resisted by switching off: 'What does he know?', whilst others took it as a direction or order and adapted their lessons to fit in with the new 'house style' without really engaging with why. A third response was to challenge the ideas that I had introduced, questioning their relevance in a particular context or their theoretical validity. I found this challenge difficult and closed it down. The senior team protected me with defensive routines reminding me that this response was from the awkward squad and could be ignored and reduced to an irrelevance.

FIONA: In what other ways did the defensive routines service the senior managers' view?

PAUL: I suppose that with this action the senior managers were signalling their importance to me. They were demonstrating that they agreed with me, and were showing me that they could manage out the blocks and contradictions to my view. These defensive routines gave them a role in a time when they must have been nervous with the arrival of a new principal.

   It was two whole years later that I realised that not engaging with this had been a missed opportunity for genuine organisational learning. My session, although I was not aware of it at the time, did not lead to genuine collective learning. Really it was just me telling professionals how to teach. The sessions actually closed down the opportunity for genuine learning and development. In fact the conditions of freedom, equality and respect that could enable collective learning were not present. My position in the hierarchy meant that I did not expect my perspective to be challenged and the collective management routine of the college ensured that it wasn't.

FIONA: That must have been disappointing? Is there a question here about how you maintain your enthusiasm to lead this approach?

PAUL: It wasn't disappointing at the time. At the time I thought that my sessions on teaching and learning were great and I was grateful for the support and validation that I got from the other senior managers and many staff. When it finally dawned on me that I had missed an opportunity by not engaging with the dissenters, I felt very excited. It was a moment for me when I understood that I needed to change, in that sense it was very powerful and regenerative. The struggle has been to stay true to this approach and to continue to be resilient during tough conversations, listening to ideas that I don't want to hear and empowering people to be able to express those ideas.

FIONA: Some writers highlight the role of the individual leader in shaping learning organisations which includes behaving as a lead learner, modelling continuous learning and ensuring learning in all its forms is valued. This viewpoint reminds us of the visibility attributed to those in the top positions to signal ways of being to others. 'When Leaders actively question and listen to employees – and thereby prompt dialogue and debate – people in the institution feel encouraged to learn' (Garvin, Edmondson and Gino, 2008: 113). And they point out that 'When leaders demonstrate a willingness to entertain alternative points of view, employees feel emboldened to offer new ideas' (Garvin et al., 2008: 113). Such a focus may arguably undermine the complex nature in which cultural norms are communicated and reinforced. Thames and Webster (2009) provide an assessment framework for building change capability in organisations. They identify 13 core capabilities which they suggest can be evaluated and further developed to enable greater learning and adaptation to change. They argue leadership as a fully implemented capability on a maturity continuum requires the following elements:

- Diverse Leadership styles are valued and integrated at all levels of the organisation.
- Execution on the organisation's shared vision is enabled through empowered and autonomous leadership teams.
- Leaders live the Five Practices of Exemplary Leadership – Model the way; Inspire a shared vision; Challenge the process; Enable others to act; Encourage the heart.
- Formal programmes to continuously renew leadership through development and succession planning.
- Leaders and collaborators are interchangeable roles on high performance teams.
- Leadership is an attribute specified in every job description.
- A spirit of leadership 'community' is evident; leadership excellence is celebrated and rewarded

(Thames and Webster, 2009: 64)

A more critical perspective suggests that leadership is too concerned with individuals, their attributes and their ability to mobilise others. Strategic learning, argues Vince 'is increased through collective and public approaches to reflection and leadership' (Vince, 2004: 144). What he refers to as an 'uncommon definition' suggests leadership can be viewed as a product of 'human community: the collective capacity to create something of value is to critique the idea of individual influence and how it is achieved' (Vince, 2004: 145). Other writers call for leaders to be a more liberating force, 'helping free people from oppressive structures, practices and habits encountered in societies and institutions, as well as the shady recesses of ourselves' (Sinclair 2007: vx).

FIONA: You once talked about creating a more democratic organisation – can you say more about that?

PAUL: Sometimes when people reflect back to me what I say I think 'Oh, no! What was I on about?' Terms like democracy are so powerful and important that I now recoil and think I really can't claim to have thought this through with rigour. However, I can give three different examples of how I might have been able to encourage more democracy in the college. The first is that I have given up my office, so this example is about behaviour. The underlying idea here is that all the space in the college should be good enough for staff and students, the IT provision should be consistently good throughout the college and that staff and students should be able to work side by side. Through not having an office I am more often found in the college canteen, library and study areas and so on. If I need a meeting room I book it like anyone else. The second is that whenever we have an Executive Strategy Day we invite two students and two staff members who are not a part of executive. They play a full role in the strategy day. We try and link it to educative purposes too, so one year the students were business students and one of the members of staff was their tutor. They were able to think about college strategy in relation to their unit on business strategy. However, the real purpose is to ensure other voices can help shape strategy and also moderate our reified ideas. The third example is to have round-table meetings when big issues arise. So recently we had a 'crisis' when there was a big disagreement about the value and implementation of a new appraisal system. This was dealt with by a series of round-table meetings with all the key protagonists sharing their views and eventually forging a solution.

Unblocking learning

PAUL: More recently I have tried to unblock learning in the college so that individually and collectively we can learn, adapt and improve. This is underpinned by an understanding that the workforce at college is highly intelligent, highly capable and motivated by education and learning. It seems absurd not to try and use this in order to develop and improve the college. I had little idea about how difficult this would be and I do not write from the perspective of success, but in order to open up a dialogue about the challenges of developing organisational capability in this way.

I began with something manageable, with my own behaviour and way of working. What could I do to begin to learn whilst in this job? What could I do to really signal the importance of learning? I developed a definition of my role as the 'lead learner' in the college, which I shared with all staff at a staff meeting and via my staff blog.

> a lead learner should set up a framework within which their learning is possible. This might include a formal learning programme, a coach or mentor and forums where the leader can share or publish ideas. More importantly you would expect the leader to be engaged in reading, in discussing and in modelling ideas and behaviours; to be engaged in action learning for example. Fundamentally you would expect the leader to invest time in the learning of those that he or she managed through discussion, planning, investment and professional review. Most fundamentally you would expect that leader to teach.

I ensured that I lived up to all the behaviours laid out above. In particular I made time to meet and discuss things with staff members that I knew did not share my views and would give me challenge. This has been very challenging for me but also very rewarding. Other examples include undertaking significant professional development every year, which I shared with staff; ensuring that the staff that I managed had good professional development; ensuring that I taught regularly; and ensuring that I read and encouraged reading in others. I also required this of other staff particularly the other senior managers.

FIONA: You have invested in professional development for your senior team on the Aspiring Principals and Senior Leaders Programme – has that made a significant difference to the individuals and their approach to learning? How do you and they maintain a learning dialogue and sustain it?

PAUL: Any professional development has varying effects on the individuals that undertake it. That is true of all the staff in the college that have undertaken the numerous forms of leadership development that have been made available. However, what has certainly come out of the leadership development in the college is an understanding and a commitment to our core values. At the heart of these values is continuous learning. Our number one value is: Learning through continuous development and reflection – capacity is developed and continuous learning is institutionalised.

I find that maintaining the learning dialogue can be challenging. Some of it takes place informally, so those staff that were inspired or engaged by the leadership development programmes still talk about it, think about it and share ideas informally. However, in order to keep this stuff live it is essential to model good practice and to create structures where the learning dialogue can continue. I ensure that I openly reflect and commit to significant professional development. I use my blog as one medium to keep the college community up to date with what I am doing. Since becoming principal I have completed the Principal's Qualifying Programme, I have been to the Kennedy School for Government at Harvard, I have undertaken a Research Fellowship in Education through the Learning and Skills Improvement Service (LSIS) and the University of Sunderland and until recently I have continued to teach on the Aspiring Principals Programme. I regularly publish any assignments or writing that I have done on these programmes in order that staff can see my engagement. In addition to all this, I still meet with my APSLP colleagues once a year for an 'action learning set'. We have done this every year since we finished the programme eight years ago.

At the same time I try to encourage engagement throughout the college. Examples include working with LSIS to develop a bespoke Routes to Success Programme for our college that included input from senior managers at the college, developing a leadership programme with other London sixth form colleges, developing a leadership programme for our own front-line managers, encouraging shared reading and seminars and making time available for professional learning communities. A particularly powerful development has been working with academics such as Professor Frank Coffield (Emeritus Professor at the Institute of Education) and Professor John MacBeath (Professor of Leadership and Learning at Cambridge University). Both have been to the college to work with a group of staff over the course of a year, one on assessment for learning and one on leadership for learning.

FIONA: Reflection has become unquestioned as a concept in many management and professional development programmes. Being a reflective practitioner is often a prerequisite to being an effective manager and/or practitioner. Many of the participants on a leadership programme within the learning and skills sector, senior post holders, reported they were familiar with the concept of the 'reflective practitioner' but admitted that it is not common practice. Many referred to individual reflection as a 'luxury', and some felt guilty using time on the programme to reflect on their leadership practice (Mackay, 2012).

A key advocate, Schon (1983), promotes the process of reflection in experiential learning, the ability to learn from and in work. The idea of reflection-on-practice requires an individual to recreate his/her experiences through remembering events, thoughts and feelings. This individualised perspective does not adequately deal with the importance of the discursive and social dimension to learning. The assumption that reflection will lead to change, also avoids engaging in the interrelationships between an individual's self-awareness, emotional openness, ability to learn and capacity to change within a particular context.

Bradbury *et al.* discuss the ways different professions have 'taken up the mantra of reflection and reflective practice in the education and development of their members' (Bradbury *et al.*, 2010: 191). Their book acknowledges the different practices adopted by differing professions. Although within the chapters there is some discussion about shared reflection and the use of action learning and team teaching, little connection is made to organisational development. Fook, for instance, suggests that the individual and social levels of reflection are linked and provides a focus on the 'social contexts of professional practice more broadly – this includes workplaces, but also professional cultures, social political and cultural contexts' (Fook in Bradbury *et al.*, 2010: 39). By acknowledging that professional communities transcend organisational boundaries the relationship between professional learning and organisational development becomes tenuous at best. Lave and Wenger (1991) have developed the idea of situated learning, exploring how learning is a process of participation in a community of practice.

Wenger (1998) in a later publication provides a framework for thinking about learning as a process of social participation. The idea of reflexivity 'challenges the idea that learning is an internal cognitive process replacing it with the idea that learning is embodied, dialogical and existential activity, intimately tied to how we feel, what we say and how we respond to others' (Vince and Reynolds, 2004: 37).

Since reflection,

by its nature, looks back at what has already taken place, it is innately limited for anticipating assumptions, opinions, rules, and differences that are only now emerging. The mindfulness embodied in dialogue involves awareness of the living experience of thinking, not reflection after the fact about it. For us to gain insight into the nature of our tacit thought, we must somehow learn to watch or experience in action. This work would require a form of collective attention and learning. Dialogue's purpose is to create a setting where conscious collective mindfulness can be maintained.

(Isaacs, 1993: 31)

Other writers also suggest that future research should include an emphasis on reflection as a 'collective approach, which takes account of social, organisational and cultural processes' (Reynolds and Vince, 2004: 65). As Vince argues in an earlier article 'it is unlikely that reflection on individual experience in itself will produce learning and change' (2002: 2). Reynolds and Vince employ the phrase 'organising reflection', 'which is to represent our view that reflection is best understood as a socially situated, relational, political and collective process' (Reynolds and Vince, 2004: 6). They acknowledge that the implementation of collective reflection processes, 'remain[s] a poorly developed aspect of organisational experience and action (Reynolds and Vince, 2004: 4).

FIONA: How do you encourage more collective forms of sense making and reflection?

PAUL: Something symbolic that we do is question and answer staff meetings. This can be particularly powerful when there are big issues to deal with. This was useful in 2009 when we found out that our new build plans had been scuppered following the collapse of the Building Colleges for the Future Programme. Myself, the chair of governors and the regional director from the Learning and Skills Council all appeared as a panel and staff were able to ask questions. It was a very effective way of us all being able to reflect on where we now were. I have used this form of meeting several times over the last few years. The key is in the way I respond to the difficult questions and questioners, because it is essential that I am not seen to be angry or defensive, because this will send a signal that I don't really want questions.

I try all sorts of things, from my blog to sharing the strategic challenges and plan in all its stages, encouraging exercises through various meeting structures such as 'future scenario building'. When we have a 'crisis' we often come together in round-table meetings to talk the crisis through.

Learning organisation

FIONA: The concept of organisational learning has been well reviewed in the literature (Easterby-Smith, 1997; Easterby-Smith, Burgoyne and Araujo, 1999). This chapter draws on the growing interest in the social perspective on organisational learning that 'focuses on the way people make sense of their experiences at work' (Easterby-Smith and Araujo, 1999). This perspective sees organisational learning as 'socially constructed, as a political process and as implicated in the culture of an organisation' (Easterby-Smith *et al.*, 1999: 5). It also considers learning as cultural artefact: 'learning is something that takes place not in the heads of individuals, but in the interaction between people' (Easterby-Smith *et al.*, 1999: 6). This perspective enables politics to be a feature of organisational life, wherein politics and power relations facilitate how learning (and change) does or does not happen in organisations. Central to this view is that learning is viewed as social construction. The technical perspective assumes that 'organisational learning is about the effective processing, interpretation of, and response to, information both inside and outside the organisation (Easterby-Smith *et al.*, 1999: 3).

PAUL: To aid organisational reflection we developed our definition of a 'learning organisation' which we discussed in detail at a management away day and used prominently in our strategic plan:

The organisation would be one in which the majority of staff could describe themselves as learners because they were engaged in, and supported in, their learning. It would be one in which there was evidence of staff developing and progressing but also an organisation in which staff felt able to lead change and develop new ways of working; of teaching; and of learning.

It would be an organisation that wasn't afraid to address difficult questions and wasn't afraid to acknowledge that it didn't have the answers.

This began to have a significant impact on staff in the college and upon our culture. There was more staff development, including action learning projects, leadership development, sponsored higher education and research projects, links with university departments and so on. This included, for example a Leadership for Learning project with Professor John MacBeath at the Faculty of Education at Cambridge University, in which approximately 20 staff were able to spend up to five days in-year working together and with Professor MacBeath to explore how practice in the area could lead to improved learning.

Developing this learning culture in the college felt, to me, a wonderfully exciting and optimistic time for the college. Many staff were invigorated during this phase: there were several internal promotions as we began to develop staff; groups formed around particular themes developing new college processes; solving old problems, initiating new practice. However a challenge that is hard to resolve is the notion of 'in and out' groups, those that benefited from this and those that didn't. Groups who seemed rewarded and able to take advantage of this and groups that didn't. Feelings of inequality developed as some teams were seen to be doing different stuff. Who told them to do it that way? Why don't they have to do it like we do? I was faced with the leadership challenge of holding a more complex organisation together: an organisation that seemed to be developing different practices, at different paces and in different areas. I was concerned about how this seemed to students and to staff. I was concerned about the impact on the college as a whole.

FIONA: How were you able to manage that complexity – in particular support those that felt left out?

PAUL: I am not sure how successful I was at that. However, two things come to mind. The first is that I shared my thinking with key figures in the 'out group'. I had written up a lot of my thinking with regard to the learning culture as part of a research fellowship that I had at Sunderland University. I shared my writing with a number of key staff, asking them to see whether I had captured the college situation accurately. I had a meeting with each of these staff and was able to hear their criticisms and respond. As a result of this, some of the 'out group' then began to make suggestions about the kind of developments that they wanted to take forward. I was able to support some of these.

I have also developed a 'tight but loose' schematic for the college. It essentially argues that we must stay tight to the values but we can be 'loose' with regard to the specific ways that things are done in particular parts of the college, as long as it is in accordance with the values. This enables me to argue that there is consistency but also autonomy. This 'tight but loose' schematic came out of a management crisis round-table meeting, after a team were accused of having no regard for college policy.

FIONA: Pedlar *et al.* suggest the challenge for leaders concerned with organisational learning involves tackling such questions as:

- How can we create development opportunities for everyone in this organisation – no matter how humble their position?
- How can we create feedback loops based on performance as a matter of daily practice?
- How can performance management systems teach people how to use finance and other resources more effectively?
- How can we set up learning partnerships with our key business partners?
- How can we ensure what is learnt in one part of the organisation is available to other parts as and when it is needed?

(Pedlar *et al.*, 2004: 137)

As Vince suggests, organisational learning is not the sum of individual learning but organisational dynamics is:

constructed from the interaction between emotion and power that creates the social and political context within which both learning and organising can take place ... Learning primarily occurs in the context of social relations and as a result of complex interactions, which are profoundly influenced by both individual and collective emotions.

(Vince, 2001:1329)

Thames and Webster suggest that organisational learning can be evaluated and further developed; they further suggest that a fully implement capability on organisational learning is evidenced with the following elements:

- A single comprehensive shared vision for change drives the organisation forward proactively and is integrated with objectives throughout the enterprise.
- Building organisational learning capability is reinforced through reward systems and personal development programmes.
- Dialogue and commitment to foster truth and trusting organisational environment.
- A robust partnering and alliance programme is in place to further extend organisational capabilities through productive relationships with customers and vendors.
- Organisational learning elements are proactively embedded within the organisation, and continuous incremental improvement is considered a competitive advantage.

(Thames and Webster, 2009: 132)

Further lists and characteristics of the learning organisations can also be found in earlier writers, for example, Senge (1990), Watkins and Marsick (1993) and Pedlar *et al.* (1996). The lists may have developed over the years; our interest, however, is in understanding the dynamics of actually developing those characteristics.

Some writers identify the processes that need to be in place to facilitate organisational members collectively interpreting information. 'Organisational learning is the processes the organisation employs to gain new understanding or to correct the current understanding; it is not the accumulated knowledge of the organisation' (Dixon, 1999: 7).

Learning is the construction and reconstruction of meaning and as such is a dynamic process.

Dixon (1999) identifies: dialogue, equalitarian, multiple perspectives, non-expert based, participant generated database and a shared experience as the underpinning elements that contribute to organisational learning.

- Information and expertise that are distributed – 'information must be distributed among individuals engaged in collective interpretation rather than residing with one or two people' (79).
- Equalitarian values (freedom to speak openly without punishment or coercion; equality which must exist for freedom to exist; respect which must be present for equality to exist) (106) – affirmation of democratic ideals.
- The organisation's size and physical arrangement support frequent interaction between subsystems.
- Processes and skills that facilitate organisational dialogue.

(Dixon, 1999: 105)

The model she proposes suggests that hierarchy is an inhibitor to learning, and argues that power relations will influence learning. Those employed at lower levels will have less interest in learning when their managers are present and senior managers are less likely to develop as their ideas and perspectives are often unchallenged. Dixon also suggests that 'perhaps one of the reasons that there is so little organisational learning is that the conditions of freedom, equality and respect so rarely exists in organisations' (1999: 108).

FIONA: You remarked recently, drawing on a story from Linsky, that the challenge in managing change is effectively the difficulty of managing loss. What have you noticed helps staff deal with the sense of loss?

PAUL: I think it is more about accepting loss. When I was at Harvard, Professor Linsky said that it is a common comment that 'people don't like change' but in fact all sorts of people like change. Think of someone who is moving house to a better house. This is a massive change but people often revel in it. In fact they have parties in their new house, show their friends round and positively celebrate the change. So people often enjoy change, what they fear is loss. Whenever you are going through some kind of change programme you have to understand that, for some, there will be a loss. Because there are only finite resources, changing from one way of doing something to another usually involves re-allocating resources, it involves a re-prioritisation. You are really saying to some people 'We don't value what you do as much as what these others do'. This is particularly sharp during times of austerity, when resources are not only finite but are in decline. I haven't got any answers as to how I have helped with this. However, I think that the honesty that goes with looking at change in this way is helpful. You just have to be honest and say, there isn't a win-win solution here, there are going to be losses.

One obvious example is when talking with staff about our recent financial strategy. Essentially we have expanded student numbers in order to maintain income levels. Clearly this isn't a win-win situation. The loss is that there is more work. It is much better to be up front about that rather than go into a defensive routine.

FIONA: There is some interest in the concept of organisational unlearning which refers to 'the discarding of old routines to make way for new ones, if any' (Tsang and Zahra, 2008: 1437). Organisational unlearning is explored as types of organisational change, 'change that is continuous, evolving and incremental and change that is episodic, discontinuous and intermittent' (Tsang and Zahra, 2008: 1446). They cite some interesting research questions: 'How do the processes of organisational and individual unlearning relate to each other? How does the composition of the workforce affect individual unlearning? How can an incentive system be revised to motivate individual unlearning?' (Tsang and Zahra, 2008: 1454).

Starbuck and Nystrom (2006) recommend three ways that senior managers can stimulate their own continuous learning and unlearning. 'They can listen to dissents, convert events into learning opportunities and adopt experiential frames of reference' (Starbuck and Nystrom, 2006: 164).

Learning managers are more likely to be honest with themselves and others and would therefore be more inclined to openly recognise what they do not know as this would present them with possibilities they may not have considered. From my experience working with managers in the Learning and Skills sector, not knowing is uncomfortable and being seen to not know something is even worse (Mackay, 2012).

Developing organisational capability

PAUL: How do you balance the requirements of a learning organisation (the need to allow for innovation, the development of evidence-based practice, action learning, decision-making at the point of delivery) with the requirement for consistency, equality and order? In other words how can a leader help people to hold an organisation in their mind as coherent as well as holding it in their mind as dynamic and organic?

FIONA: Borrowing heavily from Heifetz, Grashow and Linsky (2009), I worked with staff to develop a set of values for the college. They outline the qualities that an organisation needs if it is going to be 'adaptive' (Heifetz *et al.*, 2009: 100). It seemed to me that these qualities were really the qualities of a learning organisation. We played with these qualities and adapted them for our purposes and developed our 'values'. Increasingly the values are used in order to make decisions, design processes and engage in dialogue with staff and students.

College values

1   Learning through continuous development and reflection – capacity is developed and continuous learning is institutionalised
2   Responsibility – responsibility for personal and organisation's future is shared
3   Honesty – elephants in the room are named and staff and students can speak truth to power
4   Independence – independent judgement is expected and respected
5   Excellence – achievement and progression

The values have become the way of knitting the chaos together. The values are relevant to staff and students. They are designed to support the development of a learning organisation; they allow us to be consistent at the level of values whilst allowing different practice at the technical level. They are designed to provide consistency at a deep level but allow for different types of innovative practice to develop across the college. Increasingly in the college we talk about being 'tight' to our values and therefore being able to be 'loose' with regard to exactly how things are done in particular parts of the college. Thus the Maths team can have a different attendance policy to the Creative Arts and Media team as long as they are both committed to excellence.

The values have been particularly useful in enabling difficult organisational learning over the last couple of years. In particular, they can be used in order to orchestrate real organisational learning. Recently this has been done on a number of occasions when staff in different areas have been angered or frustrated by the actions of staff elsewhere. Previously, pre-values I think that this 'anger' would have been treated very simply. I would have taken a side in the debate and the staff that were 'wrong' would have been directed to change their practice. However, painful as it has been, the values have enabled us to bring the staff together to discuss openly what is happening here. Why the anger? Why the variance in practice? On several occasions this has led to deeper understanding and autonomous sustained improvements. Painful as it is!

FIONA: Garvin, Edmondson and Gino (2008: 111) provide a tool structured around the three building blocks of the learning organisation: (1) a supportive learning environment, (2) concrete learning processes, (3) leadership behaviour that reinforces learning. The supportive learning environment has four characteristics: psychological safety, appreciation of differences, openness to new ideas and time for reflection. They argue that the ability to think analytically and creatively is compromised in contexts that are overly stressed by deadlines and scheduling pressures.

Dialogue is acknowledged as the key element of communication involved in generating organisational learning. Issacs acknowledges that much:

> organisational conversation around tough, complex and challenging issues lapses into debate. In debate one side wins and another loses; both parties maintain their certainties, both suppress deeper inquiry.
>
> (Isaacs, 1993: 24)

Dixon identifies the methods through which the distribution of information is regularly obstructed in organisations: message routing; message summarising, message delay and message modification (1999: 100).

A leader's ability not only to communicate well and support the collective sense-making process is crucial. Relationships in working environments require attention to a complex mix of motivation, trust, feelings, emotions, group norms, knowledge acquisition, learning and sense-making. How leaders are seen to respond in challenging circumstances will affect their employees and followers. Dutton takes the argument further by suggesting that a leader's ability to enable a compassionate response can affect the organisational ability to maintain high performance in difficult times. 'It fosters a company's capacity to heal, to learn, to adapt and to excel' (Dutton *et al.*, 2002: 56). Dialogue seeks to have people learn how to think together and to contrive a situation where people are consciously participating in the creation of shared meaning. (Dutton *et al.*, 2002: 26).

Leaders need to develop the confidence to engage in a process of public debate and sense-making about the challenges the organisations face. This includes being able to explain the situation, the task, the intent, the concerns and ask for feedback, thus providing a shared framework that can foster organisational resiliency and embrace a future of recovery and growth (Weick, 2003: 76). 'This field suggests a new range of skills for managers that involve learning how to set up environments or "fields" in which learning can take place' (Isaacs, 1993: 31). The question may be the extent to which leaders under pressure can remain mindful and open, suspending immediate judgements when reading and analysing challenging organisational situations. Weick and Sutcliffe (2007) draw our attention to the concept of mindfulness and suggest that the capabilities of inquiry, interpretation and action are encouraged by distinctive organisational processes including preoccupation with failure, reluctance to simply interpretations.

Challenges with this approach

PAUL: Developing organisational capability in this way is not easy, there is no guarantee of success and there is certainly no straight-line correlation between input and impact. Many factors work against this approach, including short-term need for impact, inability to acknowledge failure or deal with the fear of failure and staff desire for a return to the 'clear old days' when everything was simple. The complexity involved in developing a learning organisation is substantial. People usually want either/or answers to their questions: So either you support staff or you don't, so why are you using a capability procedure? Either we do it this way or that way, so why is there variable practice? Either this improves things or that does, so why don't you decide? These either/or ways of looking at things are very seductive, simple and our default position. A member of staff addressed me recently 'I need some clear leadership on this' she said; what was meant was 'You need to tell me exactly what to do, so that I can do it without any responsibility'.

On the other hand, if I ever get this right I am convinced that the rewards are great. I have seen it in areas of the college where teams have developed a culture in which they can continuously improve, where there is a feeling of responsibility and honesty as well as the courage to innovate and develop. In these areas, the student achievement is improving and the staff are happy and engaged. There is a healthy culture.

FIONA: The challenges to organisational learning have been documented (Argyris and Schon, 1978; Vince and Reynolds, 2004). Argyris differentiates between organisations with and without the capacity to learn using Model 1 and Model 2. Argyris in particular is famed for showing how individuals and organisations protect themselves from the unpleasant experience of learning by engaging in individual and organisational defensive routines. These are both self-reinforcing and undiscussable and provide a major barrier to learning, particularly where this involves looking at underlying values or culturally reinforced behaviour. In his article, 'Teaching smart people how to learn', Argyris explores how professionals avoid learning. He argues that the very success of professionals at education can explain why the problems with learning occur. He explains that many:

have experienced success in their lives, they have not had to be concerned about failure and the attendant feelings of shame and guilt. But to exactly the same extent, they also have never developed the tolerance of feelings of failure or the skills to deal with these failings. This in turn has led them not only to fear failure but also to fear the fear of failure itself.

(Argyris, 1991: 103)

Vince (2002) too reminds us of the role emotion can play in blocking out learning opportunities through our inability to tolerate the levels of anxiety uncomfortable learning experiences can generate. The current climate of uncertainty may provide further blocks to learning and the stories of corporate greed have also heightened our interest in the darker side of organisational life and in particular, toxic leaders. The book *The Allure of Toxic Leaders*, is disturbing reading and provides frightening insights into why so many destructive leaders gain power and the role of followers in maintaining them in power (Lipman-Blumen, 2005).

Organisational learning has been criticised for making the assumption that organisations are undifferentiated entities and for playing down the impact of competing groups and competing professional identities have in undermining learning. In providing a review of the earlier writers on organisational learning Burgoyne suggests a second generation of learning organisation can be developed. In a short article he acknowledges that 'companies have to become more aware of the internal politics they must tackle if they are to become learning organisations' (1999: 41). The 'learning organisation' (Pedlar *et al.*, 1996) assumes a shared vision and values within the organisation. However, the experience of organisations suggests that group identities are not necessarily shared, mindsets are diverse and conflict not uncommon. Vince and Reynolds (2004) remind us that organisations are comprised of a complex system of inter-group relations and networks. It is feasible to argue that different groups will 'know' different things and relate in different ways. For leaders then, 'the task of those who manage organisational learning is therefore to reconcile group social identities with wider organisational identity, this can pose a significant challenge'.(Vince and Reynolds, 2004: 540).

In particular they argue that this is essential to:

1 establish constructive relationships between various participating groups based on trust and psychological safety;
2 search for acceptable goals that integrate the participant's efforts and provide a sense of direction for the learning process.

Managing group differences and power imbalances, real or imagined, requires generating common experiences and collaborative and shared reflection opportunities for all. This requires a culture that fosters mutual trust. Leaders, too, need to understand that investing in collective sense is necessary despite not fully knowing its future benefits.

Garvin *et al.*'s research suggests further insights,

- Leadership alone is not sufficient – the cultural and process dimensions of learning appear to require more explicit, targeted interventions.
- Organisations are not monolithic 'managers need to be sensitive to local cultures of learning, which will vary across units'.
- Learning is multi-dimensional.

(Garvin *et al.*, 2008: 115–16)

Final thoughts

PAUL: The values and the organisational learning approach have never been more valuable than they are in tough times. I have been able to be honest and name my piece of the mess. I have been able to take responsibility and commit to various actions such as reducing my external commitments. I have been able to demonstrate a commitment to learning by publicly sharing my issues with two other college principals and using an 'action learning set' structure to work through those issues. I have been able to commit to excellence by reminding staff that we must aim for better. I have been able to back independence by releasing an in-year quality improvement fund to support ground-level staff ideas. However, more than any of these individual things, I think that the hard times can be faced honestly with staff because we understand the values. This year self-assessment, appraisal and improvement planning have been more honest and powerful than ever before.

FIONA: One continual question we should be asking is how best to support learning managers, staff and leaders, all of whom face such challenging circumstances. Arguably learning managers are not only those who continuously develop themselves, but are also in a sense 'emotionally competent' and see the development of their teams as important. Leadership development should be concerned to build the capacity of people to learn (not what to learn) and enable others to learn and flourish, thus linking individual and organisational learning. Critical reflection encourages individuals to look more closely at what they think they know and the assumptions on which this is based. The capacity for critical reflection provides leaders with the ability to question the continuing relevance of their assumptions in situations where organisations are constantly changing. Antonacopoulou and Bento (2004) propose an approach to learning leadership which emphasises the continual learning and adaptability of leader and follower alike. An interesting challenge is whether learning can be enabled across roles, professional disciplines and seniority.

The APSLP was designed to have a developmental, predominantly experiential focus, and included five residential meetings encouraging a significant element of social learning. The programme design promotes leadership learning as a process of social participation, experimentation, reflection and feedback. As Grint acknowledges, drawing on Wenger's (1998) notions of communities of practice, 'both learning and leading are social rather than individual events' (Grint, 2005: 119). Leadership development interventions focus increasingly on the extent to which an awareness of the self and context, together with the ability to work with the complexities of organisational interactions, are recognised as essential dimensions towards effective leadership behaviour. This emphasis draws attention to the extent to which a leader is a lifelong learner. 'Learning to lead can be achieved through leading to learn' (Grint, 2005: 119). However, whilst the social nature of an organisation can be partially modelled within any group of peers much development is delivered and assessed privileging the individual. Boud (2010) also acknowledges that professional courses 'have typically been designed on the assumption of individual practice. That is, the individual professional makes autonomous decisions and engages in their own practice uninfluenced by anyone other than occasionally senior colleagues' (Boud in Bradbury *et al.*, 2010: 30). If we re-focused on the imperative of developing organisational capability we would insist on a greater focus on collective rather than individualistic learning and development initiatives.

What new insights have we generated? What light does this shed on the learning organisation, its limitations and prospects for the future?

FIONA: I think that we have been concerned to be both critical of theory and to put critique into action as a tool for further understanding organisational learning. The process of engaging with Paul has reminded me that principals and leaders have an opportunity to engage in a powerful learning process through honest and questioning reflections on their practice. I think Paul's voice is a testament to that. On the APSLP the facilitator team worked with a great many senior leaders which revealed the challenges of maintaining learning as a central aspect of their leadership practice. Senior leaders acknowledged the ways in which their 'theories in use', to use Argyris' term (Argyris and Schon, 1978), contradicted those theories that they espoused. I realised how critical it was for leaders to encourage and importantly model continuous learning as it can't be assumed or guaranteed. We are expecting principals and senior staff to positively engage with the concept and practice of organisational learning and to do so they need an element of faith in order to manage the bumps along the way. On the APSLP many of the senior staff were overly stressed (Mackay, 2012) working in organisations that were overly stretched. We need to work with individuals to develop a greater capacity for resilience, for adaptability and positive responses in the face of trauma. We know the challenges faced by individuals and organisations in the sector. And yet we know that serious threats, whether perceived or real from outside the organisation can result in rigid limiting and fearful responses (Drewe and Cooper, 2012). Working with individual leaders is very rewarding but as the focus from individual leaders shifts to developing leadership so too must any intervention shift from individuals to developing organisational learning capability.

PAUL: The interesting learning for me is around the 'undiscussable'. Why, despite my focus on developing organisational learning, aren't things better? Underlying this is the real 'undiscussable', 'Is this approach the right one?' The truth about this is that I am not sure. However, I know that working on this chapter with Fiona has inched my thinking forward on this. What has become apparent is the complexity of organisational learning and the significant challenges there are to enabling organisational learning. The hard times that we are facing at the moment in these austere years are truly a new level of challenge. It seems to me that given this level of challenge, the only sustainable response is to continue to work on developing organisational capacity, through developing organisational learning. This goes beyond the contribution of any particular individual and must develop and sustain itself without relying on a particular principal or chief executive. I suppose that the true measure of success will be the college providing high-quality education that meets the needs of the community, for years to come. This task, in my view, has never been more challenging than right now. The framing of this challenge as a challenge of developing an organisation through developing the capacity to learn is a way of enabling me to stay in the game. For now.

Chapter 7

Professional learning and vocational pedagogy

Sue Crowley

> Paradoxically, it is easier to construct a coherent story when you know little, when there are fewer pieces to fit into the puzzle. Our comforting conviction that the world makes sense rests on a secure foundation: our almost unlimited ability to ignore our ignorance.
>
> (Daniel Kahneman)

Introduction

This chapter sets out to explore what insights may be gained from a critical comparison of the different approaches and language used to describe effective professional learning and effective vocational learning. In relation to professional learning it draws on the thinking explored in previous chapters and for vocational learning and pedagogy it draws primarily on work carried out by the Institute for Learning (IfL) (Harkin, 2012) and a report commissioned by the City & Guilds Centre for Skills Development (Lucas, Spencer and Claxton, 2012) to support the Commission on Adult and Vocational Teaching and Learning. Harkin's work draws heavily on the voices of 120 vocational teachers and trainers as well as learners across the full spectrum of the FE and skills sector whilst the Lucas *et al.*'s work is derived from a thorough review of current national and international literature related to vocational learning and expert opinions of specialists in the field of vocational education including academics and policy analysts.

Professional as opposed to vocational learning implies that the learners have some professional status already, some expertise recognised usually through a qualification at or around degree level. This implies some age relatedness and that professional learning is unlikely to occur prior to age 19. It also implies the person carrying out the learning is likely to be already in employment and this situation influences that learning in context, content and process. So professional learning suggests higher levels of learning and an expectation that the learning is more frequently related to the requirements of current and future employment rather than anticipated or contrived employment.

The definition of 'adult' in the context of CAVTL is not entirely clear but whilst many 14–16 year-olds are taught subjects with an emphasis on application within the FE and Skills arena it is probably better to assume the term refers to students aged 16 and above. The nature and level of the curriculum taught to this student group can be very diverse from apprenticeships, National Vocational Qualifications (NVQs) (levels 1–5), Higher National Diplomas, degrees and indeed professional qualifications. Programmes will be full-time, part-time or day-release. Vocational refers to learning and teaching focused on some form of employment and the application of relevant knowledge and skills to that employment.

Are these distinguishing factors sufficient to suggest a requirement for different approaches to learning?

As mentioned in the introduction to this book, professional learning may be considered as a subset of vocational learning. One definition of vocation is 'a sense of fitness for, a career or occupation' which surely includes professionals who are remunerated for their professional work. Whilst there has been substantial attention paid to effective professional learning there has been less focus on effective approaches to vocational learning. Recently, however, there has been an enthusiastic interest in vocational learning and a drive to develop a framework for vocational pedagogy that is created through an analysis of the evidence base for effective vocational learning.

The Department for Business Innovation and Skills (BIS) in mid-2012 set up an independent Commission on Adult Vocational Teaching and Learning (CAVTL) chaired by Frank McLoughlin, a principal of a further education (FE) college supported by both the Learning and Skills Improvement Service and the IfL. It is 'tasked with raising the quality, and improving the outcomes and impact of adult vocational teaching and learning in the further education and skills sector for learners and employers (www.excellencegateway.org.uk/cavtl) and is due to report in early 2013. The Commission will explore appropriate curricula, effective pedagogies and consider how to raise 'the status of adult vocational teaching and learning beyond the FE and skills sector'. Current interest has been aroused by the recognition that high-level skills development may be crucial in supporting the nation's economic recovery 'people with the right skills are critical to national and global economic renewal' (www.excellencegateway.org.uk/cavtl).

In 2012 government also set up the Richards Review of Apprenticeships, which focuses more on the nature of the curriculum, qualifications and systems as opposed to pedagogy, although clearly there will be areas of overlap.

The focus throughout this text has been on the enhancers and barriers to effective professional learning and how can they be addressed. This chapter considers the similarities and differences and potential for vocational and professional approaches to learning to further inform one another. It also considers the language used to describe each type of learning and the messages that the use of these languages might impart to the status of each. 'Discourses create discursive frameworks which order reality in a certain way. They both enable and constrain the production of knowledge in that they allow for certain ways of thinking whilst excluding others' (Bradbury *et al.*, 2010: 84).

Background

Apprenticeship and the academy were both originally based on the concept of irrefutable knowledge and skills that are to be learnt through transmission from expert to novice (the novice had nothing to teach the expert so the role was of a passive recipient with an associated unequal power relationship). Knowledge transfer and thinking were central to both types of learning with a notion that additionally there was reading for academics' professional learning and doing for apprentices' vocational learning. Teaching was between the individual and their teacher but otherwise learning was a comparatively lone activity.

Futures, certainly in the shorter term, were predictable. Bodies of knowledge around medicine, law, science, masonry, carpentry, etc. were all considered as mostly incontestable. There was some professional debate amongst those who became experts and probably some reflection on practices as an individualised activity.

Within the academy, because knowledge was irrefutable, it was possible to design programmes of study that groups of individuals could be taught and thus knowledge could be passed on to others. This approach was subsequently deployed at all stages of 'educating people' whether in schools, private or public or in universities. This rather technical/rationale approach to learning can only work for that which is 'known'. Although knowledge transfer is a legitimate approach to learning, it rarely, by definition, leads to innovation or knowledge creation as this always requires challenging the status quo and is more likely to come from activities such as experiential learning, reflection on practice or professional debate and dialogue. Whilst clearly there was innovation and knowledge creation this was a much more sedate affair as the pace of change was much slower.

Purpose and outcomes

The purpose of both vocational and professional learning may be summarised as learning to improve the service or product for the end user; but are the expected outcomes for the learners any different?

In the report commissioned by the City & Guilds Centre for Skills Development, Lucas *et al.* (2012) suggest that vocational learning has 'six specifically desired outcomes':

1 Routine expertise: mastery of everyday working procedures in the domain.
2 Resourcefulness: having the knowledge and aptitude to stop and think effectively when required.

3   Functional literacies: adequate mastery of literacy, numeracy and digital literacy.
4   Craftsmanship: an attitude of pride and thoughtfulness towards the job.
5   Business-like attitudes: understanding of the economic and social sides of work.
6   Wider skills for employability and lifelong learning: having an inquisitive and resilient attitude towards constant improvement – the 'independent learner'.

(Lucas *et al.*, 2012: 9)

An equivalent set of outcomes for professional learning drawn from the previous chapters in this current text might be:

1   high levels of expertise
2   commitment to individual and collective, reflective practice and dialogue
3   earned autonomy
4   intrinsic motivation and curiosity with a drive for continuous improvement
5   recognition for work that is in the public interest
6   capacity for rigorous self-regulation and accountability.

Are the desired outcomes of professional learning and vocational learning fundamentally different? Let us look at each in turn.

1   Both forms of learning are designed to lead to expertise. Whilst the levels for each may be different due to age profile and assumed experience, the aspiration for both forms of learning is expertise.
2   'Resourcefulness; having the knowledge and aptitude to stop and think effectively' suggests that expertise alone is not sufficient and that something else is required that allows an individual to apply that knowledge to new situations and to collect appropriate new knowledge to assist problem-solving by drawing on their own resources and those of others. This process aligns very well with Schon's descriptions of reflection on and in action associated with professional learning (Schon, 1983) particularly if considered as both an individual and collective activity. There is no explicit reference to collective thinking and learning, a central tenet of professional learning but Lucas *et al.* do refer to the social dimension in their more detailed description of this outcome. Some teachers in the Harkin report do refer to the necessity for collaborative learning and problem-solving and the ability to apply knowledge and skills in a real-world context but perhaps it would be useful to consider how to develop learner capacity for reflective practices as a way of developing such resourcefulness and deepening their understanding of metacognition.
3   Functional literacies are usually taken as a given in the context of professional learning, however this is not always the case. This has been a constant

challenge within initial FE teacher education where some have found it difficult to reach the required levels of functional literacies, particularly if they do not hold graduate status. As revealed by IfL surveys many teachers still feel their levels of digital literacy are insufficient and this may partly reflect the older age profile of FE teachers and trainers. This phenomenon may be less obvious in professional areas where graduate status is a prerequisite but levels of digital fluency are not confined to this professional area.

4   'Attitude of pride and thoughtfulness towards the job' is the language used for vocational learning which surely equates to the 'intrinsic motivation … for continuous improvement'. Lucas *et al.* suggest that this comes primarily from role-modelling and being in a culture where striving for excellence is the norm and supportive constructive peer critique is commonplace. We have described elsewhere the way in which intrinsic motivations are restricted by an atmosphere of compliance and control and the impact this can have on approaches to professional learning. In Chapter 1, we considered a spectrum of teacher maturity where some teachers may be control-orientated in their approach to teaching and learning whilst others are more autonomy-orientated. There is considerable evidence established over many years that teachers who are autonomy-orientated tend to encourage greater self-esteem and intrinsic motivation in their learners and achieve greater learner outcomes and that:

> Just as children need autonomy-orientated classrooms to be intrinsically motivated and to perceive themselves as competent, teachers need autonomy-orientated contexts within which to benefit from feedback about their own orientation.
>
> (Deci *et al.*, 1981: 649)

> Best teaching and learning methods (see work of Frank Coffield, 2007 and 2012) need to adopt models of learning that are more empowering for both learners and teachers, rather than pressuring them to meet targets. The participation model of learning needs to be given more prominence over the current oriented, acquisition model of learning.
>
> (Harkin, 2012: 23)

5   Lucas *et al.* suggest that business-like attitudes will include a basic understanding of the practices required in running an organisation that produces services or products as well as what they refer to as the softer skills associated with effective communications.

> Ultimately business sense would include the ability to manage peers, subordinates and even superiors, and to motivate the team into giving their best for the business and working effectively together.
>
> (Lucas *et al.*, 2012: 53)

This seems to reflect not only the professional notion of working in the public interest but also claims leadership capabilities as and when required.

One might challenge the term 'independent learner' and suggest an interdependent or networked learner may imply a more expansive learning approach and this is certainly more appropriate for professional learning. It may be that the educational level and age profile in vocational learning requires a recognition that the transition from dependent learner to networked learner may be in the earlier stages for most vocational learners. These wider skills for growth required by employers as Lucas *et al.* suggest include problem-solving, team-work, resilience and entrepreneurship and are encouraged as learners take responsibility for their own learning. This is about encouraging an earned autonomy.

So the outcomes for vocational learning and professional learning are closely aligned although the language that describes them may be different. Is there anything within the discourses associated with the one that might usefully inform the other? To summarise, this comparison has highlighted that:

- Perhaps vocational learners might profit from an exploration of the concept of reflective practice and how this might be accomplished individually and, more importantly, collectively. This would also increase their understanding of metacognition and hence their capacity for learning.
- Levels of functional literacies should not be avoided within professional learning but recognised as a skills gap for some that should be addressed.
- Intrinsic motivation is associated with high levels of self-esteem and high levels of aspiration and is a desirable aspect of both professional and vocational learning but requires a learning environment that is expansive where compliance and control are minimised whilst retaining accountability.
- Many professionals react against ideas of being 'business-like' possibly because they connect these ideas with new public management (NPM) and a lack of autonomy. They may be more comfortable with ideas of leadership development, emotional intelligence and wider communications skills.
- The transition from dependent to interdependent learning can rely on both the individual and the teacher as the agent for change. Teachers need to consider how reluctant they may be to give up the ownership of their students learning, why that might be and how justifiable it is. Students' understanding of this transition, made explicit though discussion, might well help them accomplish it. The spectrum of teacher maturity described in Chapter 1 could be reflected in a similar spectrum for students.

Approaches to professional and vocational learning

The IfL report by Harkin did not address the issue of effective vocational learning but it did ask teachers, trainers and learners what the key qualities of an effective vocational teacher might be. Interestingly several respondents had asked their students this question. The findings were summarised by the following list compiled at a students' regional seminar but reflecting both teachers' views and researchers' findings:

- Open and friendly 'like talking to a colleague with respect'; having a teacher you can talk to and ask for help
- Teachers who engage in discussion that's related to real life
- Lecturers that make the subject interesting by relating content to real and current events – the Olympics was given as an example by business students
- Give one to one time to students and take time out to help individually
- Treating students as adults
- Teachers who are positive and like their subject; 'passionate about being a teacher'
- One who will go over anything as many times as necessary.

(Harkin, 2012: 40)

Whilst expertise is a requirement here and relevance is also key, it is interesting that the teacher – student relationship being one of mutual respect clearly comes across most strongly.

The City & Guilds Centre for Skills Development report was more directly focused on vocational learning and pedagogy and having thoroughly analysed the current research it identifies the following:

We suggest that effective vocational teaching requires a blend of hands-on or first-hand learning with critical reflection, collaboration and feedback in a context of strong relationship between teacher and taught'

(Lucas *et al.*, 2012: 116)

The best vocational education learning is broadly hands-on, practical, experiential, real-world as well as, and often at the same time as, something which involves feedback, questioning, application and reflection and, when required, theoretical models and explanation.

(Lucas *et al.*, 2012: 9)

This places a much greater emphasis on the need for collaborative dialogue as an aid to learning than the teachers or learners identified in the IfL report although teachers and trainers in the IfL reviews of continuing professional development (CPD) rated reflective practice and dialogue as central sources of professional learning. Some teachers seem reluctant to increase the ratio of student talk to teacher talk. There may be many reasons for this including the perceived need to 'cover' the curriculum; the need to stay in control; the fear of letting go. Teachers may do well to consider how they can encourage more student talk and less teacher talk throughout the learning process.

The emerging discourse of the previous chapters has emphasised a range of key themes and concepts that are highly significant for effective professional learning. They include:

- learning that has obvious relevance and is based in practice (in the specific case of FE and skills the relevance is to the improvement of outcomes and well-being of the students)
- critical reflection on practices individually and collectively must be an integral part of the process (Boud in Bradbury *et al.*, 2010)
- professional dialogue that promotes deep learning and asks powerful questions (Dixon, 1998; Isaacs, 1999)
- learning that is a personalised process but with a heavy emphasis on learning as a social activity
- experiential learning (Kolb, 1984) explored through communities of practice (Lave and Wenger, 1991).

There is a very strong emphasis on collective professional learning encouraging power shared with colleagues as opposed to unequal power relationships (Ginsberg, 1996). Assumption of comparatively equal power relationships means there is little mention of teaching other than peer to peer, coaching and mentoring.

Is pedagogy, i.e. the teaching approaches, merely the stimulus for learning? Does the actual deep, meaningful learning come from the dialogue, feedback, reflection or experimentation that those stimuli may or may not encourage? This is not to deflect from the importance of the teacher's role in promoting dialogue, offering feedback, reflection, experimentation and truth seeking but to highlight the importance of the learning and to suggest that the learning is often pushed aside to make way for the teaching in a way that teachers themselves rightly resist when similar approaches are adopted for their professional learning. Are we denying our students the space needed for learning through reflection and dialogue that we are demanding ourselves? Does this detract from giving the learners the skills to be self-directive and autonomous, networked learners? If so, why? Are we afraid of losing the power base that our expertise affords us? Do teachers assume that their professional learning is somehow superior or at least different to the vocational learning of their students? Even if this is not the case this may be the inadvertent communication to not just the learners but a range of other stakeholders. Teachers often intervene because they want to support and help their students' learning but intervention is sometimes not the best way to achieve such learning and this is often a display of control orientation that may deny the learner autonomy, self-esteem and confidence. Adult learners often react negatively to imposed ways of learning, and personalised learning means that you have to do it yourself albeit with help and guidance. Exploration of power relationships in effective professional and vocational learning requires an understanding of the interplay between agency and systems.

Relevance

A characteristic of adult learning, well documented over many years is the need for the learning to be relevant and this is clearly reflected in the work of Harkin and Lucas *et al.* Unless the learner can see how the learning relates to the context in which they want to use it, their motivation for learning diminishes. Teachers and other professionals need to be confident that the learning will improve their practices and as professionals they are often best placed to determine this. Vocational learners may need the relevance to be made clear to them by their teacher or trainer; unless the teacher is able to do this by calling on their own vocational experience or relating it to the learners own work experience, their credibility and the learners' motivation are both in danger.

Reflective practice

Reflective practices as a component of professional learning has been advocated as far back as the 1920s with the work of John Dewey. It was given greater prominence in the earlier 1980s with the work of Donald Schon. Paradoxically, the development of reflective practices as introduced by Donald Schon in 1983 as integral to professional practices parallels the development of NPM, possibly as a reaction to the reductionist approach to professional practices. Reflective practices have been thoroughly interrogated most recently by Bradbury *et al.* (2010).

Reflective practice as a concept arose from a need to acknowledge that expertise was more than just knowing the facts or completing the task. Two people could follow the same programme of learning and achieve the same outcomes but one of them could be significantly better than the other in the way they practised. The suggestion was that one was able to continuously consider what they had done, how well they had done and how they might be able to do better in future; because of this they were often able to pre-empt problems by learning through reflecting on their previous experiences and practices. Reflective practice can be an individual activity and some of us are more capable of carrying out this individual activity than others; reflective practice is usually more effective and less challenging for most of us if pursued as a collective activity.

The individualised idea of reflective practice that has been prevalent through both the Dewey and Schon eras has required individuals to think alone about their practices and perhaps to capture that thinking in words through a reflective diary. The difficulty here is that, in my experience with large numbers of individuals on both teacher education and leadership development programmes, many of us find this challenging, are reluctant to do it and our criticality is limited without external agency. Consequently we avoid reflective practices unless there is a strong extrinsic motivator such as a course requirement. This resistance also acts as a barrier to deep learning from the process as compulsion often leads to tokenism. However give us space and time to discuss our practice in a safe, supportive environment with others who understand the challenges we are grappling with and it is hard to stop the conversation! To make the experience more powerful we need to ensure that the conversation is focused on improvement of practice, individuals within the group respect each other, they can bring different perspectives to bear and are happy to challenge each other with powerful questioning in order to really address the issues and surface what might be otherwise undiscussable. This requires a strong sense of common purpose and high levels of trust. It is not easy but the rewards can be substantial. 'If the best moments are always found with others, then for maximum impact every teacher and trainer needs to discuss, critically reflect and co-construct their professional learning with colleagues' (IfL, 2012a: 24).

Through the reviews of CPD carried out by IfL, teachers emphasised that, at best, CPD was a stimulus for professional learning that actually came from the subsequent collective reflection and dialogue it stimulated. This means that it is talking, not teaching, that is the main powerhouse for learning. Unfortunately all too often the space and time for such talking is often unavailable.

IfL's review of CPD for 2010–11 shows that when asked which activities would lead to brilliant teaching, training and learning reflective practice topped the table. However, the feedback back from the national focus groups suggested that, 'there needs to be some interrogation of what reflection means' (IfL, 2012a: 18). This implies multiple interpretations of the meaning of reflective practice and more importantly some confusion as to how to do it.

This comment reflects the findings of Bradbury *et al.* They suggest that reflective practice has been sabotaged by a technico-rationale approach that denies the complexity and destroys the efficacy of the strategy. They suggest that reflective practice needs to be reframed in the light of the changing context of practice. Boud in Bradbury *et al.* suggests that this reframing needs to take account of the changing context of practice and highlights three important features of this practice as now being more:

a) collective in nature
b) transdisciplinary in character and
c) regularly with 'an increasing emphasis on practice being co-produced with whom it is conducted'.

(Boud in Bradbury *et al.*, 2010:30)

Interrogating practices with a view to improvement with a group of others, including the 'end-users' of that practice who bring different perspectives to bear, requires a more sophisticated approach to a complex activity and can be highly challenging.

Collective reflective practice is then seen as a powerful learning approach to professional learning. Whilst Lucas *et al.* (2012) do identify it as a desirable component of vocational learning it is given little attention by vocational teachers or learners. Exploring the potential of reflective practice in vocational teaching and learning may be a very productive exercise.

So how do we carry out critical reflection on practice?

Dialogue and the use of powerful questioning

> Dialogue is an affirmation of the intellectual capability of not only the individual but the collective. It acknowledges that everyone is blind to his or her assumptions and needs the help of others to see them. It acknowledges that each person, no matter how smart or capable, sees the world from a perspective and that there are other legitimate perspectives that could inform that view.
>
> (Dixon, 1998: 66)

Dialogue in this context is not merely about having a conversation. It is about exploration, challenge, suspending judgement and developing deep self-aware-ness. Each participant brings different perspectives to the table and the novice does have the ability to teach the expert enabling a more democratic approach to teaching and learning with the accompanying shift in power relationships. Others help to extend our zones of proximal development (Vygotsky, 1978) and they often do this through open questioning. We often don't know what we don't know but constructive rigorous dialogue can reveal this for us. Others can intro-duce different 'ways of seeing' that can be very illuminating, developing and extending our existing practices. The capacity for engaging in effective dialogue comes through the use of powerful questioning, e.g. Why do I/we do it that way, what other ways might there be and why don't I/we use them? What would be the consequences of a different approach? This may require looking for proposi-tional theory to support or challenge our current thinking and dialogue can take place between the individual and the theoretical concepts found in books. It may require some 'unlearning'. Our answers need to be evidence based where possi-ble and involve the use of diverse impact measures that are truly valid and reliable when taken together so, for example, use of the harder measures such as reten-tion and achievement along with student and peer feedback. The purpose of dialogue is not to create consensus but to gain understanding and value diversity. This narrative of the use of powerful questions is common in relation to profes-sional learning but absent from vocational learning. Developing vocational learn-ers' capacity for dialogue and the use of powerful questioning should be a natural part of their development and can be facilitated by teachers. The challenge for teachers, however, is to ask more and tell less. Not only does this help learners to engage with one another in developing critical thinking skills it also enables them to take more responsibility for their own learning and that of their colleagues. This then develops skills to be used to connect classroom and workplace learning, homework and group interaction, theory and practice. One of the greatest challenges for teachers, however, is creating the space and time for a substantial increase in learner talk.

Courses and conferences and online development programmes acknowledge that transmission approaches to learning and updating still have a role to play in learning that is based on empirical knowledge, the existence of which can be proved or disproved. But we know that much knowledge is more contestable than previously assumed. In many areas of vocational and professional expertise this is still the most predominant approach to professional learning, even though the nature of the learning is no longer based on what could be construed as empirical knowledge; the approach to learning has not kept up with the nature of that which is to be learnt.

Recent work that addresses this problem of creating time and space for learner dialogue revolves around the idea of the flipped classroom as advocated by Sal Khan and others (www.khanacademy). This suggests that the task of homework and class work is reversed. For homework, learners use the Internet to learn the concept, theory, ideas required and they come to the classroom to consider the application, resolve misunderstanding, receive feedback and internalise the learning through collaborative learning and dialogue. This approach holds many attractions. Younger students are comfortable with using the Internet to search for information but have not developed the skills of discrimination that allow them to determine what evidence is valid and reliable and what is not to be trusted. Testing the evidence gained from searches with teachers and other students will develop those skills. Students can learn from each other, share their thinking, challenge each other's ideas thus developing their capacity for critical thinking as well as freeing the teacher up to give more personalised feedback.

Communities of practice

Communities of practice are also considered central to effective professional learning. They are a way of describing the collective through which collaborative professional learning takes place. The term is used to describe a group of people drawn together by some common purpose and practice. (In the case of teachers in the FE and skills sector to develop, extend and improve learning and teaching experiences or subject expertise.) Some will be long-established members of that community with substantial expertise and experience in the practices of that community; others may be new to the community, its practices and its purpose. Metaphorically those experienced members are situated at the centre of that community whilst the new members occupy a more peripheral position and will normally defer to the more experienced members. As the newer members gain expertise and experience they move to more central positions within that community. Sometimes new members bring a new and fresh light to the community and an expansive community will recognise and capitalise on this fresh perspective so the community's practices grow, develop and extend. When applying the concept to professional learning there is usually an assumption that the members of the community belong to a similar occupational or professional practice grouping, e.g. they are all teachers and trainers in the FE and skills sector or engineers, caterers, bricklayers, etc. However, we recognised in Chapter 1 the need for a more interdisciplinary approach to professional learning and we acknowledge that all adults bring to the learning process different skills knowledge and expertise even those we consider our students. It is therefore possible to envisage a community of practice whose main purpose and practices are to extend, develop and improve learning and teaching experiences that include a wider membership than just the teachers and trainers, which extends to other support staff, potential or current employers and the students themselves. Communities of practice are not usually associated with vocational learning although their original explorations lie in apprenticeship-like systems (Lave and Wenger, 1991). Could teachers and trainers of vocational learning see their communities of practice encompassing their students? Could their students bring new and fresh perspectives to the vocational content and processes? Is there a focus in vocational learning on such communities perhaps with a different name or is there no place for them in vocational learning? Could the concept of communities of practice help metacognition for vocational learners?

Coffield and Williamson suggest that such communities should exist through their 'communities of discovery' which act as vehicles for learning for both students and their educators and therefore create a more equal power relationship.

> The issue that lies behind all the discussion so far is power. In communities of discovery, power is openly, widely and more equally shared among the members of those communities ... That will mean confronting the old elitist model, which still flourishes in our leading universities, as well as the business model that has taken over so many of our schools and colleges.
>
> (Coffield and Williamson, 2011: 12–13)

Communities of practice do exist in the workplace and perhaps using this concept might enable learners to understand the structure of the workplace more clearly.

Assessment for learning

Assessment for learning (AfL) is not often addressed in discourse about professional learning yet it is central to the discourse about student and vocational learning. Constructive feedback rigorously executed is one of the most powerful strategies for promoting successful learner outcomes (Wiliam and Black, 2006, Hattie, 2009). The use of powerful questioning within a community of practice may be the way to bring about assessment *for* learning and to promote critical thinking about one's own learning, promoting double-loop learning (Argyris, 1991). Approaches to professional learning could usefully focus more on the use of assessment for learning and feedback. From previous chapters we can see that professional learning is beginning to address issues of impact and its evaluation; should this be a discourse for vocational learning too?

Summary

There are many similarities in approaches to effective professional and vocational learning. Both need to demonstrate the relevance of the object of the study. Both rely on a respectful relationship between the teacher and the taught. Both are more effective in a more expansive learning environment characteristic of a learning organisation. However, perhaps more can be learnt to the benefit of both from the apparent differences. The discourse around professional learning emphasises reflective practice and dialogue, the evaluation and measurement of impact and the development of autonomy. Introduction of these key areas could inform and improve the practice of vocational learning. Vocational learning places much greater emphasis on teaching, assessment and feedback and similarly professional learning might usefully pay more attention to these.

The difference in emphases may reflect a shift from dependent to interdependent learning bearing in mind the difference in age and levels of learning but it is worth considering whether the shift should happen sooner or quicker.

Lucas, Claxton and Webster (2010) suggest that we have long held the belief that vocational/practical work is somehow less worthy and less intelligent than academic work. There are many reasons why influential groups in our society may wish to keep this divide including groups of teachers but Lucas *et al.* suggest that recent brain science and the concept of embodied cognition are providing evidence that will dispel this myth. They suggest that this has profound and exciting implications for teachers and pedagogy. They advocate a 'framework for learning' that:

> provides a common language for thinking about how both artisans and scholars go about their business of learning and problem-solving. We think that the development of such a language is crucial if we are to dispel the pernicious differential of esteem in which these different kinds of accomplishment have traditionally been held. The tacit assumption that generically different models of learning and teaching apply to practical and academic kinds of learning has helped perpetuate that dysfunctional imbalance.
>
> (Lucas *et al.*, 2010: 15)

Does the role of context and situation have a different impact on professional as opposed to vocational learning? Do we demand expansive learning environments for ourselves and remain content with a restrictive one for our learners, thus perpetuating our power over as opposed to power with our learners? Does the difference in use of language illustrate different processes and concepts to be applied or does it signify other, more pervasive/sinister factors at work? 'Once we used the same language to describe all forms of learning, we see how false it is to distinguish between "academic" and "practical" learning: just as false as the idea that the mind and the body are separate' (Lucas *et al.*, 2010: iii).

Chapter 8

Maintaining the challenge and the learning

Sue Crowley

> The idea is there, locked inside. All you have to do is remove the excess stone.
> (Michelangelo)
>
> Structures of which we are unaware hold us prisoners.
>
> (Peter Senge)

Introduction

Each of the chapters in this book have drawn on theory, research, practice and evidence to make sense of different aspects of challenging and supporting high-quality professional learning not just as applied to the further education (FE) and skills sector but across a range of professions. The Institute for Learning (IfL), its membership and its challenges as a comparatively new professional body were the catalyst for the compiling of this text.

Whilst the rhetoric is comparatively easy to pull together, its application or as Vivienne Porritt describes it 'putting knowledge to work' has brought with it a whole range of potential blocks to learning and application for all leaders of teachers at all levels within and across organisations, whether for senior leaders trying to lead learning within the organisation, teacher educators trying to develop effective practices in professional learning or professional bodies trying to articulate a workable future model of professionalism and professional learning. Each chapter challenges definitions and orthodoxies and, through that, the power structures that are currently reducing teachers' responsibility to pedagogy and the responsibilities of other professions towards their disciplines. There is an argument that the power of learning of any kind is being systematically diminished by a managerialist approach to organisational development and that this has a stultifying effect on learning, innovation, entrepreneurship and improvement. The reader may conclude that the book has raised more questions than answers but for this I feel no need to apologise; the book's title was carefully chosen. Too many answers and not enough questions have often been part of the problem; control orientation, even if originating from the best of intentions, restricts our ability to enable improvement and learning.

Initiatives have been around in abundance but apparent urgency and short-termism have led to the drive for implementation before understanding and deep learning, causing such initiatives to flounder and professionals to become exhausted by initiatives and more worryingly dismissive of sound, evidence-based practices. This situation is not only prevalent in the FE and skills sector, we have seen it in the health sector and other public services as well as in private sectors such as the legal services.

This final chapter therefore is not a concluding one but one that prompts those interested to carry on the dialogue in order to develop deeper learning and understanding of the attributes needed for powerful learning that has real impact. It hopes to do this by exploring a range of recurring themes that have surfaced through the construction of the text and examines each through a variety of lenses including the lens of the individual professional practitioner, the professional practice team, the whole organisation and a representative professional body. I have chosen the following key themes that stand out for me, you may have others:

1   Personalised and collective learning
2   Leadership and responsible, earned autonomy
3   Resourcing CPD
4   Measures of impact and success
5   Learning cultures and expansive learning environments.

Personalised and collective learning

The vast majority of adults prefer their learning to be relevant and contextualised and to build on that which they already know, understand and can do (Bruner, 1966; Knowles, 1980). This acknowledges who they are and values what they already have to contribute. What they need to learn will depend on what they know already, their past experiences and this will be different for each person; denying their current valuable knowledge and skills undervalues not just what they can contribute but who they are, their identity. Consequently by its nature what one adult learns will be different to the next even within the same learning session, i.e. learning *is* personalised even if teaching is not. However this personalisation can be capitalised upon by ensuring the learners' prior knowledge and experience is acknowledged as an asset by both the teacher and the learner, both recognising the value of what each brings to the learning process and that the learning to be done is negotiated so that the learner understands and acknowledges its relevance and value to them. This is equally true for the teacher and the learner relationship and for the practitioner engaged in professional learning.

Irrefutable knowledge can be passed on passively and carried out as a lone activity but most of what we need to know is contestable as is whether we need to know it or not and that is one reason why social learning, involving collective reflective practices and high-quality professional dialogue, is so important to the learning process. We need to clarify our preconceptions and assumptions and how they influence our knowledge and understanding in any domain. Unless we tell others what we think how can they learn from us and how can they expand our current understanding? This is why we have a professional obligation to profess and therefore engage in dialogue, to lead our own learning and development and assist that of colleagues. This sounds easy but it is not. The art of engaging in high-quality dialogue has been dealt with elsewhere (Bohm, 1996; Dixon, 1998; Isaacs, 1999). All writers on this subject recognise it as a complex and valuable skill. To get better at it we need to practise.

All the evidence suggests that the course, programme of study, online learning, reading, etc. have the potential to stimulate learning and development and cause impact but it is not a given, as many professionals have reported. Evidence suggests that very few implement what they may have learned from a continuing professional development (CPD) activity and this undermines its potential value. It has to be followed up with thinking and discussion, feedback, dialogue and application. As Nonaka and Takeuchi (1995) suggest, it is the internalisation of the newly acquired knowledge and the making of tacit knowledge explicit that allows it to become embedded and sustained in the practice of all and to have impact. Internalisation takes time and is often difficult; it implies deep learning and it often requires unlearning. However as John MacBeath so concisely puts it: 'Out of self-knowledge and evidence of improvement, accountability can flow as a natural consequence' (MacBeath, 2009: 146).

From a team perspective the dialogue and collective approach to learning not only explores different approaches to practice but allows new members of the team to share their different experiences and expertise and to understand the cultural and behavioural norms of the team and how they, as a unit, engage with their learners or clients. Collective learning within the team means shared responsibility for professional practices and learner/client outcomes and necessarily promotes a no-blame culture, a commitment to continuous improvement, an expansive learning environment where everybody is supported in their learning and development, all are teachers and learners. Learning is a valued good.

Organisations can, and some have, found ways to promote the feedback, the dialogue and the collective learning often by allowing the professionals to determine the stimulus they need themselves as communities of practice, disciplinary teams and inter-disciplinary teams. This does not threaten or deny the need for accountability and is best accomplished when some measures of success are determined prior to engagement in the professional learning. It can be a highly effective way of giving leadership responsibilities to appropriate individuals within the organisation rather than reverting to hierarchies. Some organisations have restructured their organisational spaces to promote sharing, interaction and collective learning and knowledge management. Some have done this with the creative use of virtual learning spaces. Leaders of organisations do have an important role to play here and Paul Wakeling in Chapter 6 outlined his personal approach and the challenges it posed. Leaders of organisations can make things happen particularly by acting as role models and by listening, responding and asking questions more than giving solutions.

Professional bodies also have a key role to play. Professionals are busy people; they cannot always devote time to researching the latest thinking and developments in the policy and practices of their profession, be it in law, engineering, health or teaching and learning. Southworth (2011) suggests that many educational leaders and practitioners themselves do not have the knowledge and skills to promote effective professional learning and this is likely to be the case in other professions. He suggests national agencies should produce 'succinct and accessible information' that can be made available to leaders:

> National agencies, research universities and government departments should liaise and jointly produce succinct and accessible information about teaching, latest evidence and research, inspection findings and so on. Currently much of this material remains piecemeal and scattered.
>
> (Southworth, in Robertson and Timperley, 2011: 82)

Professional bodies play a key role in professional knowledge management and dissemination by promoting professional dialogue with their membership. Organisational interests are often immediate and less often futures thinking; professional bodies can encourage professionals to think beyond their current practices and explore national and international dimension to their practice.

Leadership and responsible, earned autonomy

Autonomy is a concept strongly associated with professionalism; several contributors have qualified this term with the notion of earned autonomy that comes from a commitment to maintain a high level of expertise, experience and understanding that allows the professional to make informed decisions confident in the knowledge that they have consulted widely, interrogated the evidence base and considered carefully a range of implications and consequences. They are effectively networked. By demonstrating such responsible professional actions individuals are demonstrating leadership and generating a reassured and confident followership and public. The leadership role may be held by one individual in one circumstance and another in another circumstance and perhaps leadership is better seen as a process than either an individual or group trait. The key point here is that all professionals need to be ready and able to show leadership as the need arises.

Gemmill and Oakley (1997) explore the concept of leadership as a socially alienating myth that many of us in organisations collude with as it shifts the responsibility for dealing with ambiguity and uncertainty from us to the leader or the leadership and encourages what is referred to as learned helplessness.

> The social construct of leadership is viewed as a myth that functions to reinforce existing social beliefs and structures about the necessity of hierarchy and leaders in organisations ... Because the myth is undiscussable

by members, self-sealing non learning about the dynamics of the myth is constantly reinforced. As long as faults, imperfections and hopes can be attributed to leadership, the social system itself remains unexamined and unchanged.

(Gemmill and Oakley, 1997: 108–12)

Gemmill and Oakley are concerned that unless we recognise the 'collective unconscious assumptions' we all make about leadership then we deny our individual leadership roles and relinquish our professional autonomy. Many talk of dispersed or distributed leadership and 'empowerment' where the trick of the designated leader is to know when and how to give leadership away thus promoting leadership and autonomy in others. This is not always easy as outlined in Chapter 6. Many members of organisations see this as a way of the 'leaders' shifting responsibility and blame whilst still maintaining an unequal power relationship but it can also be perceived as members' reluctance to take on a legitimate leadership role. Whilst many claim autonomy as one of the valued attributes of being a professional they may simultaneously reject the inevitable responsibility that comes with it. This is the path to stalemate, distrust and inertia within an organisation. Yet it is in the gift of professionals and leaders to recognise their interdependence and help to generate expansive learning environments and a learning culture where learning and innovation can flourish and, consequently, so can all who learn therein.

This section I believe highlights the unavoidable tensions between the concept of professionalism and new public management identified by Andy Boon and Toni Fazaeli as well as Denis Gleeson. Professional bodies may be well placed to mediate this tension. New public management (NPM) is inappropriate for the current global context and needs to be replaced by different organisational systems, structures and processes. By modelling approaches to organisational development and professional learning and defining a concept of professionalism, professional bodies may help to shift organisational emphasis more towards professionalism and away from managerialism.

Resourcing CPD

Professional learning and development does require resources in terms of time, space and stimulus material. The big challenge is to determine who stands to gain from this development, in what proportions and therefore who should pay what proportion of the cost or indeed whether the benefits are outweighed by the costs.

Organisational contributions

A key issue for organisations in determining the type and volume of professional learning and development must be value for money. Benchmarking statistics suggest that most larger organisations spend between 1–2.5 per cent of their annual turnover on staff development. This however is a measure of the more traditional and explicit forms of prescribed interventions, described in terms of inputs rather than outcomes such as sending staff on development programmes. Many organisations also set up their own in-house opportunities for their staff to engage in CPD, usually events. There may be an evaluation of such programmes and events but these rarely focus on the impact of the event in terms of learning or changes in behaviours for the individual, the collective or, indeed, the impact on the students/clients. There is the suggestion that much of this approach to professional learning and development (PLD) has very little impact at all and is often resented by staff. Would a stronger focus on outcomes help to determine cost benefits and value for money?

Feedback to the IfL has shown an increased commitment by individual members to share their CPD with others but this is still a long way from reaching its potential. Many staff will engage in external programmes often including some research that no other person in the organisation gets to hear about, let alone reflect upon, learn from or evaluate. Many staff attending the Learning and Skills Improvement Service (LSIS) Aspiring Principals and Senior Leadership Programme reported that neither the executive team nor the principal ever discussed with them their learning from the programme or how their learning might suggest improvements in individual or organisational practices and many were happy for this to remain the case. They often felt they might be ridiculed for returning from a programme with new ideas for revised practices rather than stimulating discussions about how improvements might be enabled. This is hardly a sound return on investment. It represents a huge missed opportunity and betrays a culture that has an element of anti-learning.

So how can organisations maximise the impact, efficiency and effectiveness of CPD? Evidence suggests that organisations could be much more efficient and effective in the use of CPD resources if they consulted and negotiated more with the staff as to what CPD is required, how it might be enabled, what are the expected outcomes over what period of time and how can it be shared to ensure maximum staff and student/client benefit. More time and resources need to be directed towards identifying what specific improvements are necessary and possible, how they might best be achieved, what a realistic time-frame might be, what impact is required, what the measures of success should be and how the learning might be disseminated more widely. A greater emphasis on measuring and evaluating impact would ensure better value for money.

Time and space are regularly seen as crucial in allowing for effective professional learning and perhaps this is where organisations can be most helpful. This time and space may need some scaffolding initially to ensure that staff realise its potential. Time and virtual space have been creatively harnessed by some organisations for feedback and professional dialogue within and across teams so that organisational learning is dispersed.

An illustrative example saw a large organisation giving every member of staff an iPad as a Christmas present. Imagine how each individual member of staff felt receiving an apparently generous Christmas present from their employer (who presumably struck a very good deal with the supplier)! There will have been some sceptics amongst the staff but many will have felt valued and rewarded in a time of austerity. Many staff were probably uncertain of how to use it but they would know many others who were in the same boat so would have been comfortable asking for help, sharing their limited knowledge, having a laugh: engaging in professional dialogue. Many staff in the sector may still be quite technophobic but this would ensure the skills of this staff would be updated in a very non-threatening way; some would go home and ask children or grand-children for help and be delighted with their new found skills. All members of staff regardless of their position in the organisation received the gift. This com-municated a strong message about equality and respect, essential components of a learning organisation.

Did that CEO have a measure of success in mind? Did they know what the impact was that they wanted? How could a cost benefit analysis be determined or estimated? What risks were involved? What was the impact on organisational, team and individual learning? How might it impact on the learner experience?

The above examples are provided to illustrate the sometimes small ways different organisations have tried to shift the emphasis away from control and compliance to allowing professional staff their autonomy to do what they do best whilst maintaining accountability.

CPD that meets organisational goals it would seem should be supported by the employer.

Individuals' contributions

If individuals see professional learning as an imposition that has little value for them or their learners/clients then any motivation to participate will be extrinsic and begrudged; commitment will be minimal and being asked to pay for the privilege is probably unworkable. Individuals are intrinsically motivated to improve through professional learning because they have a substantial say in the process and are likely to see the benefits for them and their learners/clients. The learning gained from this latter approach helps the practitioner improve their view of themselves, their self-image and so they are prepared to invest more in it.

The role of the professional body

Professional bodies must work directly with their individual members but this can also be to the advantage of the whole organisation: interrogating the CPD car-ried out by members across the whole sector to establish effective practices can provide organisations with vital information about the efficiency and efficacy of their approaches too. Research and development in partnership with individuals can promote rigorous action research, the findings of which can be fed back to the employing institution to inform practice. Professional bodies (PBs) can set up virtual communities of practice to enable sharing and developing ideas and learning across the sector. PBs can establish partnerships with higher education institutions (HEIs) for wider research and development projects which can again feed back information on evidence-based practices. PBs can ensure that individuals and their employers have access to the latest national and international findings. Through their membership PBs have access to large amounts of data and a key role of PBs can be to interrogate and interpret this data to develop new knowledge to feed back to its membership and the sector in which they practice. A good PB should be able to offer up to date evidence of effective practices. Organisations with a commitment to developing a learning culture and an expansive learning environment are more likely to encourage staff to engage with their PB as an additional source of learning and development if they believe the PB is creating these opportunities for its members. They are also more likely to support staff in maintaining that membership financially or otherwise if they have considered how the PB can can add value to the organisation as a whole as well as the individuals.

For the long-established PBs payment of subscription by individuals is custom and practice, although some employers do subsidise this, as originally there was no employer intermediary or state intervention. For PBs established more recently this direct relationship is less straightforward with both employer and state positioned in between. There is a danger that where the employer is strongly attuned to NPM they may perceive the PB as intruding on their territory and undermining their control and subsequently they may positively discourage staff from engaging with such a body. This can severely restrict the individual and organisational learning and the potential value that a PB can add.

Measures of impact and success

Talk of value for money is almost futile if there is no rigorous and sustainable measurement of impact and success. The impact of professional learning, as Colquhoun and Kelly as well as Porritt describe, is rarely rigorously addressed by practitioners and their leaders in the FE and skills arena and this is by no means uncommon in other arenas. Whilst there may be a received wisdom that professional learning 'is a good thing' there seems to be little attempt at determining why and how it might be a good thing. Early review of CPD declarations at IfL showed that practitioners often lost sight of the relationship between CPD and improvement in their professional practices and this must be partly because CPD was separated from its potential impact.

Are the measures of success and evaluation of the impact of professional learning different for the individual, the team, the whole organisation and the PB?

Porritt argues that not only should there be rigorous evaluation of impact but that in considering impact as a prerequisite to professional learning the evaluating process becomes a learning tool in itself. The Joyce and Showers (1980) findings that only 10 per cent of teachers implemented what they learn from CPD activities may explain why much of the CPD activity is perceived as a waste of valuable time and money by the participants and sometimes treated as tokenistic by their leaders and managers. The challenge is how to put the knowledge gained to work; it is not so much the CPD activity but what we do with it that counts. Establishing what success would look like and how to evaluate it enables teachers not only to choose areas for improvement that they deem important but gives them ownership of the learning they need to develop that improvement. The frameworks proposed by Guskey (2002b), Earley and Porritt (2009) and Timperley (2011) do help in, as Timperley's book title suggests – *Realising the Power of Professional Learning.*

We should not underestimate how challenging and demanding a process this can be. However, evaluating and recording the impact made by CPD can be very empowering for the individual, the team and the organisation. Not only does it provide a clear focus for professional learning and a better understanding of what needs to be learnt and what the outcomes might be for the professional and their learners/clients (in itself motivating) but it also justifies the approaches individuals, groups and organisations take to continuous improvement and demonstrates their ability to improve and rigorously self-assess.

Chapter 3 describes how the first generation CPD for professionals was based on an input model that at its most crude described CPD in terms of the numbers of hours of CPD delivered. This is easy to measure, arguably reliable but hardly valid. Chapter 4 explored the challenges that IfL met when trying to develop an outcome model for CPD that was based on the impact it might have on the practices of professionals and their learners. It revealed the lack of knowledge and skills practitioners and their leaders had about how to measure and evaluate impact – an outcomes model for CPD. Chapter 5 showed how impact could be measured and evaluated at the individual, team and organisational levels. Valid measurement and evaluation of impact is a central challenge of effective professional learning. Many professional bodies are working to develop more effective approaches to professional learning and they need to consider what responsibilities they might have for supporting individual teachers and their organisations on filling this crucial knowledge and skills gap. They might also need to consider what success would look like if they truly enable individuals and organisations to evaluate the impact of their professional learning and then review and reflect on how to get even greater impact in their future professional learning; a virtuous upward spiral.

Learning cultures and expansive learning environments

A common theme throughout the text is the need for dialogue to facilitate the learning process. However, Dixon comments on the paradox of dialogue:

In order for organisational members to risk engaging in dialogue, the organisation must have a climate that supports the development of the individual as well as the development of the organisation. Yet that climate is unlikely to come into being until individuals are able to engage in dialogue.

(Dixon, 1998: 68)

It is this climate that is described by Fuller and Unwin (2004b) as existing along a continuum from restrictive to expansive in its potential to promote learning. Although they are concerned mostly with apprentices learning at work the parallels with a learning organisation are very similar and their alignment is reflected in Chapter 7. An expansive learning environment is one where individuals not only are able to engage in dialogue but positively embrace the opportunity. Such dialogue can be a risky business if others dismiss your contributions; where contributions lead to mistakes that are punished either overtly or covertly, where outcomes of such dialogue are not valued or are just ignored. How do individuals know whether these negative outcomes are likely to happen? Just being told that contributions are welcomed will not work if previous experience suggests that the espoused theories of practice by others in the organisation do not match the theories in action (Argyris, 2010). The experiences that inform individuals about organisational culture are often based on implicit messages that are picked up through use of language, artefacts, protocols and organisational routines as much as the behaviours and we should all be mindful of them and the messages they impart. Dempster and Bagakis in (MacBeath and Dempster, 2009) offer five prompts to enable an expansive learning environment within a school that transfer well to other organisations:

The culture should nurture the learning of everyone …

Everyone should have opportunities to reflect on the nature, skills and processes of learning …

Physical and social spaces should stimulate and celebrate learning …

Safe and secure environments enable everyone to take risks, cope with failure and respond positively to challenges …

Tools and strategies are used to enhance thinking about learning and the practice of teaching.

(Dempster and Bagakis in MacBeath and Dempster, 2009: 92–99)

This learning culture is at the heart of what is referred to as a learning organisation and as Watkins and Marsick suggest must include 'creating continuous learning opportunities, promoting enquiry and dialogue, encouraging collaboration and team building, establishing systems to capture and share learning, empowering people towards a collective vision and connecting the organisation to its environment' (Watkins and Marsick, 1993: 262).

The above examples help indicate what a learning culture or an expansive learning environment might look like but the challenge is in how to create it. It is easy to suggest that it is the role of the leadership to promote such an environment and it is true that the leadership has an important role to play but leadership can be exerted at all levels within the organisation including through individuals and teams.

Individuals can have an impact on shaping a learning culture. Developing a learning culture can be facilitated through appropriate systems and protocols but essentially it is about establishing trusting and respectful relationships. This depends on individuals, and as mentioned before, developing trust can only come through taking risks. This may require individuals to:

- ask for and value the help and opinions of others.
- admit our mistakes and ignorance and share what can be learnt from them. Learning from mistakes, our own or someone else's, is often much more powerful than learning from others 'good practice'.
- publicly acknowledge the strengths and capabilities of others and give consideration to how such capabilities can become part of your own practice.
- ask others to comment on your practices with a view to improvement (including learners or clients).
- share readings that you believe can inform practice.

Such actions will encourage others to mirror these behaviours and your sphere of influence expands.

Teams within organisations can also model such practices and then take them beyond the bounds of that team in an attempt to find out how other teams extend and develop. Observing the practices of others is always food for learning whether their practices are better, worse or just different.

Leaders' behaviours are crucial to creating learning organisations as outlined in Chapter 6 but they cannot do it alone; everybody needs to commit. What leaders can do is to create the incentives that make the changes to behaviours clearly worthwhile, acting as a role model and a lead-learner, and to be comfortable with giving leadership away as appropriate while reminding the organisation of its purpose.

The final thought

The last challenge is really an extension of the undiscussable raised in Chapter 6. If we know what makes for effective and efficient professional learning and development, why is it so difficult to implement? Some of the potential answers have been offered throughout this book. This leads us back to the question of trust; trust in ourselves as professionals, trust in our colleagues, trust in our managers, trust in our leaders, trust in our organisations, trust in our professional bodies. We are all hampered by managerialism, both managers and professional practitioners. Maybe it is time we all took a risk and did things differently?

Glossary

ACLEC	The Lord Chancellor's Advisory Committee on Legal Education and Conduct
AELP	Association of Employment and Learning Providers
AfL	Assessment for Learning
AoC	Association of Colleges
ATLS	Associate Teacher Learning and Skills
BECTA	British Educational and Communications Technology Agency
CPD	Continuing Professional Development
DBIS	Department for Business, Innovation and Skills
DCSF	Department for Children, Schools and Families
DIUS	Department for Innovation, Universities and Skills
DFE	Department for Education
DTLLS	Diploma in Teaching and Learning, Learning and Skills
EERJ	European Educational Research Journal
EPPI	Centre for Evidence Informed Policy and Practice in Education
ESRC	The Economic and Social Research Council
FE	Further Education
FEG	Further Education Guild – now named The Education and Training Foundation
FENTO	Further Education National Training Organisation
HE	Higher Education
HEI	Higher Education Institution
ICT	Information and Communications Technology
IfL	Institute for Learning
INSET	In-service Education and Training
IoE	Institute of Education
IPE	Initial Professional Education
ITE	Initial Teacher Education
ITT	Initial Teacher Training
LA	Local Authority
LCLL	London Centre for Leadership in Learning

LLUK	Lifelong Learning United Kingdom
LSDA	Learning and Skills Development Agency
LSIS	Learning and Skills Improvement Service
NPM	New Public Management
NIACE	National Institution for Adult and Continuing Education
OECD	Organisation for Economic Co-operation and Development
OFR	Outcomes Focused Regulation
Ofsted	Office for Standards in Education, Children's Services and Skills
PB	Professional Body
PD	Professional Development
PGCE	Post Graduate Certificate in Education
PL	Professional Learning
PLD	Professional Learning and Development
QTLS	Qualified Teacher Learning and Skills
REL	Registered European Law
SFA	Skills Funding Agency
SRA	Solicitors Regulation Authority
SSC	Sector Skills Council
SVUK	Standards Verification United Kingdom
TDA	Training and Development Agency
TLRP	Teaching and Learning Research Project
VET	Vocational Education and Training
WBL	Work-based Learning

Bibliography

Academy of Medical Royal Colleges (2010) *The Effectiveness of Continuing Professional Development, Final Report*, London: College of Emergency Medicine.

ACLEC (1996) *First Report on Legal Education and Training*, London: ACLEC, p. 96, para. 6.29.

ACLEC (1997) *Continuing Professional Development for Solicitors and Barristers: A Second Report on Legal Education and Training*, London: ACLEC.

AELP/AoC (2012, December) *Further Education Guild; Briefing Document*, London: Association of Employment and Learning Providers and Association of Colleges.

Antonacopolou, E. R. and Bento, R. F. (2004) Methods of 'learning leadership' taught and experiential, in Storey, J. (ed.) *Leadership in Organisations: Current Issues and Key Trends*, London: Routledge.

Argyris, C. (1990) *Overcoming Organisational Defenses*, New Jersey: Prentice Hall.

Argyris, C. (1991) Teaching smart people how to learn, *Harvard Business Review*, May–June: 99–109.

Argyris, C. (2010) *Organisational Traps: Leadership, Culture, Organizational Design*, Oxford: Oxford University Press.

Argyris, C. and, Schon, D. (1978) *Organisational Learning, 11*, Reading, MA: Addison-Wesley.

Avis, J. (2009) *Education, Policy and Social Justice*, London: Continuum Books.

Ball, S. (2003) The teachers' soul and the terrors of performativity, *Journal of Education Policy* (18)2: 215–28.

Barnett, R. (1997) *Higher Education: A Critical Business*, Buckingham: Open University Press.

Bar Standards Board (2011) *Review of CPD: Report of the Working Group*, London: Bar Standards Board.

Bar Standards Board (2012) *Handbook for Continuing Professional Development* (draft for consultation), London: Bar Standards Board.

Bathmaker, A-M. (2006) Alternative futures: professional identity formation in English further education, in Bathmaker, A. Satterwaite, J., Martin, W. and Roberts, L. (eds) *Discourse, Resistance and Identity Formation*, Stoke-on-Trent: Trentham Books.

Bebeau, M. J. (2008) Promoting ethical development and professionalism: insights from educational research in the professions, *University of St. Thomas Law Journal* 5(2): 366–403.

Beck, J. (2009) Appropriating professionalism: restructuring the official knowledge base of England's modernised teaching profession, *British Journal of Sociology of Education* 1: 3–14.

BECTA (British Educational and Communications Technology Agency) (2008) *Measuring E-maturity in the FE Sector*, London: LSN.

Bernstein, B. (1996) *Pedagogy, Symbolic Control and Identity*, London: Taylor & Francis.

Bindman, D. (2010) Testing times, *The Legal Executive Journal* June: 24–6.

Bohm, D. (1996) *On Dialogue*, London: Routledge.

Bolden, R., Hawkins, B., Gosling, J. and Taylor, S. (2011) *Exploring Leadership: Individual, Organisational and Societal Perspectives*, Oxford: Oxford University Press.

Bolton, J. (2002) Chiropractors' attitudes to, and perceptions of, the impact of continuing professional education on clinical practice, *Medical Education* 36(4): 317–24.

Boon, A. (2010) Professionalism under the Legal Services Act 2007, *International Journal of the Legal Profession* 17(3): 195.

Boon, A. and Levin, J. (2008) *The Ethics and Conduct of Lawyers in England and Wales*, 2nd edition, Oxford: Hart Publishing.

Boon, A. and Webb, J. (2008) Legal education and training in England and Wales: back to the future?, *Journal of Legal Education* 58(1): 79–118.

Bottery, M. (1996) The challenge to professionals from new public management: implications for the teaching profession, *Oxford Review of Education* 22(2): 179–97.

Bottery, M. (2003) The management and mismanagement of trust, *Educational Management and Administration* (31)3: 245–61.

Boud, D. (2010) Relocating reflection in the context of practice, in Bradley, H., Frost, N., Kilminster, S. and Zukas, M. (eds) *Beyond Reflective Practice: New Approaches to Professional Lifelong Learning*, London: Routledge.

Bourdieu, P. (1998) *Practical Reason*, Cambridge: Polity Press.

Bradbury, H., Frost, N., Kilminster, S. and Zukas, M. (2010) *Beyond Reflective Practice: New Approaches to Professional Lifelong Learning*, London: Routledge.

Brand, P. (1992) *The Origins of the English Legal Profession*, Oxford and Cambridge, MA: Blackwell.

Brighouse, T. and Moon, R. (2013) www.newvisionsforeducation.org.uk/2013/01/10/taking-teacher-development-seriously-a-proposal-to-establish-a-national-teaching-institution-for-teacher-professional-development-in-england, accessed 15 January 2013.

Brown, G. (2008) *Excellence and Fairness: Achieving World Class Services*, Cabinet Office, London: HMSO.

Brown, G. (2009) *Working Together – Public Services on Your Side*, Cabinet Office, London: HMSO.

Bruner, J. S. (1966) *Toward a Theory of Instruction*, London: Belknap/Harvard.

Bubb, S. (2009) Coaching in a special school, in P. Earley and V. Porritt (eds) *Effective Practices in Continuing Professional Development: Lessons from Schools*, London: Institute of Education and TDA.

Bubb, S. and Earley, P. (2007) *Leading and Managing Continuing Professional Development*, 2nd edition, London: Sage.

Burgoyne, J. (1999) Feature: the learning organisation, *People Management*, 3 June: 40–4.

Cambone, J. (1995) Time for teachers in school restructuring, *Teachers College Record* 96(3): 512–43.

Campbell, C. and Levin, B. (2012) Developing knowledge mobilisation to challenge educational disadvantage, paper written for Evidence in Action seminar, Educational Endowment Foundation, England.

Cervero, R. M. (2000) Trends and issues in continuing professional education, *New Directions for Adult and Continuing Education* 86: 3–12.

Clarke, J. and Newman, J. (2009) Elusive publics: knowledge, power and public service reform, in Gewirtz, S., Mahony, P., Hextall, I. and Cribb, A. (eds) *Changing Teacher Professionalism: International Trends, Challenges and Ways Forward*, London: Routledge.

Clementi, Sir David, (2004) *Review of the Regulatory Framework for Legal Services in England and Wales.* Available at http://webarchive.nationalarchives.gov.uk/+/http://www.legal-services-review.org.uk/content/report/index.htm, accessed 16 May 2013.

Clow, R. (2001) Further education teachers constructions of professionalism, *Journal of Vocational Education and Training* (53)3: 407–19.

Coffey, M. (2012) *Annual Report 2011/12,* video transcript report, London: Ofsted.

Coffield, F. (2008) *Just Supposing that Teaching and Learning Became the First Priority …* London: Learning and Skills Network.

Coffield, F., Edwards, S., Finlay, I., Hodgson, A., Spours, K., Steer. R. and Gregson, M. (2007) How policy impacts on practice and how practice does not impact on policy, *British Educational Research Journal* (33) 5: 723–41.

Coffield, F. and Williamson, B. (2011) *From Exam Factories to Communities of Discovery: The Democratic Route,* London: IoE publications.

Coldwell, M. and Simkins, T. (2011) Level models of continuing professional development evaluation: a grounded review and critique, *Professional Development in Education*, 37(1): 143–57.

Colley, H., James, D., Diment, K. and Tedder, M. (2003) Learning and becoming in vocational education and training: class, gender and the role of vocational habitus, *Journal of Vocational Education and Training* (55)4: 471–98.

Colley, H., James, D. and Diment, K. (2007) Unbecoming teachers: towards a more dynamic notion of professional participation, *Journal of Education Policy* (22)2: 173–93.

Corcoran, T. C. (1995) *Transforming Professional Development for Teachers: A Guide for State Policymakers,* Washington, DC: National Governors' Association.

Cordingley P, Bell, M., Evans, D., Firth, A. (2005) The impact of collaborative CPD on classroom teaching and learning. Review: What do teacher impact data tell us about collaborative CPD? In *Research Evidence in Education Library.* London: EPPI-Centre, Social Science Research Unit, Institute of Education, University of London. Available at http://eppi.ioe.ac.uk/cms/Default.aspx?tabid=274, accessed 29 May 2013.

Cordingley, P., Bell, M., Isham, C., Evans, D., Firth, A. (2007) What do specialists do in CPD programmes for which there is evidence of positive outcomes for pupils and teachers? Report. In *Research Evidence in Education Library.* London: EPPI-Centre, Social Science Research Unit, Institute of Education, University of London. Available at http://eppi.ioe.ac.uk/cms/Default.aspx?tabid=274, accessed 29 May 2013.

Cordingley, P., Bell, M., Rundell, B., Evans, D. (2003) The impact of collaborative CPD on classroom teaching and learning. In *Research Evidence in Education Library.* London: EPPI Centre, Social Science Research Unit, Institute of Education, University of London. Available at http://eppi.ioe.ac.uk/cms/Default.aspx?tabid=274, accessed 29 May 2013.

Cordingley, P., Bell, M., Thomason, S., Firth, A. (2005) The impact of collaborative continuing professional development (CPD) on classroom teaching and learning. Review: How do collaborative and sustained CPD and sustained but not collaborative CPD affect teaching and learning? In *Research Evidence in Education Library*. London: EPPI-Centre, Social Science Research Unit, Institute of Education, University of London. Available at http://eppi.ioe.ac.uk/cms/Default.aspx?tabid=274, accessed 29 May 2013.

Courtney, S. (1992) *Towards a Theory of Participation in Adult Education*, London: Routledge.

Deci, E. L., Schwartz, A. J., Sheinman, L. and Ryan, M. R. (1981) An instrument to assess adults' orientation towards control versus autonomy with children: reflections on intrinsic motivation and perceived competence, *Journal of Educational Psychology* 83(5): 642–50.

Deem, R., Hillyard, S., Reed, M. and Johnson, R. (2007) *Knowledge, Higher Education and the New Managerialism: The Changing Management of UK Universities*, Oxford: Oxford University Press.

Department for Business, Education and Skills (2009) *Skills for Growth,* London: The Stationery Office.

Department for Business, Innovation and Skills (2010) *Skills for Sustainable Growth*, London: The Stationery Office.

Department for Business, Innovation and Skills (2012a) *Professionalism in Further Education: Interim Report of the Independent Review Panel*, London: DBIS.

Department for Business, Innovation and Skills (2012b) *Professionalism in Further Education: Final Report of the Independent Review Panel*, Chair Lord Lingfield. Available at http://www.bis.uk, accessed 10 November 2012.

Department for Education and Skills (2002) *Success for All*, London: The Stationery Office.

Department for Education and Skills (2006) *Further Education: Raising Skills, Improving Life Chances*, London: The Stationery Office.

Department for Innovation, Universities and Skills (2007) *The Further Education Teachers' Qualifications (England) Regulations 2007.*

Dixon, N. M. (1998) *Dialogue at Work: Making Talk Developmental for People and Organisations*, London: Lemos and Crane.

Dixon, N. M. (1999) *The Organisational Learning Cycle*, Brookfield, VT: Gower.

Drewe, P. and Cooper, C. (2012) *Well-Being and Work*, New York: Palgrave Macmillan.

Dreyfus, H. L. and Dreyfus, S. E. (1986) *Mind over Machine*, Oxford: Basil Blackwell.

Dutton, J., Frost, P., Worline, M., Lilius, J. and Kanov, J. (2002) Leading in times of trauma, *Harvard Business Review*, January: 56.

Earley, P., and Porritt, V. (eds) (2009) *Effective Practices in Continuing Professional Development: Lessons from Schools*, London: Institute of Education and TDA.

Easterby-Smith, M. (1997) Disciplines of organisational learning: contributions and critiques, *Human Relations* 50: 1085–93.

Easterby-Smith, M. and Araujo, L. (1999) Organisational learning: current debates and opportunities, in Easterby-Smith, M., Burgoyne, J. and Araujo, L. (eds) *Organisational Learning and the Learning Organisation*, London: Sage, p. 4.

Easterby-Smith, M., Burgoyne, J. and Araujo, L. (eds) (1999) *Organisational Learning and Learning Organisations*, London: Sage.

Eraut, M. (1994) *Developing Professional Knowledge and Competence*, London: The Falmer Press.

Eraut, M. (1995) Developing professional knowledge within a client-centred orientation, in Guskey, T. R. and Huberman, M. (eds) *Professional Development in Education: New Paradigms & Practices*, New York: Teachers College Press.

Eraut, M. (2000) Non formal learning: implicit learning and tacit knowledge, in Coffield, F. (ed.) *The Necessity of Informal Learning*, Bristol: Policy Press.

ESRC/TLRP Programme (1999–2009) ESRC/TLRP Projects, IoE: London.

Etzioni, A. (1969) *The Semi-Professions and Their Organisations: Teachers, Nurses and Social Workers*, New York: Free Press.

Eun, B. (2011) A Vygotskian theory-based professional development: implications for culturally diverse classrooms, *Professional Development in Education*, 37(3): 319–33.

Fairhurst, G. (2007) *Discursive Leadership: In Conversation with Leadership Psychology*, London: Sage.

Fleisher, D. S. (1974) Priorities and data bases: their relationship to continuing education, in US Department of Health, Education and Welfare *Fostering the Growing Need to Learn*, Washington, DC: US Government Printing Office.

Foster, A. (2005) *Realising the Potential: A Review of the Future of Further Education Colleges*, London: Department for Education and Skills.

Foucault, M. (1997) *Discipline and Punish*, Penguin: Harmondsworth.

Frechtling, J. A., Sharp, L., Carey, N., Vaden – Kiernan, N. and Westat. (1995) *Teacher Enhancement Programs: A Perspective on the Last Four Decades*, Washington, DC: National Science Foundation Directions for Educational and Human Resources.

Freidson, E. A. (1988) *Profession of Medicine: A Study of the Sociology of Applied Knowledge*, Chicago: University of Chicago Press.

Friedman, A. L. (2011) *CPD – Lifelong Learning of Millions*, Abingdon: Routledge.

Frost, N. (2010) Professionalism and social change: the implications of social change for the 'reflective practitioner', in Bradley, H., Frost, N., Kilminster, S. and Zukas, M. (eds) *Beyond Reflective Practice: New Approaches to Professional Lifelong Learning*, London: Routledge.

Frost, D. and Durrant, J. (2003). *Teacher-led Development Work*, London: David Fulton.

Fuller, A. and Unwin, L. (2003a) Learning as apprentices in the contemporary UK workplace: creating and managing expansive and restrictive participation, *Journal of Education and Work* 16(4): 407–26.

Fuller, A. and Unwin, L. (2003b) Fostering workplace learning: looking through the lens of apprenticeship, *EERJ*, 2(1): 41–55.

Fuller, A. and Unwin, L. (2004a) Young people as teachers and learners in the workplace: challenging the Novice Expert Dichotomy, *International Journal of Training and Development* 8(1): 31–41.

Fuller, A. and Unwin, L. (2004b) Expansive learning environments: integrating personal and organisational development, in Rainbird, H., Fuller, A. and Munro, A. (eds) *Workplace Learning in Context*, London: Routledge

Gane, N. (2012) Surveillance and neoliberalism, *The Sociological Review,* 60(4): 611–34.

Garvin, D., Edmondson, A. and Gino, F. (2008) Is yours a learning organisation?, *Harvard Business Review*, March: 109–13.

Gemmill, G. and Oakley, J. (1997) Leadership: an alienating social myth, in Grint, K. (ed.) *Leadership,* 83(9): 108–16, Oxford: Oxford University Press.

Gewirtz, S., Mahony, P., Hextall, I. and Cribb, A. (eds) (2009) *Changing Teacher Professionalism: International Trends, Challenges and Ways Forward*, London: Routledge.

Ginsberg, M. B. (1996) Professionalism or politics as a model for educators' engagement with/in communities, *Journal of Education Policy* 12: 5–12.

Gleeson, D. (2010) The professional imagination: remaking professionalism in a neoliberal context, in Green, A. (ed.) *Blair's Educational Legacy: Thirteen Years of New Labour*, London: Palgrave Macmillan.

Gleeson, D., Abbott, I. and Hill, R. (2011) Governing the governors: a case study of college governance in English further education, *British Educational Research Journal*, iFirst, July 1–16.

Gleeson, D. and Knights, D. (2006) Challenging dualism: professionalism in 'troubled times', *Sociology* (40)2: 277–95.

Gleeson, D. and Mardle, G. (1980), *Further Education or Training? A Case Study of the Theory and Practice of Further Education*, London: Routledge and Kegan Paul.

Gleeson, D. and Shain, F. (1999) Under new management: changing conceptions of teacher professionalism and policy in the further education sector, *Journal of Education Policy*, 14(4): 445–62.

Gold, J., Thorpe, R., Woodall, J. and Sadler-Smith, E. (2007) Continuing professional development in the legal profession, *Management Learning* 38(2): 235–50.

Goodall, J., Day, C., Harris, A., Lindsey, G. and Muijs, D. (2005). *Evaluating the Impact of Continuing Professional Development*, Nottingham: DCSF.

Grace, G. (1995) *School Leadership: Beyond Education Management*, London: Routledge Falmer.

Green, A. (ed.) (2010) *Blair's Educational Legacy: Thirteen Years of New Labour*, London: Palgrave Macmillan.

Grint, K. (2005) *Leadership: Limits and Possibilities*, Basingstoke: Palgrave Macmillan.

Guskey, T. (2000) *Evaluating Professional Development*, Thousand Oaks, CA: Corwin Press.

Guskey, T. (2002a) Does it make a difference? Evaluating professional development, *Educational Leadership*, 59(6), 45–51.

Guskey, T. (2002b) Professional development and teacher change, *Teachers and Teaching: Theory and Practice* 8(3): 381–91.

Guskey, T. (2005) Evaluating professional development: an interview with Dr Thomas Guskey, Ohio University.

Hara, N. (ed.) (2009) *Communities of Practice: Fostering Peer-to-Peer Learning and Knowledge Information Sharing in the Workplace*, Berlin: Springer.

Hargreaves, A. and Fullan, M. (2012) *Professional Capital*, London and New York: Routledge.

Harkin, J. (2005) Fragments stored against my ruin: the place of educational theory in the professional development of teachers in further education, *Journal of Vocational Education and Training* (57)2: 164–79.

Harkin, J. (2012) *IfL Preparatory Research to Inform the Work of the Commission on Adult and Vocational Learning*, London: Institute for Learning.

Hattie, J. (2009) *Visible Learning: A Synthesis of over 800 Meta-Analyses Relating to Achievement*, Abingdon: Routledge.

Hattie, J. (2012) *Visible Learning for Teachers: Maximizing Impact on Learning*, Abingdon: Routledge.

Heifetz, R., Grashow, A. and Linsky, M. (2009) *The Practice of Adaptive Leadership; Tools and Tactics for Changing Your Organisation and the World*, Boston, MA: Harvard Business Press.

Hobby, R. (2012) *If we know how to make CPD more effective, why isn't it happening?* Teacher Development Trust Blog, July, 2012.

Hoggett, P. (1996) New modes of control in the public service, *Public Administration*, 74(1): 9–32.

Hood, C. (1991) A public management for all seasons?, *Public Administration*, 69: 3–19.

Hopkins, D (2009) The changing landscape of school improvement, *School Leadership Today* 1(4): 29–31.

Houle, C. O. (1980) *Continuing Learning in the Professions*, San Francisco and London: Jossey-Bass.

Hoyle, E. and Wallace, M. (2007) Educational reform: an ironic perspective, *Educational Management, Administration and Leadership* (35)1: 9–25.

Illingworth, S. (2009) Developing coaching as an effective method of CPD, in Earley, P. and Porritt, V. (eds) *Effective Practices in Continuing Professional Development: Lessons from Schools*, London: Institute of Education and TDA.

Institute for Learning (IfL) (2007) *Guidelines for Your Continuing Professional Development (CPD)*, London: Institute for Learning.

Institute for Learning (IfL) (2009) *2008–09 IfL Review of CPD – Making a Difference for Teachers, Trainers and Learners*, London: Institute for Learning.

Institute for Learning (IfL) (2010a) *2009–10 IfL Review of CPD – Excellence in Professional Development: Looking Back, Looking Forward*, London: Institute for Learning.

Institute for Learning (IfL) (2010b) *Brilliant Teaching and Training in FE and Skills: A guide to effective CPD for teachers, trainers and leaders*, London: Institute for Learning.

Institute for Learning (IfL) (2011) *IfL Supporting Professionalism Update for 2011–14*, London: Institute for Learning.

Institute for Learning (IfL) (2012a) *2010–11 IfL Review of CPD – CPD for the Future: The Networked Professional*, London: Institute for Learning.

Institute for Learning (IfL) (2012b) *Professionalism – Education and Training Professionals across Further Education and Skills*. Available at http://www.ifl.ac.uk/__data/assets/pdf_file/0006/28572/2012_IfL_professionalism_paper_word_doc.pdf, accessed 29 January 2013.

Isaacs, W. N. (1993) Taking flight: dialogue, collective thinking, and organizational learning, *Organizational Dynamics* 22: 24–39.

Isaacs, W. N. (1999) *Dialogue and the Art of Thinking Together*, New York: Doubleday.

James, D. and Biesta, G. (2007) *Improving Learning Cultures in Further Education*, London: Routledge.

James, D. and Diment, K. (2003) Going underground? Learning and assessment in an ambiguous space, *Journal of Vocational Education and Training* (55)4: 407–22.

Jamous, H. and Peloille, B. (1970) Changes in the French University Hospital System, in Jackson, J. A. (ed.) *Professionalization*, London: Cambridge University Press.

Jephcote, M., Salisbury, J. and Rees, G. (2008) Being a teacher in further education in changing times, *Research in Post-Compulsory Education* (13)2: 163–72.

Johnson, T. J. (1997) *Professions and Power*, London: Macmillan.

Johnson, T. J. (1972) *Professions and Power*, London and Basingstoke: Macmillan Press Ltd.

Joyce, B. and Showers, B. (1980) Improving inservice training, the messages of research, *Educational Leadership* 37(5): 379–85.

Keep, E. (2007) State control of the English vocational education and training system: playing with the biggest train set in the world, *Journal of Vocational Education and Training*, 58(1): 47–64.

Keep, E. and Mayhew, K. (2010) Moving beyond skills as a social and economic panacea, *Work, Employment and Society*, 24(3): 565–77.

Kirkpatrick, D. (1959) The Kirkpatrick model for training evaluation, *The Journal of the American Society of Training Directors*, 3, August.

Kitchener, M., Kirkpatrick, I. and Whipp, R. (2000) Supervising professional work under new public management, evidence from an 'invisible trade', *British Journal of Management*, 11(3): 213–26.

Knights, D. and Wilmott, H. (1999) *Management Lives, Power and Identity in Work Organisations*, London: Sage.

Knowles, M. S. (1975) *Self-directed Learning: A Guide for Learners and Teachers*, Englewood Cliffs, NJ: Prentice Hall.

Knowles, M. S. (1980) *The Modern Practice of Adult Education: From Pedagogy to Andragogy*, Englewood Cliffs, NJ: Prentice Hall.

Kolb, D. (1984) *Experiential Learning, Experience as the Source of Learning and Development*, New Jersey: Prentice Hall.

Larson, M. S. (2013) *The Rise of Professionalism: Monopolies of Competence and Sheltered Markets*, New Brunswick, NJ: Transaction Publishers.

Lave, J. and Wenger, E. (1991) *Situated Learning: Legitimate Peripheral Participation*, Cambridge: Cambridge University Press.

Legal Services Policy Institute (2009) *The Accreditation of Learning Programmes Leading to Professional Legal Qualifications*, London: College of Law.

Leitch, S. (2006) *Prosperity for All in the Global Economy: World Class Skills*, London: HM Treasury.

Levin, B. (2012) Innovation, transformation and improvement in school reform, *School Effectiveness and Improvement Research, Policy and Practice*, London: Routledge.

Lipman-Blumen, J. (2005) *The Allure of Toxic Leaders*, New York: Oxford University Press.

LSIS (Learning and Skills Improvement Service) (2011) *Further Education and Skills Sector: Summary Workforce Diversity Report 2011*, Coventry: LSIS.

LSIS (Learning and Skills Improvement Service) www.excellencegateway.org.uk/cavtl, accessed 17 May 2013.

Lucas, N. (2004) The FENTO fandango: national standards, compulsory teaching qualifications and the growing regulation of FE teachers, *Journal of Further and Higher Education* 28(1): 36–51.

Lucas, B., Claxton, G. and Webster, R. (2010) *Bodies of Knowledge: How the Learning Sciences Could Transform Practical and Vocational Education*, Winchester: Edge/Centre for Real World Learning.

Lucas, N. and Nasta, T. (2010) State regulation and the professionalization of further education teachers: a comparison with schools and HE, *Journal of Vocational Education and Training*, 62(4): 441–54.

Lucas, W., Spencer, E. and Claxton, G. (2012) *How to Teach Vocational Education: A Theory of Vocational Pedagogy*, London: City & Guilds Centre for Skills Development.

Lucas, N. and Unwin, L. (2009) Developing teacher expertise at work: in-service trainee teachers in colleges of further education in England, *Journal of Further and Higher Education* 33(4): 423–33.

MacBeath, J. (2009) *Connecting Leadership and Learning: Principles for Practice*, Abingdon: Routledge.

Mackay, F. (2012) 'I don't have to be like my principal': learning to lead in the post-compulsory sector, *Educational Management Administration and Leadership* 40(3): 392–409.

MacIntyre, D. (1994) preface to M. Eraut *Developing Professional Knowledge and Competence*, London: The Falmer Press.

Madden, C. A. and Mitchell V. A. (1993) *Professions, Standards and Competence: A Survey of Continuing Education for the Professions*, Bristol: University of Bristol.

Mulholland, M. (2009) Motivating with maths, in Earley, P. and Porritt, V. (eds) *Effective Practices in Continuing Professional Development: Lessons from Schools*, London: Institute of Education, pp. 91–100.

Newman, J. and Nutley, S. (2003) Transforming the probation service: 'what works', organisational change and professional identity, *Policy and Politics* (31)4: 547–63.

Newman, J. (2007) Rethinking 'the public' in troubled times, *Public Policy and Administration* 22(1): 27–47.

Nicolson, D. (2006) Making lawyers moral?: ethical codes and moral character, *Legal Studies* 25(4): 601.

Nonaka, I. and Takeuchi, T. H. (1995) *The Knowledge-Creating Company: How Japanese Companies Create the Dynamics of Innovation*, Oxford: Oxford University Press.

Nuffield Foundation (2008) *14–19 Review: Final Report*, London: Nuffield Foundation.

O'Brien, J. (2012) The potential of continuing professional development, *School Effectiveness and Improvement Research, Policy and Practice*, London: Routledge.

Ofsted (2006) *The Logical Chain*, London: Ofsted.

Ofsted (2010) *Good Professional Development in Schools*, London: Ofsted.

Ofsted (2012) *Annual Report*, London: Ofsted.

O'Leary, M. (2012) Surveillance, performativity and normalised practice: the use and impact of graded lesson observations in further education colleges, *Journal of Further and Higher Education*, ifirst 1–21.

O'Leary, M. and Smith, R. (2012) Earthquakes, cancer and cultures of fear: qualifying as a skills for life teacher in an uncertain economic climate, *Oxford Review of Education* 38(4): 437–54.

O'Reilly, D. and Reed, M (2010) Discourses of UK public services modernisation, *Organisational Studies* 32(8): 1079–101.

Parker, C. and Aitken, L. (2011) The Queensland 'workplace culture check': learning from reflection on ethics inside law firms, *The Georgetown Journal of Legal Ethics* 399–441.

Pedder, D. and James, M. (2012) Professional learning as a condition for assessment for learning, in Dylan Wiliam (ed.) *Assessment and Learning*, 2nd edition, London: Sage Publications.

Pedder, D., Opfer, V. D., McCormick, R. and Storey, A. (2010) *Schools and Continuing Professional Development in England: The State of the Nation Study*, London: TDA.

Pedlar, M., Burgoyne, J. and Boydell, T. (1996) *The Learning Company: A Strategy for Sustainable Development*, Maidenhead: McGraw-Hill.

Pedlar, M., Burgoyne, J. and Boydell, T. (2004) *A Manager's Guide to Leadership*, London: McGraw-Hill Professional.

Perkin, H. (1989) *The Rise of Professional Society: England since 1980*, London: Routledge.

Perkin, H. (1996) *The Third Revolution: Professional Elites in the Modern World since 1945*, London: Routledge.

Porritt, V. (2005) *London's Learning: Developing the Leadership of CPD, Section 7*, London: Department for Education and Skills.

Porritt, V. (2009a) Evaluating the impact of professional development, *Education Journal*, 116.

Porritt, V. (2009b) Coaching to improve teaching and learning and to develop leadership capacity, in Earley, P. and Porritt, V. (eds) *Effective Practices in Continuing Professional Development: Lessons from Schools*, London: Institute of Education, pp. 60–9.

Porritt, V., Episcopo, K. and Wybron, S. (2006) London's learning: developing the leadership of CPD in London schools, *Professional Development Today* 9(1): 7–11.

Porritt, V., Mulholland, M. and Iiyambo, R. (2011) How to ... ensure ownership of professional learning leads to school improvement, *Professional Development Today* 13(3).

Reed, M. I. (2002) New managerialism, professional power and organisational governance in UK universities: a review and an assessment, in Amaral, A., Jones, G. A. and Karseth, B. (eds.) *Governing Higher Education: National Perspectives on Institutional Governance*, Dordecht, Netherlands: Kluwer Academic.

Reynolds, M. and Vince, R. (eds) (2004) *Organising Reflection*, London: Ashgrave Publishing Limited.

Robertson, J. and Timperley, H. (eds) (2011) *Leadership and Learning*, London: Sage.

Robinson, B., Hohepa, M. and Lloyd, C. (2009) *School Leadership and Student Outcomes: Identifying What Works and Why*, Wellington, New Zealand: Ministry of Education.

Robson, J. (ed.) (1996) *The Professional FE Teacher*, Aldershot: Avebury.

Robson, J. (1998) A professional crisis: status, culture and identity in the further education college, *Journal of Vocational Education and Training* 50(4): 585–607.

Robson, J. (2006) *Teacher Professionalism in Further and Higher Education – Challenges to Culture and Practice*, Abingdon: Routledge.

Schon, D. A. (1983) *The Reflective Practitioner: How Professionals Think in Action*, New York: Basic Books.

Schon, D. A. (1987) *Educating the Reflective Practitioner*, San Francisco: Jossey-Bass.

Sen, A. (1999) *Development as Freedom*, New York: Knopf.

Senge, P. (1990) *The fifth discipline: The Art and Practice of the Learning Organisation*, New York: Harper & Row.

Shain, F. (2013) Change and transition: Muslim boys talk about their post-16 aspirations, in Bhopal, K. and Maylor, U. (eds) *Educational Inequalities: Difference and Diversity*, London and New York: Routledge.

Shirley, L. (2010) Long past its sell-by date? *New Law Journal* 160: 1461.

Simmons, R. (2008) Gender, work and identity: a case study from the English further education sector, *Research in Post Compulsory Education* 130(3): 267–79.

Simon, W. H. (1988) Ethical discretion in lawyering, *Harvard Law Review* 101: 1083–145.

Sinclair, A. (2007) *Leadership for the Disillusioned: Moving beyond Myths and Heroes to Leading that Liberates*, Crows Nest, Australia: Allen and Unwin.

Skills Commission (2011) *Teacher Training in Vocational Education*, Skills Policy Connect, London: Edge Foundation.

Smith, R. (2007) Work, identity and the quasi market: the FE experience, *Journal of Education Administration and History* 39(1): 33–47.

Southworth, G. (2011) Connecting leadership and learning, in Robertson, J. and Timperley, H. (eds) *Leadership and Learning*, London: Sage, pp. 71–85.

SRA Solicitors' Training Regulations, 2009 Available at http://www.sra.org.uk/regulatory-framework/solicitor-training-regulations-2009.page, accessed 16 May 2013.

Starbuck, W. H. and Nystrom, P. (2006) To avoid organisational crises, unlearn, in Starbuck, W. H. (ed.) *Organizational Realities: Studies of Strategizing and Organizing*, Oxford and New York: Oxford University Press.

Stronach, I., Corbin, B., McNamara, S., Stark, S. and Wrawne, T. (2002) Towards an uncertain politics of professionalism: teacher and nurse identities in flux, *Journal of Education Policy* (17)1: 109–38.

Thames, R. and Webster, D. (2009) *Chasing Change: Building Organisational Capacity in Turbulent Environment*, London: John Wiley and Sons.

Thomas, L. (2012) *Rethinking the Importance of Teaching: Curriculum and Collaboration in an Era of Localism*, London: RSA.

Thompson, M. and Wiliam, D. (2007) Tight but loose: a conceptual framework for scaling up school reforms, paper presented at the annual meeting of the American Educational Research Association (AERA) 9–13 April 2007, Chicago.

Thompson, S. and Thompson, N. (2008) *The Critically Reflective Practitioner*, Basingstoke: Palgrave Macmillan.

Timperley, H. (2011) *Realizing the Power of Professional Learning*, Buckingham: Open University Press.

Tipton, B. (1973) *Conflict and Change in a Technical College*, London: Hutchinson.

Training and Development Agency for Schools (TDA) (2007) *Impact evaluation of CPD*. Available at http://www.tda.gov.uk/upload/resources/pdf/i/impact_evaluation.pdf

Tsang, E. and Zahra, S. (2008) Organisational unlearning, *Human Relations* (61)10: 1435–62.

Venables, E. (1968) *The Young Worker at College: A Study of a Local Tech*, London: Faber and Faber.

Vince, R. (2001) Power and emotion in organisational learning, *Human Relations* (54)10: 1325–51.

Vince, R. (2002) Organizing reflection, *Management Learning* (33)1: 63–78.

Vince, R. (2004) *Rethinking Strategic Learning*, London: Routledge.

Vince, R. and Reynolds, M. (2004) *Organizing Reflection*, London: Routledge.

Vygotsky, L. S. (1978) *Mind in Society*, Cambridge, MA: Harvard University Press.

Watkins, K. and Marsick, V. J. (1993) *Sculpting the Learning Organisation*, San Francisco: Jossey-Bass.

Weick, K. (2003) Positive organising and organisational tragedy, in Cameron, K., Dutton, J. and Quinn, R. (eds) *Positive Organisational Scholarship*, San Francisco: Berrett-Koehler.

Weick, K. and Sutcliffe, K. (2007) *Managing the Unexpected: Resilient Performance in an Age of Uncertainty*, San Francisco: Jossey-Bass.

Weiss, H and Klein, L (2006) Pathways to workforce development to child outcomes, *The Evaluation Exchange*, XI(4) (Winter): 2–4, Harvard Family Research Project, Harvard School of Education.

Wenger, E. (1998) *Communities of Practice: Learning, Meaning, and Identity*, New York Cambridge University Press, 1998.

Wiliam, D. (2009) *Assessment for Learning: Why, What and How?* London: Institute of Education.

Wiliam, D. and Black, P. (2006) *Inside the Black Box: Raising Standards through Classroom Assessment*, London: NFER Nelson.

Index

Academy of Medical Royal Colleges 44
accelerated learning 101
accountability 9, 21, 23–4
activist professionalism 13
agency, and structure 4, 24
altruism 8, 13
apprenticeships 121
Argyris, C. 114
Aspiring Principals and Senior Leaders
    Programme (APSLP) 98, 104, 116,
    117, 139
Aspiring to Leadership Programme 95–6
asserted evidence 93–6
assessment for learning (AfL) 66–7, 131–2
Associate Teacher Learning and Skills
    (ATLS) 37, 42–3
Association of Colleges 43
Association of Employment and Learning
    Providers 43
attitudes 17; business-like 122, 123–4;
    pride and thoughtfulness towards the
    job 122, 123
audit 9, 21, 24–5, 44
austerity 28–9
autonomy xvi, 72; government policy and
    21, 25, 30; professionalism 8, 9, 13, 18;
    protection by professional bodies 50;
    responsible, earned autonomy 137–8
autonomy orientation 14, 16, 123

Bagakis, G. 143
Bar Standards Board 37, 38, 41, 42
Barnett, R. 7
barristers 36, 37, 41–2
baseline 85, 88; baseline and impact
    approach to evaluation 89–93
becoming 22–8
Biesta, G. 99

Bolden, R. 100
Bottery, M. 9, 13, 19
Boud, D. 117, 128
Boydell, T. 100–1
Bradbury, H. 105–6
Brighouse, T. 1
Burgoyne, J. 100–1, 115
business-like attitudes 122, 123–4

Callaghan, J. 18, 21
Campbell, C. 79
capability: for change 102; organisational
    111–14
career plan 39
centralised deregulation 28
centralised self-regulation 28
Cervero, R.M. 35
challenging circumstances 98–9
change: capability for 102; legal profession
    and FE teachers 41–3; managing loss
    and managing change 110–11
charismatic leadership 100
clarity of purpose 89–93
Claxton, G. 119, 132
coaching 89, 90
codes of ethics 37
Coffield, F. 13–14, 105, 131
collaborative learning 15, 45–6, 77–8,
    122; mandatory CPD 59, 60, 61–2;
    Professional Formation 71, 74
collaborative reflection xiv–xv, 34, 39
collective learning 3, 116–17, 122, 126,
    135–7
collective reflection xiv–xv, 106–7, 126,
    128–9
college values 111–13, 116
colleges 26
combination 81

command and control management 99
Commission on Adult and Vocational
    Teaching and Learning (CAVTL) 6,
    119, 120
communication 46–7
communities of discovery 131
communities of exploration 15
communities of practice 15, 61–2, 68,
    106, 136; professional bodies 45, 46;
    vocational pedagogy 126, 130–1
competence 32, 44, 47, 48, 65, 66
compliance 47–8, 74
compulsory evidencing of CPD 54, 55–64
confidence deficit 63
continuous learning 3, 19, 104, 112
control orientation 14, 16, 123, 134
craftsmanship 122, 123
creative compliance 24
creativity 1
critical reflection (introspection) 49, 116
cultural influences 3
cultures of mediation 28

Deci, E.L. 123
decisional capital 69, 72
defensive routines 101, 114
democracy 103
democratic professionalism 13–14, 28–30
Dempster, N. 143
dentists 35
deregulation 27–8
Dewey, J. 127
dialogue 78, 135–6; interdisciplinary 12;
    leadership and maintaining 104–5;
    learning organisation 110, 113, 143;
    mandatory CPD 59, 60, 61, 62; paradox
    of 142–3; Professional Formation 68,
    74; spectrum of professional maturity 15,
    17; vocational pedagogy 125–6, 129–30
disciplinary teams 136
discretion 50–1
distributed leadership 136, 138
diversity 11–12, 18
Dixon, N.M. 110, 129, 142–3
double-loop learning 56, 60–1
dual identities 25–6
dual professionalism 2, 4, 36, 65, 72, 74
Durrant, J. 85

Earley, P. 77, 85, 88, 94, 142
earned autonomy 137–8
Easterby-Smith, M. 107
ecologies of practice 24–5

economy 8–9
Edmondson, A. 112–13
Effective Practices in Continuing Professional
    Development project 85, 87–8, 91, 93–4
effectiveness 8–9
efficiency 8–9
employer-led professional learning 63
employers 26, 45–6
empowerment 138
engagement 47, 77
entry into FE teaching 22
e-portfolio 57; REfLECT 41, 58–9, 65, 67
equalitarian values 110
Eraut, M. 45
ethical framework 13
ethics, codes of 37
evaluation of impact of professional learning
    xv–xvi, 82–97; evidencing impact 89–96
evidence: compulsory evidencing of CPD 54,
    55–64; evidencing impact of professional
    learning 89–96; Professional Formation
    67; understanding evidence sources 93–6
excellence 48, 66, 112
expansive learning 29
expansive learning environments 142–4
expansive workplaces 62
experience 44–5
experiential learning 56, 57, 105, 126
expertise 8, 11, 13, 22; of clients and other
    stakeholders 12; vocational pedagogy
    and professional learning 121, 122
explicit knowledge 81
external programmes 139
externalisation 80–1

failure 114
flexible approaches 35–6
flipped classroom 130
focus groups 61–2
focus of professional learning 89–93
formal learning 31
framework for learning 132
Frost, D. 85
Fullan, M. 69
functional literacies 122–3, 124
Further Education Funding Council 27, 36
Further Education Guild (FEG) 27, 43,
    45–6, 64
Further Education workforce 22–3

Garvin, D. 112–13, 115
Gemmill, G. 137–8
Gino, F. 112–13

Ginsberg, M.B. 12
Gleeson, D. 10
globalisation 10–12, 18
goal of professional learning 89–93
Gold, J. 44–5
government policy xvi, 21, 23–8, 42–3
government regulations of 2007 37, 54, 74; revoked 42–3, 63
Grint, K. 116
group identities 115
Guskey, T. 83–4, 87, 142

Hargreaves, A. 69
Harkin, J. 119, 123, 125
Hartley, D. xiv
Harvard Family Research Project 86
health service 11
high-trust strategy 41
Hobby, R. 78
honesty 112
'hot action' 45
Houle, C.O. 35, 49
human capital 69, 72
humanistic education, ethic of 13
humility, ethic of 13

Iiyambo, R. 91, 92
impact of professional learning xv–xvi, 5–6, 38–9, 44–5, 75–97, 141–2; achieving impact 76–82; evaluating impact xv–xvi, 82–97; evidencing impact 89–96
in-house CPD 45–6, 49, 52
'in' and 'out' groups 108
independence 50, 112
independent learner 122, 124
individuals' contributions to resourcing CPD 140
informal education 31–2
information and communication technologies 18
information explosion 10–11
infrastructure 50
initial teacher qualification regulations 37, 43
initial teacher training/education (ITT/E) 25–6, 33–4, 64, 65, 72
innovation 1
input-based impact evaluation 82–3
input models of CPD 33–4, 37–8, 39–40, 45, 51, 142
INSET 76
inspection 21, 24
Institute for Learning (IfL) 2, 5, 36–7, 76, 134, 142; ATLS 37, 42–3; code of

practice 37; defining CPD 79; model of CPD 40, 56–7; monitoring CPD under regulations of 2007 38–9, 45, 56–64; Professional Formation 54, 64–74; professionalism 4, 16, 18; QTLS 37, 42–3, 54, 64, 67, 69, 73–4; reflective practice 128; registration of teachers 37, 42, 47; role 46–51
interactive professionalism 15–16, 17
interdependence 12–13, 18
interdependent learner 124
interdisciplinary dialogue 12
interdisciplinary teams 136
internalisation 81, 136
Internet 10–11, 130
interpersonal trust 19
intrinsic motivation 123, 124
introspection (critical reflection) 49, 116
invisible pedagogies of power 25
iPad gifts 140
Isaacs, W.N. 106, 113

James, D. 99
James, M. 68
Joyce, B. 79, 142

Kahneman, D. 119
Kaizen Primary School, Newham 91–3
Khan, S. 130
knowledge: body of esoteric knowledge 36; changing nature of 11, 18; explicit 81; putting knowledge to work 79, 80–1, 134; tacit 34, 78, 81
knowledge conversion process 80–1
knowledge transfer approach 121, 130

laggards 40, 49
law 21, 32; CPD compared with FE teaching 32–3, 35–6, 36–51
Law Society 36, 38, 46
Law Society Training Committee 39
lead learner 104
leaderism 10
leadership xiv–xv, 6, 98–118, 136; challenges with the organisational learning approach 114–15; developing organisational capability 111–14; learning organisation see learning organisations; personal learning as a leader 101–3; and responsible, earned autonomy 137–8; unblocking learning 103–7
leadership development 116
Leadership for Learning project 108

learned helplessness 137–8
learning cultures 29, 142–4
learning dialogue *see* dialogue
learning organisations xv, 1, 98, 100–1,
    107–18, 143–4
learning and skills agenda 22, 30
learning style 14, 15
Legal Education and Training Review 42
Legal Services Act 1990 43
Legal Services Act 2007 41
Legal Services Board 41, 42
lesson observation 25–6
Levin, B. 79
licensure 40–1
lifelong learning 19
Lingfield Report 27
London Centre for Leadership Learning
    (LCLL) 76–7
longitudinal analysis 86–7
Lord Chancellor's Advisory Committee for
    Education and Conduct (ACLEC) 38
loss, managing 110–11
low-trust model 40–1
LSIS 23
Lucas, N. 25, 26
Lucas, W. 119, 121–2, 123, 124, 125, 132

MacBeath, J. 105, 108
macro level of trust 19
Madden, C.A. 35
managerialism 1, 8–10, 18, 25–6, 43–4,
    134–5, 138; resisting 10, 50
mandatory CPD 2, 37, 38, 76; practitioner
    response to compulsory evidencing of
    CPD 54, 55–64
marginalisation 28
market regulation and governance 21,
    23–6, 28–30, 43
Marsick, V.J. 143
mathematics 92, 94
McLoughlin, F. 6, 120
medicine 21, 32, 36
meso level of trust 19
middle managers 10
mindfulness 113
Mitchell, V.A. 35
models of CPD: IfL model and areas of
    professional learning 56–7; input
    models 33–4, 37–8, 39–40, 45, 51,
    142; output/outcome models 38–9,
    40, 51–2, 142; professional bodies and
    33–4, 38–40, 44, 45, 51–2

monitoring 40–1; IfL *see* Institute for
    Learning; self-monitoring 49
Moon, R. 1
Mulholland, M. 92, 94
multiculturalism 11–12, 18

Nasta, T. 26
nature, and nurture 14–17
neo-liberalism 21
networked learner 61–2, 124
'new discourse of FE' 22
New Public Management 1, 8–10, 18,
    25–6, 43–4, 134–5, 138
Nonaka, I. 80–1
non-standard teaching approaches 71
nurture, and nature 14–17
Nystrom, P. 111

Oakley, J. 137–8
objectives model 99–100
O'Brien, J. 86
Ofsted 24, 85
O'Leary, M. 25–6
opportunities for professional learning 77–9
organisational capability 111–14
organisational contributions to resourcing
    CPD 138–40
organisational culture 16, 108; learning
    cultures 29, 142–4
organisational knowledge 80–1
organisational learning xv, 1, 98, 100–1,
    107–18, 143–4
organisational unlearning 111
organising reflection 106
'out' and 'in' groups 108
outcomes: evaluating impact and outcomes/
    impact 87–8; professional learning and
    vocational pedagogy 121–4; student
    outcomes and evidencing impact 89–93
Outcomes Focused Regulation (OFR)
    41–2, 44
output-based impact evaluation 83
output/outcome models of CPD 38–9,
    40, 51–2, 142
ownership 77

partnerships between schools
    and FE/HE 20
Pedder, D. 68, 85
Pedlar, M. 100–1, 109
peer review: and feedback 57, 59–60;
    Professional Formation 66, 67

performance indicators 24–5
performative tools 25–6
personal learning, as a leader 101–3
personalised learning 126, 135–7
phone interviews 60–1
policyism 28; *see also* government policy
political influences 3
poor professional practice 8
Porritt, V. 77, 84, 85, 88, 92, 94, 142
portfolios 47; e-portfolio 41, 57, 58–9, 65, 67
power 126–7; invisible pedagogies of 25
power with 12
powerful questioning 129–30
pride 122, 123
priorities 47–8
proactive professionalism 15–16, 17, 75
process model of leadership 100
processes 87–8
products 87–8
professional bodies 1, 5, 31–53, 137, 138; changing environments 41–3; context 33–6; forms of CPD 37–9; models of CPD 33–4, 38–40, 44, 45, 51–2; monitoring and licensure 40–1; professional histories and trajectories 36–7; resourcing CPD 140–1; role of 46–51; *see also under individual names*
professional capital 69, 72
professional development: conceptualising 76–7, 79–82; distinction from professional learning 55
professional dialogue *see* dialogue
Professional Formation 54, 64–74; how and why of 66–74; opportunities of 64–5
professional identity 4, 20–30; becoming 22–8; democratic professionalism 28–30
Professional Improvement Plans (PIPs) 92
professional learning 5, 54–74; compulsory evidencing of CPD 54, 55–64; conceptualising 76–9; Professional Formation 54, 64–74
professional learning opportunities 77–9
professional maturity spectrum 14–17, 70, 123
professional society 43
professionalism 4, 7–19; globalisation and professional attributes 10–12, 18; historical perspective 8–10; nature and nurture of 14–17; nineteenth-century image of 32; professional bodies and

promoting 50–1; redefining 51; reframing 12–14
professionality 29
public interest 8, 9
purposes 47–8; clarity of purpose in evidencing impact 89–93; vocational pedagogy and professional learning 121–4
putting knowledge to work 79, 80–1, 134

qualifications 33, 36, 37, 42–3, 64
Qualified Teacher Learning and Skills (QTLS) 37, 42–3, 54, 64, 67, 69, 73–4
question and answer staff meetings 107
questioning, powerful 129–30

reactive professionalism 15–16, 17
recession 28–9, 30
REfLECT 41, 58–9, 65, 67
reflection and reflective practice 65, 77, 126; collaborative xiv–xv, 34, 39; collective xiv–xv, 106–7, 126, 128–9; leadership 105–7; professional bodies 34, 39; professional maturity spectrum 15, 17; vocational pedagogy and professional learning 124, 126, 127–9
reflective integrity, ethic of 13
reframing professionalism 12–14
registration 37, 42, 47
regulations *see* government regulations of 2007
regulatory reform periods 27–8
relevance 126, 127
research-based professionalism 13
resistance 10, 24, 101
resourcefulness 121, 122
resourcing CPD 138–41
responsibility 112; to others 15
responsible, earned autonomy 137–8
review panel on professionalism 27, 63
Reynolds, M. 106, 115
Richards Review of Apprenticeships 120
routine 45; defensive routines 101, 114

scaffolding 68
scholarly activity 8
Schon, D.A. 34, 105, 127
school and FE/HE partnerships 20
scope 47–8
sector-led professionalism 27–8
self-direction 35, 50
self-monitoring of practice 49
self-regulation 28

senior managers xiv, xv, 26
Shain, F. 10
sharing outcomes of CPD 59, 60, 61–2
Showers, B. 79, 142
situated learning 45–6, 106
Skills for Growth 42
Skills for Sustainable Growth 42
Smith, R. 25–6
social capital 69, 72
social construction, learning as 107
social influences 3
social learning theory 98
socialisation 81
solicitors 36, 37–8, 39–40, 40, 41–2, 45
Solicitors' Regulation Authority (SRA) 37, 41, 46
sources of evidence 93–6
Southworth, G. 137
space 49–50, 139
spectrum of professional maturity 14–17, 70, 123
Spencer, E. 119
stakeholders 12
standards 25–6; role of professional bodies in setting 48
Starbuck, W.H. 111
strategic compliance 24
strategic leadership 93–6, 97
strategic learning 102–3
strategy: college strategy 103; role of professional bodies in strategy for CPD 48–9
structure, and agency 4, 24
student talk/teacher talk ratio 126
student-teacher relationship 125
subcontractors 24
subjectivity, ethic of 13
substantiated evidence 93–6
success, measures of 141–2
supportive learning environment 112–13

tacit knowledge 34, 78, 81
Takeuchi, T.H. 80–1
teacher-student relationship 125
teacher talk/student talk ratio 126
Teaching and Learning Research Programme (TLRP) 99
technical rationalist approach 15, 17
Thames, R. 102, 109
Thomas, L. 13

Thompson, M. 89
thoughtfulness 122, 123
'tight but loose' schematic 108–9
time 139; timescale for impact evaluation 91–3
Timperley, H. 55, 80, 82, 85, 86, 142
toxic leaders 115
Training and Development Agency for Schools (TDA) 84–5
training records 40
transmission model of teaching and learning 121, 130
trust 8–9; levels of 19
truth disclosure, ethic of 13
Tsang, E. 111

unblocking learning 103–7
uncertain future 11
underground working practices 25
understanding impact evaluation 93–6
unemployment, youth 28–9
United States (US) 35
Unwin, L. 25, 26

values 17, 18; college 111–13, 116
Vince, R. 103, 106, 109, 115
vocational pedagogy 6, 29–30, 119–33; approaches to professional and vocational learning 125–7; assessment for learning 131–2; communities of practice 126, 130–1; dialogue 125–6, 129–30; purpose and outcomes 121–4; reflective practice 124, 126, 127–9; relevance 126, 127
voluntaristic approach 27

Watkins, K. 143
Webster, D. 102, 109
Webster, R. 132
Wiliam, D. 66–7, 89
Williamson, B. 13–14, 131
Wolf review of vocational education 73
Wordle pictures 95–6
workplace-based CPD 45–6, 49, 52
World Wide Web 10–11
writing 92–3

youth unemployment 28–9

Zahra, S. 111